LINCOLN
and
SHAKESPEARE

Lincoln and his son Tad. John Hay Library, Brown University.

LINCOLN
and
SHAKESPEARE

Michael Anderegg

University Press of Kansas

© 2015 by the University Press of Kansas
All rights reserved

Published by the University Press of Kansas (Lawrence, Kansas
66045), which was organized by the Kansas Board of Regents and is
operated and funded by Emporia State University, Fort Hays State
University, Kansas State University, Pittsburg State University, the
University of Kansas, and Wichita State University

Library of Congress Cataloging-in-Publication Data

Anderegg, Michael A.
Lincoln and Shakespeare / Michael Anderegg.
pages cm
Includes bibliographical references and index.
ISBN 978-0-7006-2129-3 (cloth : alk. paper)
ISBN 978-0-7006-2148-4 (ebook)
1. Lincoln, Abraham, 1809–1865—Books and reading.
2. Shakespeare, William, 1564–1616—Influence. I. Title.
E457.2.A543 2015
973.7092—dc23

2015023665

British Library Cataloguing-in-Publication Data is available.

Printed in the United States of America

10 9 8 7 6 5 4 3 2 1

The paper used in this publication is recycled and contains 30
percent postconsumer waste. It is acid free and meets the minimum
requirements of the American National Standard for Permanence
of Paper for Printed Library Materials Z39.48-1992.

For Jeanne

CONTENTS

PREFACE

In an early scene of John Ford's 1939 film *Young Mr. Lincoln*, Ann Rutledge responds to Abe's recital of his inadequacies by saying, "But you've educated yourself, you've read poetry, and Shakespeare, and now law."[1] References to Shakespeare almost inevitably pop up in the fictional and semi-fictional representations of Abraham Lincoln that have been appearing since at least the beginning of the twentieth century. Having Lincoln quote, cite, or discuss Shakespeare became a certificate of authenticity, a detail so well-known that it could stand in for much that could not be referenced or easily incorporated into a Lincoln portrait. Many such allusions to Shakespeare are fanciful, but almost all have a source in the vast "archive" of Lincoln lore. In his quasi-historical *Lincoln, the Unknown*, Dale Carnegie embroiders Ann's point, telling his readers that Lincoln "would walk back and forth under the trees, declaiming Hamlet's instruction to the players, and repeating Antony's oration over the dead body of Caesar."[2] One novelist even has Lincoln say to the pregnant Mary, "If it's a boy . . . let's call him William—after Shakespeare."[3] An imagined Lincoln can be counted on for a few lines from *Macbeth* or *Hamlet* or *Julius Caesar* at the drop of his stovepipe hat, even if neither the context nor the tone seems quite right.

John Drinkwater, in his 1918 play *Abraham Lincoln*, invents this unlikely exchange between the president and Secretary of State William Seward:

LINCOLN: "There is a tide in the affairs of men . . ." Do you read Shakespeare, Seward?
SEWARD: Shakespeare? No.
LINCOLN: Ah![4]

Never mind that the real Seward, who had enjoyed a formal education the president lacked, would almost certainly have recognized the allusion. At least the line from *Julius Caesar* is one that Lincoln, according to his law partner, William Herndon, particularly liked to recite. At another point in Drinkwater's play, John Hay reads aloud to Lincoln the passage beginning "Our revels now are ended" and ending "rounded with a sleep" from *The Tempest*, a moment further elaborated in the 1952 *Studio One* television adaptation of *Abraham Lincoln*, which has Mary read the lines as Lincoln silently

mouths the words. At the end of the teleplay, as Lincoln walks off to his des-
tiny at Ford's Theatre, the camera closes in on a page from (one presumes)
Shakespeare's works on a reading stand as in voice-over Lincoln recites over
rising music, "We are such dreams as dreams are made on, and our little life
is rounded with a sleep" (slightly fumbling the lines).[5] There is no evidence
that Lincoln ever read or saw *The Tempest,* but Shakespeare's words unde-
niably provide a moving close to the drama. In a better-known play, Robert
Sherwood's *Abe Lincoln in Illinois,* Lincoln does not directly quote or cite
Shakespeare, but the character Joshua Speed is made to say of his friend,
"He can split rails, push a plough, crack jokes, all day—and then sit up all
night reading 'Hamlet' and brooding over his own fancied resemblance to
that melancholy prince."[6] Poetic license, perhaps, but not unreasonable.

In other Lincoln-inspired poetry and prose, the Shakespeare reference can
be inappropriate or simply puzzling. For poet Delmore Schwartz, identifying Lincoln with Hamlet is a way of debunking him: he calls Lincoln "This
Hamlet-type" and adds,

> O how he was the Hamlet-man, and this,
> After a life of failure made him right,
> After he ran away on his wedding day,
> Writing a coward's letter to his bride.[7]

The Lincoln of Irving Stone's 1954 novel *Love Is Eternal,* speaking of the am-
bitions of his rival Stephen Douglas, comments, "I can only think of the line
in Julius Caesar: 'He doth bestride the narrow world like a Colossus, and
we petty men walk under his huge legs, and peep about to find ourselves
dishonorable graves.'"[8] Though Lincoln almost certainly knew *Julius Caesar,*
the quoted passage is an odd one for the tall, long-legged Lincoln to apply
to the short, squat Douglas. Among the handful of references to Shakespeare
sprinkled throughout Gore Vidal's 1984 novel *Lincoln,* the president several
times cites or refers to *Macbeth.* In conversation with Edwin Stanton, Elihu
Washburne, and others, he says of the play, "I have never seen it in a version I
liked, not that I've seen all that many plays, of any sort."[9] The first part of this
remark has no source, but the second tells us that Vidal had read a famous
letter from Lincoln to the actor James Henry Hackett in which he similarly
played down his experience. Although references to *Macbeth,* a play Lincoln
knew well, are not surprising, Vidal's other Shakespeare reference is less au-
thoritative. As Lincoln prepares to go ashore on his visit to Fort Monroe, he
remarks, "We shall be well-met by moonlight,"[10] a somewhat bizarre refer-

ence to a play, *A Midsummer Night's Dream,* that Lincoln very probably had not read and almost certainly never saw.

The screenplay by Tony Kushner for Steven Spielberg's 2012 film *Lincoln* several times has the president quote Shakespeare, each time grabbing the words more or less out of thin air. Speaking to Secretary of State Seward's factotums, Lincoln is made to say, "We have heard the chimes of midnight, Master Shallow" (slightly misquoting *Henry IV, Part 2*); all he means is that time is getting short. When Seward tells him that he has to choose between passage of the Thirteenth Amendment or accepting a Confederate peace, Lincoln, quoting from *Macbeth*, somewhat petulantly replies,

> If you can look into the seeds of time
> And say which grain will grow and which will not,
> Speak then to me,

a convincing enough allusion given Lincoln's well-known fondness for the play, though it is hard to imagine that he would address his secretary of state with Macbeth's words to the Weird Sisters. A more meaningful moment comes in the conversation with Elizabeth Keckley, a former slave and Mary Lincoln's dressmaker and friend, when Lincoln paraphrases a line from *King Lear*: "Unaccommodated, poor, bare, forked creatures such as we all are," associating himself, and all mankind, with the people he has helped rescue from slavery. When he recounts a dream, Lincoln cites *Hamlet*: "I could be bounded in a nutshell and count myself a king of infinite space . . . were it not that I have bad dreams," an oblique way of alluding to Lincoln's oft-remarked-upon fascination with his own dreams.[11]

The impulse of novelists, poets, playwrights, and filmmakers to associate Lincoln with Shakespeare, sometimes felicitous, sometimes awkward and self-conscious in execution, is founded on a substantial body of evidence. Lincoln's affection for Shakespeare's plays was frequently mentioned by his contemporaries and has become a notable part of Lincoln lore, helping define his personality and character in a manner overlapping with but distinct from his penchant for jokes and comic stories. Throughout his life, and particularly in the years of his presidency, Lincoln turned to Shakespeare's plays not only for the pleasure he took in the poet's language and fund of dramatic incident but also for relief from the cares of state and even for solace when faced with personal disappointment. His Shakespeare was, inevitably, a partial Shakespeare, a Shakespeare adopted early on as an honorary American, shaped by the sensibilities of a new world and made palatable to the democratic, leveling impulses of the American nation. The tragedies and histories, in particular, appealed to Lincoln at least in part because they appealed to America. These plays again and again illustrated the dangers of inordinate ambition, the devastation of civil war (no less than eight plays are concerned, directly or indirectly, with the Wars of the Roses), and the corruptions of illegitimate rule. In addition to these thematic issues, the oratory of Shakespeare's characters, the speeches and soliloquies, were well suited to a highly oratorical age. Politicians and other public figures quoted or cited Shakespeare in their speeches and writings. Lincoln's interest in Shakespeare can only be understood fully when placed in the context of nineteenth-century American culture.

Although quotations from and citations to Shakespeare's plays are not abundant in Lincoln's own writings, he often read from and alluded to Shakespeare in conversation with friends, secretaries, family members, and other visitors and bystanders who recorded their impressions in diaries and letters as well as, in later years, essays and memoirs. We also have testimony to Lincoln's interest in Shakespeare from newspapers and other more or less "official" sources contemporary to the events they describe or report. In the pages that follow, I strive to separate plausible evidence from myth without undermining my central contention that Lincoln was throughout his life fascinated by and engaged with Shakespeare's plays. I then explore the question of how Lincoln came to know Shakespeare, including a consideration of what editions of the plays he may have owned or had access to at various points in his life. Particular interest is paid to *Hamlet* and *Macbeth,* the plays that figured most prominently in Lincoln's imaginative life. I explore as well various aspects of nineteenth-century Shakespearean theater as Lincoln might have experienced it from his youth to the years of his presidency. Here, I examine what theatrical venues would have been available to Lincoln in Springfield as well as in other places to which he traveled before 1861, including New Orleans and Chicago. The American theater in general underwent a significant transformation in the period from when Lincoln would have first encountered it to his years in the White House. As a young man on the frontier, he would have had small occasion or opportunity to attend the theater; by the time he was elected president, theater all over America was a thriving institution.

When President Lincoln wrote to the actor James H. Hackett in the late summer of 1863, he revealed his enthusiasm for Shakespeare and initiated a friendship of sorts that gave him much pleasure, at least for a time. Hackett was one of the most popular comic actors in America, famous for his many years of portraying Shakespeare's Sir John Falstaff. Lincoln saw Hackett play Falstaff on several occasions, and Hackett from time to time visited the White House and discussed Shakespeare with the president. Beginning with Hackett's Falstaff, Lincoln would see a variety of Shakespeare productions featuring the leading actors of his day. I describe the Shakespeare performances of Edwin Booth, Charlotte Cushman, Edwin Forrest, and others that Lincoln saw. Of particular interest are the observations of people who either accompanied Lincoln to the theater or were simply there at the same time and took note of his responses. Lincoln may have preferred reading to seeing Shakespeare, as some have suggested, but he still liked measuring his understanding of the plays against the interpretations of professional actors. While he certainly read and enjoyed other writers, from poets like Robert Burns and Lord Byron to satirists like Petroleum V. Nasby and Artemus Ward, it was to Shakespeare's dramatic universe that Lincoln turned again and again for intellectual nourishment, emotional support, and sheer pleasure he could find nowhere else.

When quoting from nineteenth-century documents, I have kept the original spelling and punctuation without indicating apparent errors and anomalies unless the meaning was unclear. The word "Shakespeare," for example, is variously spelled in the sources (Shakspeare, Shakespere, Shakspere, etc.), and I have not attempted to regularize the usage.

ACKNOWLEDGMENTS

Although the Internet has made research on both Lincoln and Shakespeare easier than was once the case, libraries and librarians remain invaluable. I would particularly like to thank Georgianna Ziegler and Betsy Walsh at the Folger Shakespeare Library; Patrick Kerwin, Lewis Wyman, and Sarah Duke at the Library of Congress; Alison Reynolds at the University of Rochester; Susan Alpert at Harvard's Houghton Library; Holly Snyder at the John Hay Library, Brown University; Jane E. Gastineau of the Lincoln Financial Foundation Collection; and the staffs of the Wilson Library at the University of Minnesota, the St. Paul Public Library (especially the helpful folks in the Dayton's Bluff branch), the Library of the Minnesota Historical Society, the Georgetown University Library, and the Huntington Library.

A number of scholars generously shared the results of their research. Terry Alford provided me with information from his forthcoming biography of John Wilkes Booth, Thomas A. Bogar sent me a chronology of Lincoln's Washington, D.C., theatergoing, and Jon White allowed me to see his forthcoming article on Lincoln's dream of his own death. Daniel J. Watermeier interrupted his work on Edwin Booth to read and comment on portions of my manuscript. Friends and fellow writers and scholars Sharon Carson, Ron Engle, Laurence Goldstein, and James McKenzie helpfully looked at drafts of several chapters. Michael Burlingame, who read my manuscript for the University Press of Kansas and whose knowledge of Abraham Lincoln is unrivaled, made valuable suggestions and saved me from mistakes large and small. It is not necessary to add that the remaining errors are my own.

At the University Press of Kansas, Michael J. Briggs enthusiastically responded to my proposal. I am grateful as well for the help and support of Kathy Delfosse, Larisa Martin, Rebecca J. Murray, and Michael Kehoe.

I am fortunate that both of my children live in Washington, D.C., where the Folger Library and the Library of Congress are located. My son Niles worked for a time as a historical interpreter at President Lincoln's Cottage and one day casually told his boss, Callie Hawkins, that his dad would be happy to give a talk on Lincoln and Shakespeare—before his dad had even thought of linking those names together. I eventually gave the talk, and my other son, Timothy, who heard it, remarked afterward, "So, Dad, are you writing a book?" I guess I was. I thank them both, and I thank Callie for the invitation and encouragement.

Jeanne, once again, gave me her love and support in every way, and I can only repeat what I have said before: as wife, partner, and dearest friend, she helped in all sorts of ways, not the least of which involved reading my drafts and keeping me honest.

LINCOLN
and
SHAKESPEARE

Abraham Lincoln and America's Shakespeare

> *All that Shakspeare says of the king, yonder slip of a boy that reads in the corner feels to be true of himself.*
>
> Ralph Waldo Emerson, "History," *Essays, First Series*

The image of young Abraham Lincoln reading by the light of a fireplace, especially as captured in Eastman Johnson's 1868 painting, has become a significant part of America's imaginative understanding of its most beloved historical figure: the humbly born, self-educated frontier boy who grows up to be president holds an iconic force thoroughly embraced from Lincoln's time to our own. If we were asked what Lincoln is reading in this fanciful depiction of his youthful studies, the answer would probably be the plays of William Shakespeare, though the Bible, John Bunyan's *Pilgrim's Progress*, and Parson Weems's *Life of Washington* might also be suggested. That Lincoln read and enjoyed Shakespeare is well known. While he was alive, witnesses testified to his appreciation of Shakespeare's plays and took note of his attendance at Shakespeare performances in the years of his presidency; after his death, friends, colleagues, and acquaintances came forward with a variety of stories and anecdotes that contributed to a view of him as a Shakespeare enthusiast. In a letter to the actor James H. Hackett (discussed in detail in chapter 4), Lincoln unwittingly made public his love of Shakespeare and at the same time gave friends and enemies the opportunity to make political hay from his observations. Although he seldom quoted or cited Shakespeare in his writings and speeches (as Robert Bray notes, Lincoln "rarely refers to *any* poet, no matter what his mode of writing or his audience"),[1] he often employed allusions to Shakespeare in conversation, and he read Shakespeare's plays aloud on a number of occasions. Not surprisingly, perhaps, some of the evidence for Lincoln's Shakespearean interests is highly dubious: myth—that "vast accumulation of the apocryphal, fabulous, and spurious that began to gather about the man during his lifetime"[2]—soon came to overtake fact in Lincoln's posthumous fame. As important as it is to separate fact from fiction, however, the myth nevertheless has its own value. The desire to see Lincoln associated with Shakespeare speaks to something deep in the culture of nineteenth- and early-twentieth-century America.[3]

The conjunction of Lincoln and Shakespeare derives perhaps as much from the way we understand Shakespeare as from the way we understand Lincoln: both were boys of obscure birth who grew up to great achievement and posthumous fame. If Lincoln has become the great man as statesman, Shakespeare is the great man as author. Walt Whitman early on made the case:

> One of the best of the late commentators on Shakespeare . . . makes the height and aggregate of his quality as a poet to be, that he thoroughly blended the ideal with the practical or realistic. If this be so, I should say that what Shakespeare did in poetic expression, Abraham Lincoln essentially did in his personal and official life.[4]

Shakespeare, furthermore, could be seen to embody the "right to rise" impulse often ascribed to Lincoln. The year Lincoln assumed the presidency, the Scottish reformer Samuel Smiles, in his popular book *Self-Help*, alluded to Shakespeare as an exemplar of the self-made man.[5] For some writers, Lincoln and Shakespeare share a special, sometimes spiritual affinity. Francis Carpenter, who spent six months in the White House preparing and executing the painting *First Reading of the Emancipation Proclamation by President Lincoln*, describes Lincoln's temperament in these terms: "It has been well said by a critic of Shakspeare, that 'the spirit which held the woe of "Lear," and the tragedy of "Hamlet," would have broken, had it not also had the humor of the "Merry Wives of Windsor," and the merriment of "Midsummer Night's Dream."' With equal justice can this profound truth be applied to the late President. The world has had no better illustration of it since the immortal plays were written."[6] Lincoln could even be seen as a character out of Shakespeare's plays: "Among all the public figures in American history," Roy Basler writes, "Lincoln stands out as the character with a difference, part of this difference being that in dramatic actions as well as words, he seems to have been cast in a heroic role comparable to that of a Shakespearean hero."[7] John Drinkwater, the English poet who wrote a play about Lincoln, invented an imaginary conversation between Lincoln and Shakespeare in which he has the latter say, "A simple proposition—like this. England—a poet—with a shrewd head for affairs—good bargain and a comfortable retirement at the end. But a poet always. America—a politician, searching always for vision, vision—as the poet does. We should understand each other."[8] Lincoln and Shakespeare here combine pragmatism and idealism even as they are conjoined as symbols of Anglo-American unity and amity.

Abraham Lincoln first came to Shakespeare, as did many other Americans, through schoolbooks and oratory. Of the so-called readers available to him as a youth, some, like Lindley Murray's enormously popular *English Reader*, did not include any Shakespeare; those that did, including one Lincoln undoubtedly used, *Lessons in Elocution*, provided little more than excerpts of set speeches and soliloquies. Beyond his exposure to school anthologies, the young Lincoln, as he grew to manhood in the 1830s, would have attended lectures of various kinds; the lyceum movement, in particular, which "played an important part in American culture after 1825 by helping to extend the cultural frontier,"[9] often featured talks on Shakespeare and other writers. When lyceum speaker Ralph Waldo Emerson lectured in the 1840s, he included Shakespeare among his six "Representative Geniuses"; in 1853 he came to Springfield, where he may have given his Shakespeare lecture. Some lecturers would perform Shakespearean readings in place of or in addition to analysis and commentary. As Esther Cloudman Dunn has noted, "Readings from Shakespeare [in the early nation] were a real rival to the production of the plays as a whole."[10] "Elocutionists," as these speaker-readers were sometimes called, "argued that the practice of reading great works aloud sharpens the mind and nurtures elocutionary talent."[11] One such elocutionist, James Murdoch, performed several nights of readings from the works of Shakespeare, Charles Dickens, and other writers in Springfield in January 1861; Lincoln almost certainly attended one and may have been present at both. Lincoln himself, of course, participated in oratorical activities from early on. Apart from purely political speeches, he prepared and sometimes delivered talks on various topics, most notably when he spoke, in 1838, at the Young Men's Lyceum, a place "where aspiring young men of the town tested their rhetorical skill and improved their elocution before their peers."[12] "Whether declaiming or debating," one writer has noted, "Lincoln appeared before audiences whose ears already rang with the oscillations between the bawdy insult of the political arena and the rhetorical flourish of training in classical rhetorical modes."[13] While there is nothing of Shakespeare, or any other literary text (though there is one New Testament quotation) in Lincoln's lyceum talk, it is this oratorical culture that, at least in part, would have attracted Lincoln and his contemporaries to the rhetorical richness of Shakespeare's plays.

In addition to school readers and lectures, Lincoln would have encountered Shakespeare in the theater. Unfortunately, little is known of his youthful theatergoing experience. Only when he became president did he have the opportunity to attend plays on a more or less regular basis, though there is no definitive evidence that he did so before 1863. Lincoln was fortunate to be in Washington as that city, though physically not much changed from the time of his previous habitation in 1847–1849, was becoming something more than the cultural backwater it had been for the first few decades of its existence. Famous American Shakespearean actors frequently came to the capital in the years of his presidency, from the aging stars of an earlier era, such as Edwin Forrest, to the emerging stars of the second half of the century, such as Edwin Booth, and the evidence suggests that Lincoln saw Shakespeare's plays whenever he could. In part because that was the taste of the time, and perhaps in part because of his own inclination, he sought out tragedies and histories primarily: *Hamlet, Othello, King Lear, Macbeth, Richard III,* and *Henry IV,* along with *The Merry Wives of Windsor* and *The Merchant of Venice.* Lincoln's attendance at the theater and his reaction to what he saw and heard was reported both in the press and in the diaries and reminiscences of those who accompanied him or happened to be present at a particular performance. We have firsthand accounts of his reactions to or comments on *The Merchant of Venice* with Edwin Booth, *King Lear* with Edwin Forrest, and *Macbeth* with Charlotte Cushman. As president, Lincoln also continued to attend readings, which often included Shakespeare.[14] James Murdoch, whom he had met in Springfield, became a fund-raiser and morale booster for Union troops and engaged in readings of Shakespeare and other writers in the capital as well as in the field, and his audience several times included the president.

That Lincoln so often attended Shakespeare productions insulated him to some degree from the condemnation of those who thought theater immoral and the president's attendance indecorous. Just as presidential vacations today can be criticized as irresponsible by political enemies and defended by political friends as necessary relief from the rigors of governing, Lincoln's playgoing was both regretted and justified. Lincoln's journalist friend Noah Brooks retrospectively made the case as well as anyone: "Those who are disposed to consider that Lincoln exhibited a frivolous side of his character by his play-going should reflect that the theater was almost the only place where

he could escape from the clamor of office-seekers, and for a moment un-
fix his thoughts from the cares and anxieties that weighed upon his spirit
with dreadful oppressiveness."[15] Theater manager Leonard Grover, employing a Shakespearean phrase, noted that Lincoln, no matter what he came
to see, "was satisfied with being entertained and amused, and to have his
mind taken from the sea of troubles which awaited him elsewhere."[16] After
Lincoln's assassination at Ford's Theatre, southern sympathizers and other
mean-spirited individuals suggested that he had got what he deserved for
going to see a play on Good Friday; that he had been killed by an actor could
be seen as further evidence of heavenly judgment. But for most Americans,
the fact that Lincoln was murdered while enjoying a well-earned moment of
relaxation and celebrating the war's end added to the poignancy of his tragically premature death.

Lincoln's interest in Shakespeare necessarily belongs to the wider history
of how Shakespeare's plays were received and understood in nineteenth-
century America. What Shakespeare's works have meant to Americans over
the last 400 years cannot be recovered fully, but it is fair to say that "since the
middle of the eighteenth century ... [the English playwright] has remained a
staple in America's cultural diet."[17] Much has been made of a somewhat cav-
alier remark in Alexis de Tocqueville's *Democracy in America*, an often-cited
guide to life in the United States in the 1830s, claiming that there was "hardly
a pioneer's hut that does not contain a few odd volumes of Shakespeare."
Tocqueville adds that he "read the feudal drama of *Henry V* for the first time
in a log cabin."[18] It is not entirely flippant to wonder just how many log cab-
ins Tocqueville visited on his travels. But we do not need to take this observation entirely at face value to accept the idea that the French observer was
pointing to a phenomenon actually present in American culture. We know,
from a variety of sources, that Shakespeare was read, quoted, and performed
in America by the early 1800s, even if attitudes toward the English poet were
not entirely unmixed. Another famous foreign traveler to America in the
1830s, Frances Trollope, discussing literature with an unnamed interlocutor
"said to be a scholar, and a man of reading," is told, "Shakespeare, madam,
is obscene, and, thank God, we are sufficiently advanced to have found it
out!"[19] In any case, from the early days of the Republic, if not earlier, Americans were familiar with and often cited at least the better-known of Shakespeare's works. Bardolatry, which can be roughly dated in Great Britain from
actor David Garrick's Shakespeare Jubilee of 1769, reached the shores of New
England and elsewhere quite soon afterward. A number of the Founding
Fathers were enthusiastic Shakespeareans. George Washington, an avid the-

atergoer, staged a production of *Julius Caesar* in the executive mansion in Philadelphia,[20] and he frequently cited Shakespeare in his writings; his letters were "filled with passing references to *Hamlet, Othello, The Merchant of Venice,* and *The Tempest*."[21] That John Adams and Thomas Jefferson together visited the Shakespeare birthplace in Stratford-upon-Avon suggests that, at least to these educated Americans, that humble abode had already become a shrine. What is of particular interest in Tocqueville's observation, however, is the implication that the appreciation of Shakespeare pervaded the entire social and economic spectrum.[22]

But Tocqueville, whatever weight we want to give to his words, does not really tell us all that much about the reading habits of early-nineteenth-century Americans; after all, many a family Bible sits on a shelf unread. The possession of Shakespeare's *Complete Works,* then or now, either in a frontier cabin or in a Virginia mansion, cannot guarantee close acquaintance with the contents. The more difficult question would be, How was Shakespeare known? What, for example, does it tell us that the *Massachusetts Spy,* a newspaper in colonial America, printed a parody that begins with the words "Be taxt or not be taxt—that is the question?"[23] Are we to assume that the paper believed its readers to have read *Hamlet?* Or, much more likely, that the phrase "to be or not to be" was already common currency, a well-worn cliché, 150 years after Shakespeare's death? An allusion to Hamlet's famous soliloquy, in other words, could suggest nothing more than that Shakespeare was well enough known, at least in bits and pieces, to inspire parody and burlesque. In this context, cultural historian Lawrence Levine has remarked on the difficulty of taking "familiarities with that which is not already familiar; one cannot parody that which is not well known."[24] This may serve well enough as a general principle, but in practice parody, pastiche, and burlesque can exist even when the audience is not familiar with the original, as the jokes of Jon Stewart and other television satirists sometimes demonstrate. There is a considerable distance between a paraphrase of Hamlet's soliloquy and a genuine familiarity with Shakespeare's melancholy Dane. At the other end of the cultural spectrum, and moving to Tocqueville's era, we find John Quincy Adams engaging in a sophisticated discussion of *Hamlet, Othello,* and other plays with the Shakespearean actor and later-to-be Lincoln "friend," J. H. Hackett.[25] Certainly, Shakespeare's works were known to the educated elite of the eighteenth and early nineteenth centuries. By the 1840s, when P. T. Barnum attempted to purchase Shakespeare's birthplace and bring it to New York, America's interest in Shakespeare, we may assume, was becoming more widespread; if anyone can be said to have had a finger on the pulse of American tastes, it was Barnum.

By the 1830s and 1840s, too, a select number of Shakespeare's plays were beginning to dominate the stage, accounting for "one-fifth to one quarter of performances."²⁶ For a variety of reasons—the Puritan resistance to theater, the mainly provincial origins of the early English settlers (relatively few were from London), the absence of any theater productions in England during the 1640 to 1660 interregnum, the alienation many colonists felt toward the mother country²⁷—virtually nothing in the way of Shakespearean stagings is known before the middle of the eighteenth century. The first reported professional production of Shakespeare (*Richard III*) dates from 1750, more than three decades after the first appearance of a Shakespeare text in America.²⁸ After the Revolution, however, theatrical activity flourished, and Shakespeare soon became established as a "draw." Although Levine no doubt exaggerates when he writes that "Shakespeare actually *was* popular entertainment in nineteenth-century America,"²⁹ the evidence suggest that the plays appealed to a wide range of readers and theatergoers, low-, middle-, and highbrow alike. As Levine goes on to remark, Americans in the mid-nineteenth century "shared a public culture less hierarchically organized, less fragmented into relatively rigid adjectival boxes than their descendants were to experience a century later."³⁰ Nonetheless, it is important to note that Shakespeare's "popularity" needs to be significantly qualified when considered in the context of such forms of theatrical presentation as satire and burlesque. Much of what passed as "Shakespeare" was not really Shakespeare at all, or was only obliquely or marginally so. When audiences in the mining camps of California went to see and hear Junius Brutus Booth in *Richard III* or *King Lear*, they were drawn by the overwhelming theatrical personality of the actor as much as, and perhaps more than, the words of Shakespeare—words that, in any case, were as much from Colley Cibber's (*Richard III*) and Nahum Tate's (*King Lear*) eighteenth-century adaptations as they were from Shakespeare. One might even argue that the movement from lowbrow to highbrow that Levine traces was not so much a matter of changing audience taste as it was a change in Shakespeare: new and better editions of the texts and restorations by actors and producers of the plays more or less as originally written meant that a less easily accessed Shakespeare came to the fore, replacing, even if never entirely erasing, the "popular" Shakespeare of earlier decades.

References to Shakespeare can also be found both in the congressional debates and unofficial political discourse of the time, much of which would have been familiar to Lincoln. A number of the men who populated the halls of Congress were of the educated elite, but even members not well educated could cite Shakespeare. In the course of the debates over the Missouri Compromise, "senators and congressmen who more often than not lacked college educations spoke from the barest of notes (or none at all) for hours on end, and were confident that their colleagues and the public would understand them, in speeches that were peppered with allusions to Shakespeare, the Bible, American history, British common law, and classical literature."[31] Shakespeare allusions are employed by virtually all the major participants, either in debate or in personal correspondence: Henry Clay ("Meantime some of the Hotspurs of the South are openly declaring themselves for a dissolution of the Union, if the Wilmot Proviso be adopted," *Henry IV, Part 1*), William Seward ("You may slay the Wilmot Proviso in the Senate chamber, and bury it beneath the Capitol today; the dead corse, in complete steel, will haunt your legislative halls tomorrow," *Hamlet*), Thomas Hart Benton ("It is giving a government and leaving out the people! It is the play of Hamlet—the part of Hamlet left out!"), and Stephen Douglas (writing of Clay, "But let it be said of old Hal that he fought a glorious & a patriotic battle," *Henry IV*).[32] Lincoln's political heroes—Clay, Daniel Webster—were familiar with the plays and dropped references to them both in formal speeches and in casual conversation. Clay, like Adams and Jefferson before him, visited Shakespeare's birthplace in Stratford-upon-Avon. Alluding to the notoriety of Peggy O'Neil Eaton, the wife of Jackson's secretary of war, John Eaton, Clay quipped, "Age cannot wither, nor custom stale her infinite virginity."[33] John Eaton, too, could cite Shakespeare against a political enemy, in this instance John C. Calhoun: "The time will come when the victims of his policy shall rise before him," Eaton wrote, "like the shades which appalled the insidious and heartless usurper Richard, to disturb his slumbers and to drive peace from him."[34] We cannot, of course, entirely gauge the extent or depth of knowledge represented by this or that quotation from Shakespeare, but taken together these allusions suggest an easy familiarity with at least parts of the canon.

Allusions to Shakespeare, his plays having become by midcentury a species of cultural capital, could lend authority to any writer or speaker, serving quite different functions depending on the occasion.[35] For the political elite, an exchange of Shakespearean language was a form of mutual recognition. But Shakespeare is not always cited primarily to make points: an offhand allusion, unidentified, suggests the pervasive presence of Shakespearean sentiment that may not even enter into the consciousness of the user. An interesting example of this is the phrase "the tented field" ("For since these arms of mine had seven years' pith, . . . / they have used / Their dearest action in the tented field," *Othello*, act 1, scene 3),[36] which occurs as a passing allusion in quite different contexts. In itself an unremarkable expression, a periphrasis for "military experience" ("at the bidding of their government, they left the plough for the tented field"),[37] it nevertheless carries a certain compressed elegance of meaning. Thomas Jefferson could use the phrase as a less alarming substitute for "going to war"; if peace is not possible, he wrote, "we must again take the tented field, as we did in 1776."[38] When South Carolina congressman Robert Barnwell Rhett spoke of "the stern realities of the tented field," the phrase was a contribution to a rhetoric of secession.[39] When the president of the New York Fire Department sent Lincoln's friend Elmer Ellsworth and his First Fire Zouaves into battle with the words "We know that, whether in the midst of burning cities, or in the tented field, you will sustain your own high character, and these banners will ever wave in triumph, even though it be in the midst of ruins,"[40] it was an encouragement to quench the flames of rebellion. On a less exalted level, a comic writer Lincoln particularly enjoyed reading, Petroleum V. Nasby (the nom de plume of David Ross Locke), writes in an 1862 essay, "I see in the papers last nite, that the Goverment hez institooted a draft, and that in a few weeks, sum hunderds uv thousands uv peeseable citizens will be dragged to the tented feeld."[41] Nasby in his ironic fashion here zeroes in on the way Shakespeare's words had evolved into a pompous euphemism.

A famous moment in the history of American political debate, however, suggests a richer and more complex engagement with Shakespeare than the passing references cited above.[42] In January 1830, Senator Daniel Webster of Massachusetts engaged with Senator Robert Hayne of South Carolina in an exchange that would reverberate throughout the following decades; ostensibly about the sale of public lands, the debate came to focus on sectionalism and the value of the Union in the wake of the Nullification Crisis. Of particular note here is Hayne's First Reply to Webster. In the course of several paragraphs, Hayne quotes, cites, and paraphrases Shakespeare a half dozen times. Rhetorically questioning Webster, Hayne asks, "Has the gentleman's distempered fancy been disturbed by gloomy forebodings of 'new alliances to be formed' at which he hinted? Has the ghost of the murdered Coalition come back, like the ghost of Banquo, to 'sear the eye-balls of the gentleman,' and will it not 'down at his bidding'?"[43] It would be interesting to know what books Hayne had available to him when he prepared his reply to Webster. Did he have Shakespeare's plays? Did he have a copy of the newly published *Bartlett's Familiar Quotations*? Or was he relying on his memory? It would not need recourse to a text, certainly, to make an allusion to Banquo's ghost: *Macbeth* was one of the most popular plays on stage at that time and, like

Hamlet's "To be or not to be," the ghost at the feast can be assumed to have been well-known, both to Hayne and to his listeners. That same ghost finds its way into a political argument over slavery: in 1828, a New York congressman, arguing that slaves could not be considered property, paraphrases from *Macbeth* to ask rhetorically, "Is the ghost of the Missouri question again to be marched, with solemn and terrific aspect, through these halls? Is it again to 'shake its gory locks' at us, and, pointing with one hand to the North, and with the other to the South, and gazing its blood-shotten eye on slavery, written on the escutcheon of the Constitution, to proclaim with unearthly voice, 'out damned spot'?"[44] Horace Mann, in 1851, referring to Daniel Webster's support of the Fugitive Slave Act, wondered "whether the political Macbeth shall succeed to the Banquo he spirited away, though all the 'weird' brethren of the slave mart and of the 'Union and Safety committees' still tempt him onward by their incantations."[45]

Hayne goes on to quote from or cite other Shakespeare plays, and here we can be fairly certain that, in addition to what he might have been able to recall from earlier reading, some more recent turning of pages must have taken place. Alluding to *Henry IV, Part 1*, Hayne remarks, "I doubt not the gentleman feels very much, in relation to the tariff, as a certain knight did to, instinct,' and with him would be disposed to exclaim—'Ah! no more of that, Hal, an' thou lovest me.'" (118). A few paragraphs later, Hayne turns to *Othello*: "We solemnly declare that we believe the system to be wholly unconstitutional, and a violation of the compact between the States and the Union; and our brethren turn a deaf ear to our complaints, and refuse to relieve us from a system 'which not enriches them, but makes us poor indeed'" (119). In quick succession, Hayne cites *Julius Caesar* ("Sir, if the gentleman had stopped there, the accusation would have 'passed by me like the idle wind, which I regard not,'" 119) and *A Midsummer Night's Dream* ("But when he goes on to give to his accusation a local habitation, and a name," 119). Later, he cites a familiar *Hamlet* quotation, one that, according to William Herndon, was a favorite of Lincoln's ("But a wise and just Providence, which 'shapes our ends, rough hew them as we will,' gave us the victory, and crowned our efforts with a glorious peace," 134), but he follows it with what can only be considered a remarkably obscure and at the same time bizarre Shakespeare allusion: "It mattered not whether the gift was bestowed on Towser or Sweetlips, 'Tray, Blanche, or Sweetheart'" (138). Even someone quite familiar with Shakespeare's plays would have to jog his or her memory to remember that "Tray, Blanche, or Sweetheart" are the names of King Lear's (imaginary?) dogs. And why does Hayne mention these canines at all? The phrase comes as mere decoration: Hayne, having quoted John Randolph's observation that "the power of conferring favors creates a crowd of dependents," merely adds Shakespeare's dogs to the generic names Towser and Sweetlips. The *King Lear* reference, in short, is completely unnecessary and may simply be an example of a kind of stream of consciousness flow on Hayne's part: the reference to hounds makes him think of Lear's dogs, he recalls their names, and more or less for his own amusement, includes them in his parse of Randolph's remark. It is possible, of course, that the allusion may have meant something quite specific to Hayne's hearers that we can no longer recover. Lear's dogs, curiously enough, are mentioned in another comment on Peggy O'Neill Eaton and her husband: we read in the *Washington Globe* for July 26, 1831, that the Eatons would remain in Washington so long as "the kennel corps, Tray, Blanch and Sweetheard [*sic*], growl and bark so fiercely."[46] Even if the allusion had a meaning in the 1830s that we no longer have access to, that would in itself suggest a sophisticated employment of Shakespeare, one that goes beyond common knowledge or familiar quotation.

Hayne's literary citations and allusions also illustrate the possible pitfalls of employing Shakespeare in argument. Webster, in what is known as the Second Reply to Hayne, was quick to suggest that Hayne's references to Banquo's ghost were off the mark. "But . . . the honorable member was not . . . entirely happy in his allusion to the story of Banquo's murder, and Banquo's ghost. It was not, I think, the friends, but the enemies of the murdered Banquo, at whose bidding his spirit would not *down*."

> The honorable gentleman [Webster continues] is fresh in his reading of the English classics, and can put me right if I am wrong; but, according to my poor recollection it was at those who had begun with caresses, and ended with foul and treacherous murder, that the gory locks were shaken. The ghost of Banquo, like that of Hamlet, was an honest ghost. It disturbed no innocent man. . . . It made itself visible in the right quarter, and compelled the guilty, and the conscience-smitten, and none others, to start, with,
>
> > Pr'ythee, see there! behold—look! lo,
> > If I stand here, I saw him! . . .
>
> I have misread the great poet if those who had no way partaken in the deed of the death, either found that they were, *or feared that they should be*, pushed from their stools by the ghost of the slain, or exclaimed to a

spectre created by their own fears and their own remorse, 'Avaunt! and quit our sight!'[47]

Webster then strings together a number of citations and quotations from *Macbeth*:

Did not even-handed justice ere long commend the poisoned chalice to their own lips? Did they not soon find that for another they had "filed their mind"? that their ambition, though apparently for the moment successful, had but put a barren sceptre in their grasp? Ay, sir,

> "A barren sceptre in their gripe,
> Thence to be wrenched by an unlineal hand,
> No son of theirs succeeding."

Sir, I need pursue the allusion no farther. I leave the honorable gentleman to run it out at his leisure, and to derive from it all the gratification it is calculated to administer.[48]

Webster, with self-satisfied irony, makes it clear that a misquotation, or quoting out of context, can be dangerous, and that two can play the game of citing Shakespeare to support or clinch an argument.

Another kind of political discourse, satirical cartoons, made use of Shakespeare in the contentious politics and electoral atmosphere of the first half of the nineteenth century. The popularity of Shakespeare's history plays, *Richard III* in particular, encouraged pointed commentary associating ambitious politicians with Shakespearean monarchs. Andrew Jackson, Henry Clay, and John C. Calhoun, among others, were sometimes portrayed in cartoons depicting "Shakespearean" scenes, such as one from the 1828 election depicting Jackson as Richard with a caption reading, "Methought the souls of all that I had murdere'd came to my tent."[49] Another, captioned "The assassination of the Sage of Ashland," from 1848, shows Clay about to receive multiple dagger thrusts from his erstwhile Whig associates, who speak phrases from *Julius Caesar* as they prepare to stab him. In "The hurly-burly pot," from 1850, publisher Horace Greely, congressman David Wilmot, and abolitionist William Lloyd Garrison are portrayed as *Macbeth*'s witches, stirring the pot of disunion as they utter variations of "Bubble, bubble, toil and trouble!" while the aging Calhoun eggs them on. The witches's cauldron from *Macbeth* reappears in a cartoon print, from sometime during the presidency of James

Buchanan, captioned "A proslavery incantation scene, or Shakespeare Improved." This cartoon shows Buchanan and a group of unidentified proslavery supporters burning a variety of documents in a cauldron as they chant "Double double, Free state trouble. Till Fremont men are straw & stubble," together with a number of variations of like nature.

But no previous president or politician would be as frequently caricatured as Lincoln was, and a number of these cartoons, both pro and anti, placed him in a Shakespearean context.[50] In one of the earliest of these, "Et tu, Greely," published soon after the 1860 Republican Convention in Chicago, a very dark-skinned and proportionally small "Lincoln," the very image of a "black Republican," plays a secondary role (he is not even identified in the caption) as Pompeii's statue, overseeing the death of William (Caesar) Seward, murdered by Horace Greely and other of Seward's former supporters. Lincoln plays a larger role in a preelection cartoon from 1860, "The Smothering of the Democratic Princes," from *Frank Leslie's Budget of Fun*. Alluding to *Richard III*, the cartoonist shows "Catesby Lincoln" as one of Shakespeare's two assassins smothering presidential candidates John Bell and John C. Breckenridge with a "pillow" in the shape of Stephen Douglas labeled "Squatter Sovereignty." (The politics here are sufficiently oblique that a thirty-line poem has been appended to explain the imagery.) Almost immediately after the election, the cartoonist Henry L. Stephens, in *Vanity Fair*, drew on *Much Ado about Nothing* for "Dogberry's Last Charge," a parody of the upcoming presidential transition in which Buchanan is cast as Shakespeare's comically inept watchman, Dogberry, and Lincoln as his equally inept deputy, Seacoal; the caption includes a direct quotation from Shakespeare's play in which Seacoal is described as "the most senseless and fit man for the constable of the watch," which makes clear that, in the opinion of *Vanity Fair*, one incompetent was giving way to another.[51]

As president, Lincoln became the target of a wide variety of comic and satirical portraits, not only in the United States, in both the North and the South, but in Great Britain as well. One particularly elaborate, if at times oblique, attack from 1864 on the entire Lincoln administration is the print entitled "Behind the Scenes," purporting to be a rehearsal for *Othello* with Lincoln, in blackface (and black body), in the starring role.[52] *Othello* was one of the most frequently burlesqued of Shakespeare's plays in the nineteenth century, reflecting both the fragile balance of tragic and potentially farcical elements in the play itself and the fascination with and fear of blackness generated by the slavery crisis. Lincoln was variously portrayed either as "black" himself (as in "Et tu, Greely," mentioned above) or as burdened by various

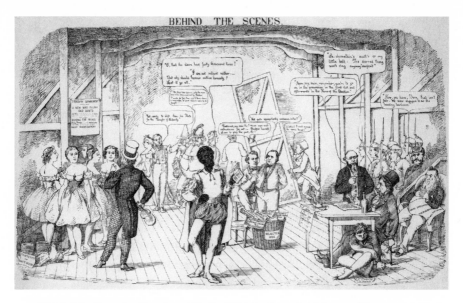

"Behind the Scenes"—Lincoln as Othello. 1864 election print. Library of Congress.

black figures either weighing him down or pulling him toward a right or wrong action, depending on the satirist. Lincoln-Othello, seemingly reading from the text of the play in his hand, here speaks several lines from different scenes: "O, that the slave had forty thousand lives! I am not valiant neither:— But why should honour outlive honesty? Let it go all." The dialogue balloons make reference to other Shakespeare plays, as when Union general Benjamin F. Butler, in a Falstaff costume, is made to say (combining disparate lines from *Henry IV, Part 1*), "We that take purses, go by the moon and seven stars; and not by Phoebus! I would to God, thou and I knew where a commodity of good names were to be bought!"—a reference to Butler's alleged rapacity. The satire is presented in a scattershot way, with members of Lincoln's cabinet and others, including Andrew Johnson, all targets of scurrilous representations. Although it cannot be precisely dated, this print is clearly aimed at Lincoln's 1864 reelection campaign. In another print from the same period, Lincoln plays a decidedly secondary Shakespearean role—Yorick's skull—to Democratic presidential candidate George B. McClellan's Hamlet. "I knew him, Horatio: A fellow of infinite jest. . . . Where be your gibes now?," McClellan says, as Peace Democrat and New York governor Horatio Seymour looks on. The immediate context may have been a story in the *New York World* accusing Lincoln of inexcusable levity when touring the Antietam battlefield, but whatever the occasion, Lincoln's reputation as jester has seldom been so cleverly and acidly presented.[53]

"I KNEW HIM, HORATIO; A FELLOW OF INFINITE JEST. * * * WHERE BE YOUR GIBES NOW?—*Hamlet, Act IV., Scene* 1.

Lincoln as Yorick's skull, with George B. McClellan as Hamlet and Horatio Seymour as Horatio. 1864 election print. Library of Congress.

Perhaps unsurprisingly, it was English publications like *Punch* that were most likely to employ Shakespearean allusions in political cartoons, particularly those featuring Lincoln. From time to time, those cartoons—at least the most negative ones—found their way into Southern newspapers; as Gary Bunker notes, "England's image makers were the primary sculptors of [Lincoln's] pejorative international reputation."[54] Several of these images are particularly memorable because they are so well executed. In a November 9, 1861, cartoon captioned "The Genu-ine Othello," John Tenniel (the illustrator of *Alice's Adventures in Wonderland*) shows a surprisingly dignified-looking black man telling both North and South, "Keep up your bright swords, for de dew will rust dem. . . . Both you ob my inclining, and de rest." Lincoln, whose expression in this first appearance in *Punch* only hints at the "malice, vulgarity, and cunning" that would sometimes characterize Tenniel's drawings of the American president, is here depicted in a "Brother Jonathan/ Uncle Sam" manner.[55] In the April 5, 1862, issue of *Punch*, Lincoln as Oberon demands of Titania (Miss Virginia) "a little nigger boy, to be my henchman" (*A Midsummer Night's Dream*, act 2, scene 1), the casual racism contrasting with the elegance of the draftsmanship. Tenniel's drawing was a comment

THE GENU-INE OTHELLO.

OTHELLO.—" *Keep up your bright swords, for de dew will rust dem.* * * * * *Both you ob my inclining, and de rest.*"

"The Genu-ine Othello"—An English View. John Hay Library, Brown University.

on Lincoln's plan for compensated emancipation, but, minus the caption, it could almost be an illustration for Shakespeare's play, even if the bearded image of Oberon clothed in a costume of stars and stripes seems a bit out of place. The specificity and ironic appropriateness of the allusion to *A Midsummer Night's Dream*, a play only infrequently presented on the American stage, testifies to the educated middle- and upper-class readership *Punch* enjoyed.

A Tenniel cartoon entitled "Scene from the American 'Tempest,'" published in the wake of the Emancipation Proclamation, shows "Caliban (Sambo)" pointing to his presumed Confederate master and telling Lincoln, "You beat him 'nough, Massa! Berry little time, I'll beat him too," a paraphrase from the play identified in the caption as "Nigger Translation." (Tenniel here anticipates the twentieth-century postcolonial interpretation of Caliban as an African slave.) Although Tenniel's drawing of Lincoln is hardly flattering, the

OBERON AND TITANIA.

OBERON (MR. PRESIDENT LINCOLN). "I DO BUT BEG A LITTLE **NIGGER** BOY,
TO BE MY HENCHMAN."

TITANIA (MISS VIRGINIA). "SET YOUR HEART AT REST,
THE **NORTHERN** LAND BUYS NOT THE CHILD OF ME."

Lincoln as Oberon. John Hay Library, Brown University.

association with Shakespeare's Prospero, an image of fair-minded if severe authority, makes it possible to see the cartoon overall as "perhaps among the most benevolent images on emancipation published in Punch,"[56] which, however, is not saying very much. Tenniel places Lincoln in a Shakespearean context one final time (August 15, 1863), presenting a particularly loutish, disreputable image of him as Brutus in his tent, the ever-popular Joe Miller joke book in hand, with a youth (Shakespeare's Lucius), a black boy with banjo and minstrelsy costume, sleeping nearby. The ghost of Caesar is an imposing black man, albeit with a stereotypically "comical" face, who tells Lincoln, "I am dy ebil genus, massa Linking. Dis child am awful Inimpressional." Though the general thrust of the cartoon perhaps refers to the failure of Lincoln's emancipation policies, the exact context is unclear. That this cartoon was reprinted in the *Southern Illustrated News* on October 31 suggests that, whatever its precise meaning, Southerners found Tenniel's satire useful to their cause.

Whether experienced in the context of politics and oratory or in the privacy of the parlor or study, the language of Shakespeare's plays was in the atmosphere Lincoln breathed while he lived on what was still considered to be the American frontier. It is possible, as Fred Kaplan suggests,[57] that Lincoln and Mary Todd read Shakespeare to each other when they were courting. In an 1841 letter to a friend, Mary, presumably alluding to Lincoln's mental state in the winter of 1840–1841, expresses the wish that "he [Lincoln] would once more resume his Station in Society, that 'Richard should be himself again,' much, much happiness would it afford me."[58] (She is, however, quoting not from Shakespeare's *Richard III* but from one of the most famous passages in Colley Cibber's adaptation.) By the time Lincoln became president, he benefited from, but was not intimidated by, being surrounded by men who were better educated than he and whose knowledge of literature exceeded his own. To take only one example, young John Hay, graduate of Brown University (where he was elected Class Poet), alluded to Shakespeare, directly or indirectly, in letters, in speeches, and even in the privacy of his diary. Commenting on a meeting between Lincoln and some Maryland disunionists, he joked that "their [the Marylanders'] roaring was exquisitely modulated." On second thought, he crosses out the whole phrase and writes, "They roared as gently as twere any nightingale," a surprising but apt use of a line from *A Midsummer Night's Dream*.[59] Writing to John Nicolay, his friend and Lincoln's chief secretary, he quotes from *Richard III* (incorporating the words of Colley Cibber): "Blair says Armstrong shall eat dirt or 'off goes his head, so much for Buckingham.'"[60] In a letter to the writer Nora Perry, a Brown University friend, he remarks, commenting on the dreariness of Springfield, that Shakespeare's Dogberry "ought to have been an Illinoisan."[61] In the course of his 1871 obituary remarks for Tad Lincoln, he remembered that as a boy Tad "was always a 'chartered libertine,' and after the death of his brother Willie, a prematurely serious and studious child," the quoted phrase a rather obscure allusion to *Henry V* (act 1, scene 1).[62] Of a California senator killed in a duel, Hay directly alludes to *Hamlet*: "But there was that within the hearts of Broderick's friends, like the anguish of the royal Dane, 'passing show.'"[63] Citing or referring to Shakespeare came naturally to Hay.

By midcentury, educated Americans like Hay had become so familiar with Shakespeare that some of them wanted to adopt him as an honorary citizen. "During the nineteenth century," Kim Sturgess writes, "Americans learnt to use the possessive pronoun 'our' when referring to Shakespeare, something not done with other foreign writers."[64] The poet William Cullen Bryant believed that "Americans may . . . claim an equal property in the great English poet with those who remained in the Old World."[65] An 1850 English edition of Shakespeare, reprinted in New York, contains this appeal to the American reader: "Shakespeare—a name which belongs as much to Saxon America as Saxon England—especially adapted to the American public."[66] Charles King Newcomb, who was associated with Emerson and other New England transcendentalists, believed Shakespeare to be, "in some respects, more of an American than he is of an Englishman." Shakespeare, Newcomb added,

> belonged to the age in which the tide of principles began to turn & swell, that, at its full, in the next age, surged to New England & was there received on the congenial shores of nascent democracy, whilst it subsided in the relatively uncongenial & hardened spheres of old England. In his English Historical Plays he showed English loyalty, English tenderness for royal tradition, & English conservatism, but, also, unbiased regard for the energy & general fitness for office which is one of the early prognostics of republicanism.[67]

"How wondrous, how universal is the fame of Shakespeare!" a newspaper theater reviewer wrote in 1855. "Generation after generation is entranced by his genius. Nation after nation rejoices in celebrating his works. . . . But in no land, not even in his own, is he so deeply loved and so deeply reverenced by so large a number as in America."[68] We can sense here an oddly divided attitude toward this greatest of English poets: on the one hand, he represents the culture and refinement of the Old World and reminds some Americans of the relative poverty of their own literary culture; on the other hand, Shakespeare is seen as not really English at all, and his plays in fact offer a critique of the undemocratic, stultifying culture of Great Britain. So *Richard III*, which presents a damning view of the English monarchy, was a perennial favorite on American stages, whereas *Henry V*, with its seeming jingoism, was seldom performed.

The question of Shakespeare's "nationality" exploded dramatically in what has come to be known as the Astor Place Riot. On the evening of May 10, 1849, the popular American-born actor Edwin Forrest (whom Lincoln would see as Lear in 1864) was playing Macbeth at the Broadway Theatre while an English visitor, William Charles Macready, was playing the same role at the Astor Opera House (a theater at that time comanaged by Lincoln's future acquaintance James H. Hackett). Not only was there personal bad blood between the two Shakespearean tragedians (Forrest had, three years earlier, loudly hissed a Macready performance of Hamlet in Edinburgh), but their rivalry also reflected the combustible class division that roiled Manhattan life at the time. Simplifying things considerably, one can suggest that Forrest, a hero of Jacksonian democracy, was popular with the working class and with immigrants, while Macready was favored by the older, nativist element and the well-to-do of the city.[69] For several nights, Forrest's followers mobbed the Astor Opera House, both inside and out, creating such a disturbance that Macready's Macbeth could not be heard. By the night of May 10, the rioting had become sufficiently threatening that the militia was called in and, in the ensuing confusion, some twenty-five to thirty or more (accounts differ) protestors were killed and many others were wounded. The Astor Place Riot has gone down in history as the most destructive public protest in the United States up to that time, and was also the first time a militia was called out to put down a civic disturbance. (It is probably no coincidence that this riot took place in the wake of the 1848 revolutions in Europe.) That such a tragic event could have been brought about by the performances of two actors in *Macbeth* says much about both the centrality and the contested nature of Shakespeare in nineteenth-century American life.[70]

Both Emerson and Whitman, eminent nineteenth-century literary and cultural figures who in different ways have been associated with Abraham Lincoln,[71] commented directly on the value of Shakespeare for America. Emerson believed that Shakespeare "wrote the text of modern life; the text of manners: he drew the man of England and Europe; the father of the man in America: he drew the man, and described the day, and what is done in it."[72] Though the syntax is somewhat obscure, Emerson seems to be claiming

Shakespeare for America and for the modernity that America exemplified. Whitman, whose comments and observations on Shakespeare, formal and informal, stretch over more than a half century, could not decide if the English poet could have value for America. On the one hand, Whitman writes, while "it seems a shame to pick and choose from the riches Shakspere has left us—to criticise his infinitely royal, multiform quality—to gauge, with optic glasses, the dazzle of his sun-like beams," Shakespeare nevertheless represented the feudal, aristocratic world that was the antithesis of America: "For all [Shakespeare] stands for so much in modern literature, he stands entirely for the mighty aesthetic sceptres of the past, not for the spiritual and democratic, the sceptres of the future."[73] Ultimately, this ambivalence, which was not Whitman's alone (Herman Melville, too, worried that an "absolute and unconditional adoration of Shakespeare [had] grown to be a part of our Anglo Saxon superstitions"),[74] would be resolved, in the words of Gail Kern Paster, in favor of "the quintessentially American belief that England's National Poet, properly understood, was a spokesman for republican values and a symbol, in his life's remarkable history and achievement, of the American commonplace that extraordinary talents might have unexpected origins."[75] Although Lincoln was perhaps unconscious of the tension at the heart of America's embrace of Shakespeare, he would, over time, find his own way of adopting Shakespeare's imaginative world into a program of self-education and personal resource that began with his boyhood on the frontier and would continue to the end of his life.

Lincoln Reads Shakespeare

"Last night . . . I went with [the president] to the Soldiers' Home," noted John Hay, Abraham Lincoln's young secretary, in his diary entry for Sunday, August 23, 1863, "& he read Shakespeare to me, the end of Henry VI and the beginning of Richard III till my heavy eye-lids caught his considerate notice & he sent me to bed."[1] Hay's amusing anecdote is one among many testifying to the enjoyment Lincoln found in reading and discussing the plays of William Shakespeare. Throughout his life, and particularly in the years of his presidency, Lincoln often turned to Shakespeare's plays for intellectual stimulation and emotional support.[2] And yet Shakespeare is only infrequently mentioned or cited in Lincoln's speeches and writings. Daniel Kilham Dodge, who was one of the first to make a thorough study of Lincoln's literary style, found that "the number of quotations from Shakspere is even smaller than that from the Bible. . . . When we consider the ample testimony of [Francis] Carpenter, [Noah] Brooks and others to Lincoln's habit of introducing passages of Shakspere in his conversation, this comparative neglect of his favorite poet in his writings is remarkable."[3] Dodge also found that "Lincoln did not, as a rule, quote freely and some of his speeches do not contain any quotation."[4] Although Dodge did not identify every Shakespeare quotation or allusion in Lincoln's writings, his general conclusion cannot be seriously challenged. Consequently, much of what we know, or think we know, of what Shakespeare meant to Lincoln necessarily derives from a mixed bag of stories and anecdotes of varying reliability. Some, like Hay's, were recorded at firsthand by close friends or associates, while others were recalled and written down many years after Lincoln's death by people far removed in time and place from the events they describe.

The evidence for Lincoln's abiding interest in Shakespeare is nevertheless extensive and, at least in its general drift, incontestable, ranging from the testimony of friends and acquaintances of his youth to that of Civil War officers, White House secretaries, theater practitioners, journalists and politicians. Many of the best-known stories were gathered and reproduced in various essays and books over the years, a number of them filled out with circumstantial detail and other adornments of little evidentiary value. Repeated over and over, these accounts, seldom seriously questioned, have taken on a life and veracity of their own and have made a notable contribution to Lincoln lore. Although similar versions of the same incident might be thought to reinforce each other, the opposite may be the case, as each story or anecdote does not so much confirm as derive from the ever-growing myth. The general and undoubted belief that Lincoln was familiar with Shakespeare gives rise to instances that support and contribute to that belief. As all students of Lincoln know, however, even the most promising firsthand account can be misleading. Without entirely dismissing what might be thought marginal evidence, I will here focus primarily on Lincoln's own words as written down by him or as recorded contemporaneously by acquaintances and associates in diaries and letters. I will also rely on public information from newspapers and other more or less "official" sources when those references are closely contemporary to the events they describe or report.[5]

We have evidence from early on in Lincoln's social life and political career that he was sufficiently immersed in Shakespeare's writings as to employ quotations and citations effectively. Like other writers, politicians, and orators of the nineteenth century, Lincoln sometimes alluded to Shakespeare in passing, citing a phrase or line so commonplace as not to require identification. Such offhand references belong more or less to what might be called a *Bartlett's Familiar Quotations* category—phrases that, long detached from context, have become so established in the language that they are transformed into "wise saws" with a meaning or meanings of their own. "Neither a borrower nor lender be," "more in the breach than the observance," "the quality of mercy is not strained," "discretion is the better part of valor"— all of these are in *Bartlett's Familiar Quotations*, the first edition of which was privately published in 1855 and which was reprinted in a more widely distributed edition in 1856. Dropping such phrases, some of them misquotations, into a text does not require a familiarity with Shakespeare's plays and poems. When in a speech in the House of Representatives, Lincoln referred to Zachary Taylor as "the noblest Roman of them all," he was simply drawing on a common currency, employing a well-worn cliché rather than consciously citing *Julius Caesar* (though the phrase, surprisingly, is not cited in the second edition of *Bartlett*, from 1856).[6] Similarly, when, in a letter to his friend Mrs. Orville Browning, Lincoln ungallantly wrote of Mary Owens, his erstwhile sweetheart (whom he does not identify), "I knew she was oversize, but she now appeared a fair match for Falstaff,"[7] he was not necessarily revealing anything about his reading of Shakespeare; Falstaff enjoyed a fame in common parlance extending well beyond his role in three of Shakespeare's plays. And Lincoln employed another familiar Shakespeare allusion in an 1848 letter alluding to the end of the Mexican War: "I suppose 'Othello's occupations gone'—All hands here seem to think the war is over."[8]

A less commonplace citation comes from Lincoln's remarks at the Great Central Sanitary Fair in Philadelphia (June 16, 1864): "War, at the best, is terrible, and this war of ours, in its magnitude and in its duration, is one of the most terrible. . . . It has carried mourning to almost every home, until it can almost be said that the 'heavens are hung in black.'"[9] "Hung be the heavens with black" is a line from one of Shakespeare's most obscure works, *Henry VI, Part 1*, but it is a play Lincoln may have read (we know, from Hay, that he read from *Henry VI, Part 3*); the phrase, in any case, was familiar enough to be in *Bartlett's*. A possible allusion to *Hamlet* appears in a line from Lincoln's poem "My Childhood Home I See Again": "Ere yet the rising god of day / Had streaked the Eastern Hill,"[10] echoing Shakespeare's "the morn in russet mantle clad / Walks o'er the dew of yon high eastward hill" (act 1, scene 1, lines 166–167). There are instances, too, when a phrase or expression seems so apropos to a particular occasion that there is no reason to assume it comes from Shakespeare at all, though it is certainly tempting to discover an allusion to *Henry V's* St. Crispin Day oration in one of Lincoln's earliest recorded speeches: "We meet here to break down that difference—to unite, like a band of brothers, for the welfare of the common country."[11] "Band of brothers" was very probably a conventional expression in Lincoln's time, particularly in political discourse.[12]

At other times, Lincoln either identifies his source or quotes a passage of sufficient length as to make his allusion to Shakespeare unambiguous. An early example, if indeed he was the author, comes from the anonymous "Sampson's Ghost" letters that some scholars believe Lincoln sent to the *Sangamo Journal* in June 1837. One letter was in the form of a burlesque entitled "A Ghost! A Ghost!" that began with a slightly garbled quotation from *Hamlet*: "Art thou some spirit or goblin damn'd— / Bringst with thee airs from heaven or blasts from hell?"[13] A rather more obscure quotation comes from a December 10, 1856, speech at the Republican Banquet in Chicago. Speaking of James Buchanan, Lincoln remarked, "He is in the cat's paw. By much dragging of chestnuts from the fire for others to eat, his claws are burnt off to the gristle, and he is thrown aside as unfit for further use. As the fool said to King Lear, when his daughters had turned him out of doors, 'He's a shelled pea's cod.'"[14] Lincoln is paraphrasing (the line is "That's a shelled peascod"; *King Lear*, act 1, scene 4), but in any case the original phrase was hardly a well-known one (it's not in the 1856 *Bartlett's*), which would suggest that he is remembering the line from his reading of the play. Exact quotations of more than a few words are rarer. Writing to a young officer court-martialed for, among other things, taking part in a duel, Lincoln writes, "The advice of a father to his son, 'Beware of entrance to a quarrel, but being in, bear it that the opposed may beware of thee,' is good and yet not the best. Quarrel not at all. No man resolved to make the most of himself, can spare time for personal contention."[15] In this instance, one can almost see Lincoln reaching for his Shakespeare. Though *Bartlett's*, which does not appear to have been in the White House library, includes parts of Polonius's speech (*Hamlet*, act 1, scene 3), it does not reproduce these particular lines. The passage is quoted exactly as it would have appeared in almost any edition of Shakespeare's plays.[16]

A carefully chosen handful of quotations from Shakespeare comes in Lincoln's crucial 1854 address in Peoria, Illinois, attacking the Kansas-Nebraska Act, which, as Dodge long ago noted, has more quotations than any other of Lincoln's speeches.[17] At one point, Lincoln employs a phrase from *Hamlet* that, though printed within quotation marks and set as a separate paragraph (evidently by Lincoln himself),[18] is not otherwise identified:

> Much as I hate slavery, I would consent to the extension of it rather than see the Union dissolved, just as I would consent to any GREAT evil, to avoid a GREATER one. But when I go to Union saving, I must believe, at least, that the means I employ has some adaptation to the end. To my mind, Nebraska has no such adaptation.
> "It hath no relish of salvation in it."
> It is an aggravation, rather, of the only one thing which ever endangers the Union.[19]

The quoted phrase is not in *Bartlett's Familiar Quotations*,[20] though by the end of the nineteenth century it does appear in dictionaries as a usage example for the word "relish." Interestingly, the line comes just after one of Lincoln's favorite passage from *Hamlet*, Claudius's soliloquy and prayer. In this speech, which exhibits more Shakespeare citations than the rest of Lincoln's speeches put together, he also cites or quotes from *Macbeth*. Dodge writes that the following words, where Lincoln countered the claim that the Nebraska bill was not intended to and would not extend slavery, "suggest" *Macbeth*: "Like the 'bloody hand' you may wash it, and wash it, the red witness of guilt still sticks, and stares horribly at you."[21] Even though the words "bloody hand" are in quotation marks, they do not appear together in *Macbeth* (though they appear together several times in *King Lear* and once in *Julius Caesar*), but Lincoln's sentence, taken as a whole, makes the allusion sure:

> Come, seeling night,
> Scarf up the tender eye of pitiful day
> And with thy bloody and invisible hand
> Cancel and tear to pieces that great bond
> Which keeps me pale.
> (*Macbeth*, act 3, scene 2)

Moments earlier in the speech, Lincoln directly quotes from the same passage: "In our greedy chase to make profit of the negro," Lincoln says, "let us beware, lest we 'cancel and tear to pieces' even the white man's charter of freedom." We can trace Lincoln's thought processes at work here. "Bloody hand" is an appropriately strong phrase to define a deception meant to extend slavery, whereas "cancel and tear to pieces," which does not have the same kind of immediate, allusive power (no listener or reader would have been likely to identify this phrase as from *Macbeth*, or even from Shakespeare), simply came usefully to hand as Lincoln either read or remembered the lines that gave rise to "bloody hand." Lincoln's imaginative engagement with the haunting language of Shakespeare's *Macbeth* would only increase as he confronted the horrors of Civil War.

The number of citations from Shakespeare in the Peoria speech (and there are other literary allusions as well) may have something to do with the process of its transmission. Historians have determined that this speech was essentially the same as the one Lincoln had delivered in Springfield two weeks earlier; the Springfield speech, however, survives not in written form but only in brief press reports and in the recollection of people who heard it. After making his Peoria address, and perhaps even before, Lincoln knew the importance of what he had said and how he had said it. The speech was, as David Herbert Donald has written, "a remarkable address, more elevated in sentiment and rhetoric than any speech Lincoln had previously made."[22] Although he had spoken for three hours without notes, Lincoln must have had the essential outline of the speech memorized, and he now took pains to write it down and, in doing so, to make it memorable and polished. He had it published in the *Illinois State Journal*, "inaugurating the practice of editing carefully his important speeches for subsequent publication."[23] And this raises the possibility that the Shakespeare quotations, which are carefully transcribed, may not have been in the speech as delivered but were added, or at the least "corrected," for publication. On the other hand, Lincoln (if we can believe a report in a pro–Stephen Douglas newspaper on the subject of the Springfield address) had been "nosing for weeks in the state library, and pumping his brains and his imagination for points and arguments,"[24] which would suggest that the Shakespeare allusions may have been there all along. There can be no doubt, in any case, that Lincoln had researched his topic assiduously, delivered the speech with passion and power, and taken great care in preparing it for publication. The literary allusions would have lent an educated sheen to Lincoln's prose, something that he may have believed of value in this, his most important published speech up to that time, but he would never again find it necessary to employ the language of Shakespeare so directly in a public forum.

These citations and quotations tell us little of the depth and extent of his knowledge of Shakespeare, but we are fortunate to have a valuable, if tantalizingly brief, piece of documentary evidence from Lincoln himself. In a letter to the actor James H. Hackett (discussed in detail in chapter 4), Lincoln writes, "Some of Shakspeare's plays I have never read; while others I have gone over perhaps as frequently as any unprofessional reader. Among the latter are Lear, Richard Third, Henry Eighth, Hamlet, and especially Macbeth. I think nothing equals Macbeth. It is wonderful."[25] (As we shall see, this list overlaps but does not duplicate the list of plays Lincoln saw during his presidency.) With the partial exception of *Henry VIII*, these are all tragedies. While it has been argued that Lincoln was particularly drawn to Shakespeare's darker plays, it needs to be said that tragedies (and to a lesser extent the histories), were the plays most valued by readers and most likely to be performed in Lincoln's time. *Henry VIII* is an anomaly for another reason: it has never been considered among Shakespeare's best plays and in the nineteenth century was infrequently performed even in Great Britain.[26] After listing his favorite plays, Lincoln adds, "Unlike you gentlemen of the profession, I think the soliloquy in Hamlet commencing 'O, my offence is rank' surpasses that commencing 'To be, or not to be.' But pardon this small attempt at criticism."[27] His letter to Hackett, widely publicized and sometimes mocked, tells us something about Lincoln's tastes and interests and also reveals a critical intelligence at work, but if we want to understand the significance of his remarks on *Macbeth* and *Hamlet* and to learn something of how he acquired his knowledge of Shakespeare's plays, we need to consider in some detail the abundant but uneven secondary evidence.

The earliest accounts of Lincoln's Shakespearean interests come from William Herndon, whose writings relating to his former law partner, and in particular the testimony he collected from the witnesses who have come to be known as "Herndon's informants," provide us with some of the most convincing evidence for Lincoln's love of Shakespeare. When Herndon began to plan a biography of Lincoln, he wrote and spoke to many of Lincoln's relatives, employees, friends, and associates, collecting a considerable wealth of firsthand, if sometimes distant, memories. Although Herndon's own reliability as a witness has been regularly questioned from his time to ours—as late as 1996, for example, he received mixed reviews from Don and Virginia Fehrenbacher in their *Recollected Words of Abraham Lincoln* (though the primary issue for them was the accuracy with which Herndon recorded Lincoln's conversation)—the tide appears to have turned in Herndon's favor. The editors of *Herndon's Lincoln*, Douglas Wilson and Rodney Davis, have recently noted that "many of the doubts and misgivings about the testimony of Herndon's informants have either been successfully addressed or put into better perspective."[28] It is, of course, one thing to conclude that Herndon was himself a reliable witness and another to determine the reliability of his sources, and doubts remain. Eric Foner, in *The Fiery Trial*, notes apropos of oral history in general that "many writers rely on recollections of Lincoln's words related long after they were spoken and often of dubious reliability."[29] As with any oral testimony, the evidence gathered by Herndon needs to be placed in context and weighed against other evidence whenever possible.

Whatever the presumed trustworthiness of this or that informant, the pattern of testimony recorded in Herndon's notes with regards to Lincoln's Shakespearean interests is quite consistent.[30] A cousin, Dennis Hanks, provides family evidence: "[Lincoln] was a great Reader of the united [*sic*] States Speaker the life of H Clay Shakespeare Rollins works."[31] James Matheny remembered that Lincoln "Loved Burns generally—Shakespear" (470), and Frances Todd Wallace added to this that "he would read generally aloud . . . would read with great warmth all funny things—humorous things &c.: Read Shakespear that way: he was a sad man—an abstracted man" (485–486). Another informant, Ninian Edwards, Lincoln's brother-in-law, claimed that "Lincoln read Shakespear Every Evening—not the Bible" (446), thereby contributing some grist to the mill of controversy over Lincoln's religious beliefs. Caleb Carman, who first met Lincoln in 1831, several times makes reference to his friend's reading habits: "He loved Burns' poetry—Shakespear—and some few other books" (374);[32] "His Conversation very often was a bout [*sic*] Books—such as Shakespear & other histories and Tale Books of all Discription in them Day" (429). Carman introduces as well the shadowy figure of schoolmaster John A. Kelso who, he tells Herndon, "loved Shakespear and fishing above all other thing. Abe loved Shakespear but not fishing—still Kelso would draw Abe: they used to sit on the bank of the river and quote Shakespear—criticise one an other" (374). Who Jack Kelso was and what the nature and extent of his relationship to Lincoln may have been remain open questions,[33] but the image of Lincoln and his friend fishing and reciting Shakespeare by a river bank is hard to resist. Whether as "schoolmaster," "vagabond poet," "village ne'er do well," or "drunkard," "fat, lazy" Jack Kelso, who Carman described as "a good Shakesperian Schollar for a western man" (374), lives on in the mythos of Lincoln's literary education.

It is at times difficult to know how to interpret much of this testimony. The claim by Lincoln's lifelong friend William H. Greene that "[Lincoln] nearly knew Shakespear by heart" (21), for example, sounds like an offhand exaggeration. And what are we to make of Joshua Speed's somewhat cryptic statement that "[Lincoln] read law History, Browns Philosophy or Paley—Burns Byron Milton or Shakespeare—The news papers of the day—and retained them all about as well as an ordinary man would any one of them—who made only one at a time his study" (498–499). And then we have John Todd Stuart's observation that "[Lincoln] never read poetry as a thing of pleasure, Except Shakespear" (519), which not only appears to contradict the considerable evidence of Lincoln's enthusiasm for the poetry of Robert Burns and Lord Byron, but also contradicts Stuart himself, who moments earlier in his interview with Herndon had said that Lincoln loved Burns and Poe's "The Raven" (519). Interestingly, Herndon seems to have taken the evidence of his informants with a grain of salt; his own remarks as quoted in the Lincoln biography he put together with Jesse Weik are guarded, as well as somewhat inconsistent. "Along with his Euclid," he notes at one point, "he carried a well worn copy of Shakespeare, in which he read no little in his leisure moments."[34] Almost immediately afterward, he tells us, "Beyond a limited acquaintance with Shakespeare, Byron, and Burns, Mr. Lincoln, comparatively speaking, had no knowledge of literature."[35] Still later, he adds, "When young he read the Bible, and when of age he read Shakespeare; but, though he often quoted from both, he never read either one through."[36] (Surprisingly, John Hay told Herndon that Lincoln "read very little," which appears to contradict what Hay records elsewhere.)[37] In spite of these contradictory statements, we have sufficient evidence to conclude that Lincoln read and recited Shakespeare in the years of his youth and early manhood; less clear is the depth and extent of his knowledge of Shakespeare's works.

As nearly everyone with an interest in his life knows, Lincoln did not receive anything like a formal education apart from a year or so of grammar school. Nevertheless, as Roy Basler writes, "In Lincoln's day anyone who had learned to read in school much beyond the alphabet could not avoid knowing some Shakespeare, for the simple reason that passages from the plays made up considerable portions of the literary textbooks which were used in the grammar schools."[38] Three of these textbooks were very probably read by young Abraham: William Scott's *Lessons in Elocution* (Lincoln's stepmother may have owned a copy),[39] Lindley Murray's *The English Reader*, and Thomas Dilworth's *New Guide to the English Tongue*. Of these, only Scott reproduces passages from Shakespeare's plays, primarily set speeches and soliloquies from *Hamlet*, *Julius Caesar*, the two parts of *Henry IV*, *Henry V*, *Othello*, and *Richard III* (other than grouping the quoted passages into general categories, Scott does not comment on or provide context for his selections). He also reprints a scene from *Henry VIII* that includes that play's best-known speech, Cardinal Wolsey's soliloquy "Farewell, a long farewell to all my greatness." If young Lincoln read this, it might have been enough to whet his appetite for the play itself, whenever it was that he acquired a collection of Shakespeare's plays. Of course, his claim to have "read" *Henry VIII*, in his letter to Hackett, may have meant little more than that he had read "into" it. For nineteenth-century America, "knowing Shakespeare" often meant knowing passages from Shakespeare. Interestingly, the *Richard III* speech that Scott reproduces is not from Shakespeare's play but from Colley Cibber's eighteenth-century adaptation; it is a hodgepodge of Cibber's own composition and some of Shakespeare's lines from another play, *Henry V*. Scott also includes a passage from *King Lear* that is not Shakespearean at all; it is from Nahum Tate's rewriting of the play, a version in which Lear and Cordelia survive at the end and which held the stage well into the nineteenth century. The balance of selections are the kind of purple passages and declamation exercises one would expect from an "elocution" textbook: Hamlet's advice to the players, Othello's address to the Venetian Senate, the orations from *Julius Caesar*, Falstaff's dissertation on sack, "All the world's a stage" from *As You Like It*, and so forth.

Attempting to assess Lincoln's acquaintance with Shakespeare beyond the contents of such school texts as *Lessons in Elocution* involves, in part, identifying the edition or editions of the plays Lincoln would have had available to him. We should perhaps be suspicious of the evidence of one Mrs. C. H. Dall who, in an 1867 article in the *Atlantic Monthly*, claimed that Lincoln first encountered Shakespeare in the house of Ann Rutledge; Dall was a friend of Herndon's, and her story helps shore up Herndon's controversial thesis that Ann Rutledge was Lincoln's one true love.[40] But the image of Lincoln riding the circuit as a young lawyer, carrying a copy of Blackstone in one saddlebag and a copy of Shakespeare in the other, early on became a significant part of the mythos and carries a good deal more weight, though probably founded on little more than a few casual words by John Todd Stuart, who, as Lincoln's onetime mentor and law partner, was in a position to know: "Mr Lincoln Commenced Carrying around with him on the Circuit—to the various Courts, books such as Shakespear."[41] Unfortunately, we can no longer recover the identity of the particular volume or set of volumes Stuart identifies as "Shakespear." Biographers and historians, Basler among them,[42] have at times pointed to a one-volume edition published in 1835 and now housed in the Folger Shakespeare Library that appears to have Lincoln's signature on the title page, but the Folger librarian, Georgianna Zeigler, notes, "We're now pretty sure that the signature . . . is not, in fact, in Lincoln's hand."[43] This does not mean that Lincoln could not have owned it, but there is no direct evidence linking him to this volume. It was only a little before the time of Lincoln's birth that American editions of Shakespeare began to appear (the first American complete works, reprinted from a 1791 Dublin edition, dates from 1795); by the mid-1860s, however, "more than one hundred fifty editions and reprints had been published in the United States."[44] Although these were mostly reprints of British editions, by the time Lincoln moved to Washington in 1861, Shakespeare scholarship in America had reached a high level of sophistication, as exemplified by Richard Grant White's carefully prepared edition of Shakespeare's works, published in twelve volumes from 1857 to 1865.[45]

Editions of Shakespeare were not cheap (which was of course true of books in general). It is not surprising to learn, from a variety of sources, that young Lincoln was more likely to borrow books than to purchase them. Lincoln's own words indirectly confirm this: speaking in Trenton, New Jersey, in 1861, he introduces comments on Parson Weems's *Life of Washington* with the words "I got hold of a small book," phrasing that suggests borrowing rather than buying.[46] When Shakespeare editions began to appear, they were issued in multiple volumes and variously priced. A Boston edition published from 1802 to 1807 was sold to subscribers for $6 and to nonsubscribers for $8 (among the subscribers were Harvard students Richard Henry Dana and

Edward Everett). "These prices," Alfred Westfall writes, "indicate that the cost of Shakespeare was high though not prohibitive." "Prohibitive," of course, is a relative matter: the average worker earned around $15 a week in 1800, and that figure would not have changed significantly by midcentury.[47] In contrast, the first edition of *Uncle Tom's Cabin* sold for $1.50 in 1852.[48] Another significant Shakespeare set, the 1805–1809 Dennie edition, was published in seventeen volumes at $1.50 a volume. In 1813 the first American one-volume Shakespeare appeared.[49] At around the same time, the relatively inexpensive method of stereotyping was replacing movable type in the printing of certain types of books; the first stereotyped American edition of Shakespeare was published in New York in 1817–1818.[50] The price of this edition is unknown, but it would probably have been more affordable than earlier multi- and single-volume editions. For someone like the young Lincoln, the cost of transporting such books to the frontier would have been included in the final price.

By the late 1830s, in any case, Lincoln, though still paying off various debts, would have been sufficiently well-off to purchase his own copy of Shakespeare's plays, and we know that around this time western "publishers and booksellers were able to offer Shakespeare's works in a variety of forms."[51] Intriguingly, what may be the earliest published association of Lincoln's name with Shakespeare appeared in the *New York Herald* on February 20, 1861, on the occasion of the president-elect's reception at New York's Astor Hotel: "Mr. *Lincoln* then bowed . . . to the several gentlemen who were . . . presented to him. . . . He mistook one old gentleman for a person who formerly used to call on him at Springfield to sell illustrated copies of '*Shakespeare*,' but was set right by some person present."[52] The thought of Lincoln buying Shakespeare's plays from a door-to-door salesman in what was still the frontier West is appealing, though the reporter may have misunderstood what he overheard, and, too, one must keep in mind the sometimes satirical view of Lincoln characteristic of the *Herald*. What is certain is that by midcentury, at the latest, a sufficient number of "editions and adaptations of [Shakespeare's] plays had been produced so that people from all economic classes would have access to them and people of all ages could understand them,"[53] which makes it reasonable to assume that the Lincolns by that time would have acquired their own copy of Shakespeare.

When the Lincolns occupied the White House, they would have found, in the library put together by Millard and Abigail Fillmore, a popular and often-reprinted seven-volume edition, *The Dramatic Works of William Shakespeare*,[54] known as the Phillips, Samson edition, anonymously edited by O. W. B. Peabody and first published in 1836 (the White House set was an 1849 reprint, purchased in 1850 for $10.50). This Shakespeare set, which advertised itself as "the most splendid edition ever presented to the American public,"[55] was, like nearly all Shakespeare editions up to the 1830s, heavily indebted for its textual and explanatory notes and other paraphernalia to an earlier English edition, edited by Samuel Singer in 1826, but Peabody "did attempt some original, independent textual work."[56] The "Advertisement" at the beginning of volume 1 asserts that "the object of the publishers has been, to prepare an edition in a handsome and convenient form, not too much encumbered with comments, nor too destitute of them, and comprehending such other advantages as the inquiries and research of the accomplished scholar, who has prepared the work for the press, have suggested."[57] The White House set was evidently already quite worn by 1862, when Mary Lincoln bought a replacement set of the Phillips, Samson edition for $12 from a New York bookseller, the volumes variously dated 1850 (vols. 1–3) and 1852 (vols. 4–7), with an eighth volume of Shakespeare's poems dated 1853.[58] (Instead of placing the new set in the White House Library, however, it appears that Mary gave it to her son Robert.)[59] The White House Library also had a copy of Mary Cowden Clarke's invaluable *Complete Concordance to Shakespeare*, a volume published in London in 1845.[60] Thus, by 1861, and perhaps earlier, Lincoln had available to him editions of and commentaries on Shakespeare informed by a high level of scholarship and critical acumen, at least by nineteenth-century standards.

Whatever effect Shakespeare's works may have had on Lincoln's thought and emotions, they do not appear to have had much in the way of direct influence on Lincoln's writing style; very little that could be described as "Shakespearean" appears in Lincoln's writings, early or late. As Douglas Wilson notes, "while frequently given credit for its clarity, [Lincoln's prose] did not rate high by the prevailing standards of eloquence, which, like the architecture of the day, valued artifice and ornament. Like his contemporaries Herman Melville, Nathaniel Hawthorne, Walt Whitman, Henry David Thoreau, and Emily Dickinson, Lincoln was effectively forging a new, distinctively American instrument . . . a prose that expressed a uniquely American way of apprehending and ordering experience."[61] Indeed, the style, syntax, and vocabulary Lincoln employs is very directly American and nineteenth century, and, in his writings at least, he is closer to us today, 200 years after his birth, than he was to Shakespeare, even if he was born 200 years after Shakespeare wrote *The Tempest*. Lincoln seldom employs figurative language; as Herbert Edwards and John Hankins note, "In an age when the whole tendency of

English prose style was toward discursiveness, verbosity, and grandiloquence, [Lincoln's] prose had an austere brevity and a stern simplicity."[62] Nor, as Kenneth Cmiel notes, is Lincoln's vocabulary in any way archaic: "The power of Lincoln's eloquence begins with his cadence, not vocabulary. Strategic repetition, antithesis, and parallelism lend mood far more than lofty diction."[63] Wilson at one point suggests that the word "withal," used by Lincoln in a letter, is "Shakespearean."[64] That claim, it seems to me, is particularly weak: the word was still in common use in the nineteenth century, and even if that were not the case, the employment of a single word—a word that Lincoln in fact used at least half a dozen times—does not count for much. This is the kind of exception, if exception it is, that proves the rule.

James Russell Lowell, attempting to characterize Lincoln's prose, claimed that "the English of Abraham Lincoln was so good not because he learned it in Illinois, but because he learned it of Shakespeare and Milton and the Bible, the constant companions of his leisure." And yet, of course, Lincoln did learn his eloquence in Illinois, as Lowell's next sentence seems to affirm: "and how perfect it was in its homely dignity, its quiet strength, the unerring aim with which it struck once nor needed to strike more!"[65] This can hardly be thought a description of Shakespeare or Milton or the Bible. Lincoln's style was not, in fact, constructed on the sort of literary, sixteenth-century foundation of either Shakespeare or the King James Bible, however familiar those books were to him and however much they had insinuated themselves into his thought and feeling. Robert Alter points out that the Gettysburg Address, Lincoln's best-known composition, has only a single phrase "explicitly biblical."[66] The opening words, "Four score and seven years ago," echo Psalm 90's "fourscore" and the more common "threescore and ten" which occurs over a hundred times in the King James Bible, and in part because of this, "Four score and seven" has a "poetic," elevated sound to it. As Alter notes, "The difference between 'eighty-seven' and 'four score and seven' is that the former is a mere numerical indication whereas the latter gives the passage of time since the founding of the Republic weight and solemnity."[67] As a lead-in to what Lincoln wants to tell us, "eighty-seven years ago" does not really work very well; indeed, it would not work in a speech today, however modern it sounds. (In earlier speeches, Lincoln had said "Nearly eighty years ago" and "Eighty-odd years.")[68] "Four score and seven" seems right, not only because that is what Lincoln wrote and we are inevitably attached to the sound of it, but because, though precise, it does not sound *too* precise, suggesting as it does the unfolding of time rather than a mere count of years. Fourscore is a nice round number, and the "and seven" resonates, I would argue, because the number seven has overtones of biblical numerology; it is a number with an "aura" attached to it. At the same time, the phrase is, to a certain extent, Shakespearean: Lear describes himself as a "foolish, fond old man, / Four score and upward." But though we may want to count this as one of the very few echoes of Shakespeare in Lincoln's writings, the biblical phrase is certainly more to the purpose.

The desire to find biblical and Shakespearean influences on Lincoln's prose is natural enough, but the allusions are subterranean at best. Jaques Barzun considered the Bible and Shakespeare's poetry to be "less influential [on Lincoln's style] than Shakespeare's prose, whose rapid twists and turns Lincoln often rivals, though without imagery,"[69] but he provides no examples. There are times when we can hear slight but telling structural echoes even of Shakespeare's blank verse in Lincoln's prose. In a speech at Bloomington, Illinois, Lincoln said, "If we could know where we are, and whither we are tending, we could then better judge what to do, and how to do it."[70] Both the cadence and the sentiment are similar to a passage from *Julius Caesar*, a play written in a notably spare, unadorned language:

> O, that a man might know
> The end of this day's business ere it come!
> But it sufficeth that the day will end,
> And then the end is known.
> (act 5, scene 1)

Carl Sandburg, for all of his sins of omission and commission as a biographer, intuited, as a poet, that Lincoln's words here, only slightly modified, could be rendered into free verse:

> If we could first know where we are,
> and whither we are tending,
> we could better judge
> what to do, and how to do it.[71]

But Lincoln's prose style, as Garry Wills has shown, was most clearly derived from the rhetorical manner of Greek and, especially, Latin oratory, with its use of such time-honored devices as isocolon, anaphora, epistrophe, zeugma, and other guides to the building of sentences and paragraphs to achieve a particular effect.[72] Shakespeare and the various authors of the King James Bible, of course, were subject to the same influences, but they employed them in quite different ways. Lincoln's lawyerly training, too, no doubt contributed to an essentially logical style of writing in which ideas are advanced, objections anticipated, secondary sources addressed, and conclusions reached.

However little Shakespeare's writings influenced Lincoln's prose, we have extensive and at times quite detailed evidence from the years of his presidency and into the following half century of his continuing interest in Shakespeare. Here, too, as with the testimony of Herndon's informants, care needs to be taken to separate what is likely from what is unlikely or even demonstrably false. In the last category are several reminiscences reported in *Lincoln's Favorite Poets* by David James Harkness and R. Gerald McMurtry. The authors cite, uncritically, a lecture (for which they provide no information) by J. B. Merwin, "a long-time friend of Lincoln,"[73] in the course of which Lincoln is quoted as saying, "Shakespeare had an unerring moral sense; a sense of justice, of what is due others, a sense of what is kind, of what is polite, of what is proper under all circumstances."[74] Quite apart from the un-Lincoln-like language and sentiment here, the words attributed to Lincoln are actually paraphrased from a volume entitled *The Shakspeare Treasury of Wisdom and Knowledge* by Charles Woodward Stearns, published in 1869: "In him [Shakespeare] we find an unerring moral sense—a sense of justice, or what is due to others; a sense of propriety, or the fitness of things; a sense of honor, or what is dignified, refined, and polite."[75] Lincoln is also quoted as saying, "What point is there of morals, of manners, of economy, of religion, that Shakespeare has not settled? What maiden has not found his teachings somewhat finer than her own delicacy? What lover is there whom Shakespeare has not out-loved? What sage has he not out-seen?" But this is a close paraphrase from Ralph Waldo Emerson's essay on Shakespeare in *Representative Men*.[76] In this instance, of course, Lincoln could have been borrowing Emerson's sentiments: as stated earlier, he very probably heard Emerson lecture in Springfield in 1853, and he certainly greeted Emerson at the White House in February 1862. (We know, too, that *Representative Men* was requested by the White House from the Library of Congress that same month.) Once again, however, this does not sound at all like Lincoln talking. Nor is it likely that Lincoln described Shakespeare as "one of those geniuses God leaves unbridled, that he might dip into the infinite as far and as deep as he liked."[77] Actually, this is a variation of a passage from a translation of Victor Hugo's *William Shakespeare*: "Shakespeare . . . is one of those geniuses that God purposely leaves unbridled, so that they may go headlong and in full flight into the infinite."[78] From Hugo, too, is this sentence that Merwin attributed to Lincoln: "What can bronze or marble do for such a man as

Shakespeare?"[79] Lincoln seldom indulged in the kind of sweeping generalities and abstract language that characterize each of these passages.

In evaluating the reported words of Lincoln, we again have to separate undoubted quotations and allusions from wording vaguely similar to something in Shakespeare or from the employment of a genuine but universally familiar "Shakespearean" phrase. In an amusing anecdote, published not long after his death, Lincoln tells of having had his photograph taken soon after his nomination in Chicago: "This stiff, ungovernable hair of mine was all sticking every way, very much as it is now, I suppose; and so the operation of [the photographer's] camera was but *holding the mirror up to nature*" (my emphasis).[80] The highlighted phrase from *Hamlet* was and is a commonplace. Similarly, when Herndon recalls Lincoln discussing Caesar and Brutus, there is no reason to assume that the reference is specifically Shakespearean. We may have a more telling, if indirect, allusion to King Henry's soliloquy on the night before Agincourt (*Henry V*, act 4 scene 1) when Lincoln, after a sleepless night of his own, tells Schuyler Colfax, "How willingly would I exchange places, today, with the soldier who sleeps on the ground in the Army of the Potomac?"[81] Here it is the situation more than the exact words that are suggestive, though Henry does muse that any one of his soldiers sleeps more soundly than he.[82] That Lincoln, receiving bad news from the front, should momentarily identify with Shakespeare's warrior king is not altogether surprising. It is tempting, as well, to hear an allusion to *Hamlet* in Lincoln's farewell to Springfield when he expresses the hope that "all will yet be well," especially since the echo ("all may be well") is from Claudius's prayer, a passage that we know Lincoln was particularly fond of, but in this instance we have to say that the specific words and the sentiments they express are hardly distinctive (Lincoln used exactly the same phrase in his Annual Message to Congress of December 1, 1862).[83] When Charles Ray, editor of the *Chicago Tribune*, has Lincoln say of Samuel P. Chase, "Take him all in all, he is the foremost man in the party," we need not assume a specific reference to *Hamlet*, though the possibility is certainly there ("Take him for all in all," Hamlet says of his father, "I shall not look upon his like again"; act 1, scene 2).[84]

A more likely Shakespearean echo is first reported by Herndon, who remembered Lincoln remarking in a Springfield lecture that "it was a common notion that those who laughed heartily and often never amounted to much—never made great men. If this be the case, farewell to all my glory."[85] Given Lincoln's claim to have frequently read *Henry VIII*, it is quite likely that he is here remembering Cardinal Wolsey's "Farewell, a long farewell to all my greatness" (the speech, as I have noted, is in *Lessons in Elocution*). Stephen

R. Capps, an Illinois merchant, heard something similar when he attended Lincoln's lecture "Discoveries and Inventions," delivered in Jacksonville in February 1859. Quoting Horace Greely to the effect that truly great men did not engage in levity, Lincoln remarks, "If Mr. Greely's definition of a great man is correct, then farewell, a long farewell to all my hopes of greatness."[86] (The letter to Mrs. Orville Browning, referred to above, includes the phrase "all my fancied greatness.")[87] An undoubted allusion to Shakespeare appears in James M. Scovel's report of an incident when Lincoln, talking about an officer dismissed for drunkenness, commented, "I dare not restore this man to his rank and give him charge of a thousand men, when he 'puts an enemy into his mouth to steal away his brains.'"[88] (Lincoln is alluding to *Othello*, act 3, scene 3: "O God, that men / should put an enemy in their mouths to steal away / their brains!") The Fehrenbachers, however, found that Scovel's recollections were "often so wildly inaccurate and improbable as to cast doubt on everything he wrote."[89] In this instance, the Shakespeare allusion may be Scovel's imaginative reconstruction rather than Lincoln's direct statement.

There are instances as well where the gist of the report sounds true but certain details seem unlikely. General Egbert L. Viele, who was with Lincoln at Fort Monroe, Virginia, in early May 1862, recalled, "[The president] would sit for hours during the trip, repeating the finest passages of Shakspere's best plays, page after page of Browning, and whole cantos of Byron."[90] Also, according to Viele, Lincoln knew "several pages" of Byron's *The Corsair* by heart.[91] As Luther Emerson Robinson notes, this is the only recorded reference to Lincoln reading Browning,[92] which, in addition to the undoubted exaggeration ("whole cantos of Byron") makes the story somewhat suspect (Robert Bray gives this story a "C"—"somewhat unlikely").[93] Viele, it should be noted, claimed an intimacy with the president not borne out by the evidence, writing, in an essay entitled "Lincoln as a Story-Teller," "I had the *entrée* to the White House. Though Senators, Congressmen and diplomats were kept waiting, I was always admitted," all of which is highly unlikely.[94] Another story, highly circumstantial in the telling, cites an event that took place in 1847 but was not set down until 1882. In the course of the trial *Case v. Snow Brothers*, Lincoln supposedly said,

> The best judge of human character that ever wrote has left these immortal words for all of us to ponder:
>
> > "Good name in man and woman, dear my Lord,
> > is the immediate jewel of their souls:

Who steals my purse steals trash; 'tis something, nothing;
'Twas mine, 'tis his, and has been slave to thousands;
But he that filches from me my good name
Robs me of that which not enriches him
And makes me poor indeed."
(*Othello*, act 3, scene 3)[95]

Though Lincoln does not mention *Othello* as among the plays he has frequently read, he is several times reported as quoting from or alluding to it, and this particular passage is included in the appendix to *Lessons in Elocution*. Nonetheless, the thirty-five-year gap between the event and its telling counts against taking the story entirely at face value.

Many Lincoln stories date from the period after the 1889 publication of Herndon and Weik's *Herndon's Lincoln: The Story of a Great Life*, and some of them, a least, were probably influenced by the volume's contents. Writing in 1909 (the centenary year of Lincoln's birth, rich in Lincoln reminiscences), James Grant Wilson recalls Lincoln visiting his office at the *Chicago Record* and noticing busts of Burns and Shakespeare. "They are my two favorite authors," he recalls Lincoln telling him, "and I must manage to see their birthplaces some day, if I can contrive to cross the Atlantic."[96] Though the story is not inherently improbable, the presence of those busts, one cannot help but feel, is a bit too convenient, and the story itself clearly relies for its effect in part on the reader's knowledge that Lincoln would never have the opportunity to follow through on his wish.[97] An even later story, first recorded in 1918 in Simon Wolf's *The Presidents I Have Known*, may nonetheless be genuine: invited to an "entertainment" celebrating Shakespeare's 300th anniversary at the Literary and Dramatic Association of Washington (of which Wolf was president) and told that *Hamlet* would be played, Lincoln, though unable to attend, remarked, "Why would I not make a splendid grave digger, for am I not quoted as a fellow of infinite jest and humor, and is not my present life typical of that vocation?"[98] Wolf kept a detailed diary, so this incident is probably based on more than memory (even though it is not the grave digger but Yorick whom Hamlet describes as a "fellow of infinite jest"); certainly, the combination of quick wit and a mournful recognition of the terrible toll the war was continuing to inflict on the nation (the so-called Fort Pillow Massacre had taken place less than two weeks earlier) is characteristic of Lincoln's at-times grim humor.

John Hay, who is among the most trustworthy firsthand witnesses we have,[99] refers several times to one of Lincoln's best-known eccentricities:

reading and reciting Shakespeare to sometimes captive listeners. In addition to the incident referred to at the beginning of this chapter, Hay also writes, "Where only one or two were present, he was fond of reading aloud. He passed many of the summer evenings in this way when occupying his cottage at the Soldiers' Home. He would there read Shakespeare for hours with a single secretary for audience."[100] In a story indirectly attributed to Hay, Lincoln (presumably in the White House) wakes Hay in the middle of the night and, sitting on the edge of his bed, begins to read from one or another poet or "a passage from Shakespeare. . . . After perhaps twenty minutes or half an hour, his mind having become calm, the tall gaunt figure would rise from the edge of my bed and start for the door and on down the dark corridor. The candle carried high in his hand would light the disheveled hair as the President in flapping night-shirt, his feet padding along in carpet slippers, would disappear into the darkness." As attractive as this story is, particularly in its circumstantial details, Hay, as far as we know, never wrote it down, at least not in these words.[101] The inspiration for the anecdote here recorded was undoubtedly the following, which Hay did write down: "He would go to bed with a volume of [the poet Thomas] Hood in his hands, and would sometimes rise at midnight and, traversing the long halls of the Executive Mansion in his night clothes would come to his secretary's room and read something that especially pleased him. He wanted to share his enjoyment of the writer; it was dull pleasure to him to laugh alone."[102] One can easily see how this incident became embroidered in the retelling, including the reference to Shakespeare and the disappearance of the lesser-known poet Thomas Hood.[103] In the process, the president's "pleasure" in sharing a laugh with his secretary is transformed into a need to calm a troubled mind; one Lincoln, melancholy, weighed down with the cares of office, takes the place of another Lincoln, always happy to share a comic story.

Simon Wolf's account of the "splendid grave digger" remark, cited above, is given at least some support from our knowledge of Lincoln's abiding interest in *Hamlet*, which, next to *Macbeth*, may have been his favorite play. He no doubt identified, at least to a degree, with the fatalism of the play's eponymous protagonist; Herndon's testimony here is convincing: "I have heard him frequently quote the couplet, 'There's a divinity that shapes our end, / Rough-hew them as we will.'"[104] Oddly enough, however, Lincoln's interest, as revealed in the Hackett letter, particularly focused on the character of Hamlet's uncle, Claudius. "Unlike you gentlemen of the profession," he tells Hackett, "I think the soliloquy in Hamlet commencing 'O, my offence is rank' surpasses that commencing 'To be, or not to be.'"[105] It may not be coincidental that both speeches appear, one after the other, in *Lessons in Elocution*. We know from other sources, in any case, that Lincoln was fond of the speech. In an account published in 1895, John Littlefield recalls that Lincoln, with whom he had studied law, "could recite whole passages from Shakespeare, notably from 'Hamlet,' with wonderful effect. He was very fond of the drama. In 'Hamlet,' he claimed that the passage commencing: 'Oh! my offence is rank,' etc., was better than the soliloquy. He said that the great beauty of Shakespeare was the power and majesty of the lines, and argued that even an indifferent actor could hold an audience by the power of the text itself."[106] If this is an accurate remembrance, it suggests that Lincoln's interest in Claudius's soliloquy and prayer was formed quite early.

The most detailed reference to Lincoln's appreciation of Claudius's soliloquy appeared in Francis Carpenter's *Six Months at the White House*, a memoir written while Carpenter was living in the executive mansion (February to July 1864) working on his painting of Lincoln presenting the Emancipation Proclamation to his cabinet. Carpenter, who is responsible for several of the most memorable Lincoln-Shakespeare anecdotes, had special access to Lincoln, and much of what he recounts rings true, though the Fehrenbachers think that Carpenter "probably exaggerated the extent of his intimacy with Lincoln, . . . [his] recollected words . . . are a mixture of what he himself heard and what he heard secondhand from others, and it is not always easy to tell the difference."[107] When Carpenter recounts a discussion he had with the president concerning *Hamlet*, we may be tempted to grant his story's credibility in part because it fits with other accounts of Lincoln's interests. "Said he,—and his words have often returned to me with a sad interest since his own assassination,—'There is one passage of the play of "Hamlet" which is very apt to be slurred over by the actor, or omitted altogether, which seems to me the choicest part of the play. It is the soliloquy of the king, after the murder. It always struck me as one of the finest touches of nature in the world.'" Carpenter then tells us that Lincoln, "throwing himself into the very spirit of the scene," began to recite the lines beginning,

> Oh my offence is rank, it smells to heaven;
> It hath the primal eldest curse upon't,
> A brother's murder. Pray can I not,
> Though inclination be as sharp as will.
> My stronger guilt defeats my strong intent.

"He repeated [the] entire passage from memory," Carpenter adds, "with a feeling and appreciation unsurpassed by anything I ever witnessed upon the stage."[108] Carpenter would have known how much Lincoln valued this speech given the wide circulation the letter to Hackett had received well before he arrived at the White House. Moreover, his comment that Lincoln's reading of the soliloquy surpassed anything he had witnessed on the stage is itself somewhat suspect, given that Claudius's speech was seldom included in nineteenth-century productions of *Hamlet*. Carpenter is probably embellishing a bit, but the incident he describes is quite believable in its outlines.

We have, as well, the evidence of James Murdoch, the "elocutionist" who claims to have discussed the "My offence is rank" speech with Lincoln in Springfield in 1861. We know that Murdoch, who crossed paths with Lincoln on several occasions, came to Springfield that January to give two public readings from Shakespeare, Dickens, and other authors. "Lincoln cosponsored and attended the second show . . . laughing heartily at the comic turns,"[109] and he may have attended the first as well. While Murdoch's account is highly circumstantial and detailed, it is well to remember that it was first recounted and published in 1882.[110] "As there was but little of the metaphysical or speculative element in Mr. Lincoln's mind," Murdoch writes, "though strong in practical philosophy, common sense, and clear moral intuitions, it was not difficult to understand and appreciate the preference he expressed, on this occasion, for the speech of King Claudius: 'Oh ! my offense is rank and smells to heaven,' over Hamlet's philosophical 'To be or not to be.'" Moreover, Murdoch continues,

> He expressed a wonder that actors should have laid so much stress on the thought contained in the latter soliloquy, and passed with such comparative indifference over the soul-searching expressions of the king, uttered under the stings of self-accusation. "The former," said Mr. Lincoln "is merely a philosophical reflection on the question of life and death, without actual reference to a future judgment; while the latter is a solemn acknowledgment of inevitable punishment hereafter, for the infraction of divine law. Let any one reflect on the moral tone of the two soliloquies, and there can be no mistaking the force and grandeur of the lesson taught by one, and the merely speculative consideration in the other, of an alternative for the ills that flesh is heir to."[111]

Again, it is intriguing to have Lincoln, while still in Springfield, talk about "actors" and how they regarded the two speeches, given what scant evidence we have of Lincoln's playgoing before he became president. Perhaps more questionable is the highly conventional and un-Lincoln-like moral he finds in the two speeches.

Though his preference for "My offence is rank" over "To be or not to be" was mildly ridiculed by the *New York Herald* ("henceforth the role of Claudius, King of Denmark, will be sought after by accomplished actors, instead of being remitted to the greatest stick in the company"), Lincoln was not alone in failing to be charmed by Hamlet's most famous soliloquy, as even the *Herald* writer acknowledged.[112] Charles Lamb, for example, found that Hamlet's well-known words had been "[so] handled and pawed about by declamatory boys and men . . . till it has become to me a perfect dead member."[113] Today we may think of this soliloquy as overworn by constant repetition, but it was already—indeed had long been—a cliché in Lincoln's time, even in America. What has made it so frequently quoted and alluded to is the generality and universality of its sentiments. There is almost no circumstance to which Hamlet's words here cannot be applied. In this, it differs strikingly from the rest of Hamlet's five major soliloquies, each of which refers to the specifics of Hamlet's situation. "To be or not to be" makes no mention of Gertrude, Claudius, or the murder of Hamlet's father; it is the one soliloquy that can be taken out of its context without losing its meaning and significance. At the same time, it is the one with the least dramatic force: it is as least as much philosophy as it is theater.

Claudius's soliloquy, in contrast, has the immediacy and drama of a mind in turmoil: it is a remarkably human speech, in which a man who has killed his own brother, thereby gaining the latter's throne and wife, nevertheless both wishes for some expiation of his sin and at the same time realizes that he cannot give up what his crime has gained for him. Lincoln, whose love of Shakespeare had much to do, I believe, with the drama of men caught up in powerful emotions, found Claudius's immediate struggle with his conscience more compelling than Hamlet's generalized speculations on suicide. "Lincoln was deeply touched by the portrait of the mind of a politician who had committed great wrongs," David Bromwich writes; "he was not equally moved by the thoughts of a hero who reproached himself for doing too little."[114] And as Allen Guelzo suggests, it may also be that Lincoln, who "remained through his entire life under the cloud of predestination," was fascinated to watch Claudius "writhe in predestination's coils, too."[115] Lincoln's preference for Claudius's soliloquy reveals a sensitive, imaginative response to Shakespeare's play.

As great as his interest in *Hamlet* may have been, Lincoln's particular admiration for *Macbeth*, a play not represented in Scott's *Lessons in Elocution*, is well attested. A comment in his letter to Hackett stands out from the generalized account of the plays he had especially studied: "Nothing equals Macbeth," he writes; "it is wonderful." The word "wonderful," as often in his writings, takes on the primary meaning of "full of wonder" (he refers to the Constitution as "wonderful"). One witness to Lincoln's interest in *Macbeth* was John Forney, who was both secretary of the Senate and publisher of the *Washington Chronicle* when Lincoln was president. The context is a discussion of Lincoln's tendency to depression: "One evening I found him in such a mood. He was ghastly pale, the dark rings were round his caverned eyes, his hair was brushed back from his temples, and he was reading Shakespeare as I came in. 'Let me read you this from "Macbeth,"' he said. 'I cannot read it like Forrest' (who was then acting in Washington), 'but it comes to me to-night like a consolation.'"[116] Lincoln then recited the "Tomorrow, and tomorrow" speech from act 5, scene 5. As Basler notes, the word "consolation" is peculiar: it is hard to see how Macbeth's despairing, nihilistic words would console anyone. On the other hand, Lincoln undoubtedly knew as well these words from *King Lear*: "The worst is not, so long as one can say 'this is the worst.'" The worst, of course, is death, when it is no longer possible to speak at all. Basler concludes, quite sensibly, "Perhaps it was the range of Shakespeare's characters from the sublime to the ridiculous and from profound pessimism to infinite hope, a range which Lincoln shared, that accounted as much as anything for Lincoln's returning again and again to Shakespeare for 'consolation' whenever he had the opportunity to read for relaxation."[117] To put the matter in another way, Lincoln turned to Shakespeare not for consolation in the usual sense of the word but, rather, for powerful, imaginative expressions of pain and loss that echoed his own feelings.

Perhaps the best-known instance of Lincoln reading from and discussing *Macbeth* is attested to by several witnesses, including the young Frenchman Adolphe de Pineton, Marquis de Chambrun, who was on a steamship returning with Lincoln and others from a visit to City Point and Petersburg, Virginia, on April 6–9, 1865. The war was all but over, and Lincoln had been both exhilarated and sobered by his visit to Richmond, the devastated capital of the Confederacy; his mood, as Michael Burlingame writes, "oscillated between hearty bonhomie and sad introspection."[118] "On Sunday, April 9th, we were steaming up the Potomac," Chambrun writes.

That whole day the conversation dwelt upon literary subjects. Mr. Lincoln read to us for several hours passages taken from Shakespeare.

Most of these were from "Macbeth," and, in particular, the verses which follow *Duncan*'s assassination. I cannot recall this reading without being awed at the remembrance, when *Macbeth* becomes king after the murder of *Duncan*, he falls a prey to the most horrible torments of mind.[119]

Lincoln, presumably, was quoting the passage that includes the lines,

> What hands are here? Ha: they pluck out mine eyes.
> Will all great Neptune's ocean wash this blood
> Clean from my hand? No: this my hand will rather
> The multitudinous seas incarnadine,
> Making the green one red.
> (*Macbeth*, act 2, scene 2)

Charles Sumner, who also traveled with the Lincoln party, gives a similar account: "In the course of the day the President read to the few friends about him, with a beautiful quarto copy of Shakspeare in his hands, the tribute to the murdered Duncan,—'Macbeth' being his favorite play,—and 'impressed by the beauty of the words, or by some presentiment unuttered,' he read the passage aloud a second time."[120] It is not surprising, of course, that reminiscences from that brief journey are shaded by the retrospective knowledge that Lincoln would be dead within the week.

An allusion to *Macbeth* appears in another story associated with Lincoln's final days. According to a witness who claims to have been present, Lincoln told his wife and others of a disturbing dream that "has got possession of me, and, like Banquo's ghost, it will not down."[121] In his dream, Lincoln sees "a catafalque, on which rested a corpse wrapped in funeral vestments. 'Who is dead in the White House?,'" Lincoln asks of one of the nearby soldiers. "'The President,' was his answer; 'he was killed by an assassin!'"[122] Though often cited and repeated, this story, to paraphrase Cole Porter, is almost too bad to be true, and the somewhat gothic circumstantial detail does not make it any more convincing. The only source is Lincoln's friend and unofficial bodyguard Ward Lamon, who, according to his daughter who wrote down the account, commented, "There was something about [the dream] so amazingly real, so true to the actual tragedy which occurred soon after, that more than mortal strength and wisdom would have been required to let it pass without a shudder or a pang."[123] And that, of course, is the problem—Lincoln's dream is too convenient, fits too easily into a pattern of premonitions and occult mysteries of one sort or another that surround Lincoln's death. Of

Lamon's memoirs in general, the Fehrenbachers found that "more than a few of its supposedly firsthand anecdotes of Lincoln were derived from Lamon's reading, rather than his experience, and that more than a little of its quotations of Lincoln was simply invented." They give this story a grade of "E"—"a quotation that is probably not authentic."[124] Lamon's account concludes with another Shakespeare reference: "In conversations with me [Lincoln] referred to [the dream] afterward, closing one [*sic*] with this quotation from 'Hamlet': 'To sleep; perchance to dream! ay, *there's the rub!*' with a strong accent on the last three words."[125]

It is, of course, quite possible that Lincoln had a dream so disturbing as to compel him to tell Mary and others close to him about it; we need not accept every detail of Lamon's account to believe that the gist of it could be true. We have credible evidence from a variety of sources that Lincoln sometimes referred to his dreams in conversation. Jonathan White, who has carefully sifted the evidence, concludes that Lamon's dream story "is an utter fabrication," and his argument is convincing.[126] My interest, in any case, is in the Shakespearean allusions, and authenticity as such does not really matter: that a story about Lincoln, which has been frequently retold over the years, should be embroidered with Shakespearean detail is telling in itself. We can note that by the time Lamon's recollections were first published (in 1895), it had long been known that *Macbeth* and *Hamlet* were the two Shakespearean plays of greatest interest to Lincoln. The quotations from Shakespeare can thus be seen to add conviction as well as color to the story. In any case, although the main point of Lincoln's dream is his premonition of his own death, the very marginal *Macbeth* allusion has been cited to support the idea that Lincoln identified with Macbeth: one historian writes of "the inescapable implication of guilt in Lincoln's statement that his dream haunted him like Banquo's ghost."[127] But, of course, this ignores the fact that it was Duncan, not Macbeth, who was assassinated.[128] As the Shakespeare allusions in the Hayne-Webster debate remind us (see chapter 1), Banquo's ghost can be summoned to appear for or against almost any argument.

The conjunction of his assassination with his interest in *Macbeth* has provoked speculation on Lincoln's overall state of mind in the closing days of the Civil War. In an essay entitled "Lincoln, *Macbeth*, and the Moral Imagination," Michael Beran argues that Lincoln identified with Macbeth himself because both were men of great ambition whose coming to power involved terrible bloodshed: "However justifiable his actions were, Lincoln knew that he had the blood of a nation on his hands: and there were times when even a conception of providential will, and a consciousness of principled ambition, did not sufficiently answer to the purpose of washing them clean."[129] This goes much further than the evidence allows. Lincoln was not Macbeth; if he was ambitious, it was not for power or for riches but for the fame that came from the performance of great deeds, and though he undoubtedly suffered over the horrible bloodshed of the Civil War, we have no evidence that he ever believed that his ambition was responsible for the carnage, however grieved he was by its extent. Don Fehrenbacher, more reasonably, found it "not altogether unlikely that in the gloom of some sleepless night [Lincoln] . . . beheld blood upon his hands or found a prayer faltering on his lips."[130] It is also possible, however, that Lincoln, if we believe the various reports of his tendency to premonitions, identified not with Macbeth but with Duncan, the slain king, murdered after having achieved a great victory over his enemies. As John Briggs comments, "We do not need to psychologize about subconscious motivations or speculate about Lincoln's deepest purposes to notice that his reading of [passages from *Macbeth*] entailed his taking on of both roles."[131] Indeed, Chambrun himself suggests as much: "Either because he was struck by the weird beauty of these verses, or from a vague presentiment coming over him, . . . he read over again the same scene."[132] To say that Lincoln responded deeply to the images of horror *Macbeth* presented is not unreasonable. The play clearly haunted his imagination throughout his presidency, and as we have seen, it was already part of his imaginative vocabulary as early as the Peoria address.[133]

His fascination with both those guilty murderers, Claudius and Macbeth, continues nevertheless to be cited as evidence of Lincoln's crushing sense of guilt over the Civil War. Adam Gopnik has again made the argument: "He recognized and understood the pain of one who, believing himself to be essentially good and capable of salvation, as Claudius does, knows that he is covered with blood—one who, having chosen to take on the weight and worry of the world, knows that he has done it and, like Macbeth, too, cannot be free of its guilt: *Help, angels! Make assay!*"[134] But such a view is too simple. Macbeth and Claudius, after all, were murderers whose crimes were premeditated and stemmed from a desire for personal gain—Claudius's "my crown, my own ambition, and my queen." And not incidentally, they were both regicides, the killers of lawful kings. Several so-called psychohistorians have argued that Lincoln identified with Claudius and Macbeth as a consequence of unresolved fratricidal and patricidal feelings. "Of all Shakespeare's creations," George Forgie writes, "Lincoln was drawn to the plays, characters, and indeed the very scenes that most vividly dramatize fratricidal ambition."[135] Forgie makes much of the fact that Carpenter described the way Lincoln, in his recitation from *Richard III*, "became" Richard.[136] "How could Lincoln have identified with the mentality of men consumed with fratricidal guilt? Was there any sense in which he also burned with repressed hate and jealousy and then committed a 'brother's murther' in order to get to power?"[137] Answering his own rhetorical questions, Forgie concludes that the "brother" Lincoln murdered, at least symbolically, was Stephen A. Douglas.[138]

Both Forgie and Dwight Anderson cite Chambrun's report that Lincoln, after reciting a passage from *Macbeth*, "paused to expatiate on how exact a picture Shakespeare here gives of a murderer's mind when, the dark deed achieved, its perpetrator already envies his victim's calm sleep. He read the scene twice over."[139] "How could Lincoln have been certain that Shakespeare's picture of the murderer's mind was exact?," Forgie asks.[140] Again, of course, the question answers itself. Anderson, who also gives a patricidal interpretation to Lincoln's dream of his own death, concludes that in reading from *Macbeth*, "Lincoln was offering a judgment on himself."[141] Neither of these interpretations is really compelling.[142] Lincoln without doubt felt deeply and continuously the pain and suffering that inevitably accompanied the great conflict in which his country was embroiled, as John Hay, who witnessed it firsthand, makes movingly clear: "The cry of the widow and the orphan was always in his ears; the awful responsibility resting upon him as the protector of an imperiled republic kept him true to his duty, but could not make him unmindful of the intimate details of that vast sum of human misery involved in a civil war."[143] If we believe the account of his secretary of the interior, James Harlan, however, Lincoln, at the end of the war, gave off an expression of "serene joy as if conscious that the great purpose of his life had been achieved. . . . He seemed the very personification of supreme satisfaction."[144] Though Lincoln must have had moments of regret for the course he had chosen, there is no reason to believe that he thought himself personally responsible for the calamities that overtook his country.

None of which is to deny that Shakespeare resonated for Lincoln in ways that went beyond relaxation or intellectual sustenance. John Hay, commenting on Lincoln's habit of reading Shakespeare aloud, noted that he "never tired of Richard the Second. The terrible outburst of grief and despair into which Richard falls in the Third Act, had a peculiar fascination for him; we have heard him read it at Springfield, at the White House and at the Soldiers' Home."[145] Lincoln's fascination with Richard's despairing words suggests how deeply he felt the weight of his responsibilities and gives evidence as well to the fatalism to which he was prone:

> For God's sake let us sit upon the ground
> And tell sad stories of the death of kings,
> How some have been deposed, some slain in war,
> Some haunted by the ghosts they have deposed,
> Some poisoned by their wives, some sleeping kill'd,
> All murdered.
> > (*Richard II*, act 3, scene 2)

At times, too, Lincoln found in Shakespeare a way of dealing with personal loss more meaningful to him than the usual church homily. One evening, soon after the death of his son Willie, he read aloud a variety of passages from Shakespeare to an army officer who was visiting him, Le Grand Cannon, concluding with the scene from *King John* where Constance bewails the loss of her son. Lincoln was very probably reading these lines:

> Grief fills the room up of my absent child,
> Lies in his bed, walks up and down with me,
> Puts on his pretty looks, repeats his words,
> Remembers me of all his gracious parts,
> Stuffs out his vacant garments with his form.
> > (*King John*, act 3, scene 4)[146]

"I noticed as he read these pathetic passages that his voice became tremulous, and he seemed to be deeply moved. When he reached the end he closed the book, laid it down, and turning to me, said: 'Did you ever dream of some lost friend, and feel that you were having a sweet communion with him, and yet have a consciousness that it was not a reality? . . . That is the way I dream of my lost boy Willie.'"[147] Shakespeare's words, though they could not be considered comforting, gave Lincoln, a man "of profound emotional reserve,"[148] a way of maintaining an imaginative connection to his own "absent child."

Throughout his life, Lincoln adapted Shakespeare to his own needs and desires, selecting a speech here or a passage there, fitting the playwright's works into his own worldview, finding moving depictions of the burden that comes with responsibility and rule, while at the same time bringing to bear a unique, thoughtful, critical understanding and indulging his well-developed sense of the dramatic. In the years of his maturity, he returned to the Shakespeare he was introduced to in his youth, building on that initial foundation of purple passages, set speeches, and familiar quotations with subsequent reading and theatergoing. Commenting on what Lincoln might have gleaned from *Lessons on Elocution*, Fred Kaplan writes, "All Scott's selections on the subject [of ambition], which includes King Henry's soliloquy from *Henry IV, Part I*, 'Uneasy lies the head that wears the crown,' and King Richard's soliloquy before his final battle in *Richard III*, extended into dramatic example what Lincoln had absorbed in his earlier textbooks: that ambition is a two-edged sword."[149] All of this is reasonable enough, but we need to consider as well Lincoln's imaginative engagement with Shakespeare's texts. The Marquis de Chambrun, in the account of the *River Queen* journey, tells us that after reading passages from *Macbeth*, Lincoln "paused ... while reading, and began to explain to us how true a description of the murderer that one was; when, the dark deed achieved, its tortured perpetrator came to envy the sleep of his victim; and he read over again the same scene."[150] Rather than taking this as evidence that Lincoln saw himself as a murderer, we might better consider that he was responding to one of the major reasons why we still read Shakespeare's works and still attend his plays: his almost uncanny ability to make us believe that his characters are feeling what they profess to feel, whether it be murderous guilt, romantic love, or foolish egotism.

Lincoln's Shakespeare, inevitably, was a nineteenth-century Shakespeare, the Shakespeare of, on the stage at least, tragedies and histories, of kings and affairs of state, rather than of the comedies. In part, no doubt, this was because the life lessons Shakespeare was thought to teach were more evident in the former. In the John Hay diary entry that begins this chapter, Lincoln reads from *Henry VI* and *Richard III*, a somewhat surprising choice given that the three plays that constitute *Henry VI*, taken together or individually, were then (and continue to be) among the least known and least performed of Shakespeare's works. *Richard III*, in contrast, was one of the best known and most frequently staged of the Bard's plays throughout the nineteenth century.[151] But Lincoln and Hay (who also knew his Shakespeare) were quite aware that the *Richard III* as acted on both the English and America stage was a drastic revision and elaboration of Shakespeare's text, cobbled together by the eighteenth-century actor and playwright Colley Cibber. Cibber's version began with scenes from part 3 of *Henry VI* tacked onto the beginning of *Richard*. In conjoining the two plays, Lincoln was, in a sense, re-creating Cibber's adaptation, which suggests that for him, as for most nineteenth-century readers and playgoers, "Shakespeare" was not a fixed, unchanging phenomenon but, rather, an evolving mix of text and performance tied to time and place. Lincoln knew the difference between the reading and acting versions of the plays and, on the evidence we have, perhaps preferred reading to playgoing.[152] Or, to put the matter somewhat differently, he liked best the Shakespearean drama he could himself create reading aloud: he was unembarrassed when it came to sharing the poetry he loved with family, friends, and even strangers. He would, nevertheless, also come to appreciate Shakespeare in the theater, possibly in his Illinois years, and certainly during his all too brief time as president, when he would see and hear the most notable Shakespearean actors of his time.

3

Lincoln at the Theater

In his letter to the actor James H. Hackett, Abraham Lincoln wrote that he had "seen very little of the drama," a tantalizingly imprecise remark. Few definite clues exist to suggest where or when Lincoln might have attended the theater before arriving in Washington in 1861; what evidence we have would suggest that he did not go much to the theater at all as president before 1863. When he might have first seen a Shakespeare play, in particular, is not known. Roy Basler thinks that Lincoln "probably saw Shakespeare acted prior to his election to the presidency,"[1] but this is no more than a hunch. Mark Neely, on the other hand, writes that "Lincoln's first opportunity to see Shakespearean plays came only when he was president,"[2] but Neely does not tell us on what he bases this claim. That Lincoln was drawn to the theater, perhaps from an early age, appears more than likely. Gertrude Garrison, who provided information on Lincoln's assassination to biographers William Herndon and Jesse Weik (she was Weik's literary agent) wrote that Lincoln "was fond of the drama. Brought up in a provincial way, in the days when theatres were unknown outside of the larger cities, the beautiful art of the actor was fresh and delightful to him. He loved Shakespeare, and never lost an opportunity of seeing his characters rendered by the masters of dramatic art."[3] Her account, however, provides no sources and was not published until 1889. A somewhat different view comes from a close acquaintance of Lincoln's, Henry C. Whitney:

> Lincoln was raised in the social wilderness; the pastimes of his neighborhood were (not balls, or hops, but) *shindigs* or hoe-downs; not concerts, operettas, or recitals, but *sings*: not theatrical representations, but charades: the light literature of his youth was not [the Sanskrit

animal fables] Pilpay, or the "Arabian Nights," or even Sara Slick; but "Cousin Sally Dillard," and "Becky Williams' Courtship," and such like trash; and no wonder, with such tuition of the fancy, when he could select for himself he should prefer a "nigger" show, to an opera; a farce, to a tragedy; a circus, to a lecture; a joke book, to Homer's "Iliad."[4]

Whitney is not an entirely reliable witness, and although he is in part echoing Herndon here, his comments seem both exaggerated and mean-spirited, even if they are part of an ostensible defense of Lincoln's love of humor and jokes.

Lincoln's interest in the theater was encouraged by Mary Todd, possibly before and certainly after their marriage. A school friend of Mary's remembered a discussion of possible future husbands: "Mary Todd stipulated that her choice should be willing and able to let her see as much of the theater as she wanted, and beyond that she did not expect to be too particular. So when I heard she had chosen a struggling young lawyer . . . I wondered how she was going to manage about the theater-going."[5] It would not be surprising, in any case, to discover that Lincoln, as a young man, had seen little or nothing of the theater, since theatrical activity was pretty much nonexistent in the small towns of Kentucky, Indiana, and Illinois where he grew up. What professional theater there was on the western frontier would have been found primarily in the river towns of Louisville and Cincinnati, where touring performers would often stop on the way to New Orleans. Even Chicago would not be much of a theater town until the 1830s; it is notable that a popular barnstorming actor like Junius Brutus Booth did not make his first appearance in Chicago until the fall of 1848 (he had, by that date, acted in places like Louisville, Kentucky; Jackson and Vicksburg, Mississippi; and Mobile, Alabama, in addition to New Orleans and the major theater towns of the eastern seaboard). What is certain is that Lincoln would have begun to experience theater at a time of explosive growth: "Throughout the United States between 1825 and 1860, the number of theatres, like the nation's cities and populations, grew at a phenomenal rate."[6]

It is tempting to consider the possibility that Lincoln attended the theater, and even saw some Shakespeare, in New Orleans when he traveled there on flatboats in 1828 and 1831. New Orleans was already a vibrant theatrical city by this time, and Shakespeare was popular there, "averaging twenty-five performances per season and doubtless rivaling any southern and many northern cities."[7] Unfortunately, although Lincoln spent a month in that city on his second trip, we have no way of knowing what he did on his visits apart from consulting a fortune-teller, if Herndon can be trusted on this point.[8] On his first trip, he could have arrived mid-May 1828, though some of the evidence suggests the subsequent winter as equally likely.[9] If the May–June date is correct, we know that "the famous Orleans Theater presented Mr. Good Fortune plus comedy and vaudeville acts ('The Cat metamorphosed into a Woman') during Lincoln's visit,"[10] but Shakespeare's plays are nowhere evident; the theater season, in any case, appears to have been over by the end of April that year.[11] If, however, Lincoln was in New Orleans in the winter of 1828–1829, he would have had the opportunity to see Junius Brutus Booth, the father of John Wilkes and Edwin, in *Hamlet*, *King Lear*, *Othello*, *Merchant of Venice*, and *Richard III*.[12] On the second trip, Lincoln would have been in New Orleans for around a month between the end of April and sometime during the first two weeks of June 1831—probably for the month of May. (The theater season generally ran from November to April but might be stretched to the last days of May.) A notice in the *New Orleans Bee (L'Abeille)* for May 24, 1831, announces *Catharine et Petruchio* ("Comédie de Shakespeare"—presumably eighteenth-century English actor David Garrick's version of *The Taming of the Shrew*) at the Theatre de la Rue de Camp.[13] Though the ad is in French (the *Bee* was a bilingual newspaper), the production was probably in English. Apart from his stay in New Orleans itself, Lincoln may have had the opportunity to see Shakespeare on the journey down and back. Richard Campanella has uncovered the reminiscences of John A. Watkins, who described "one operation that [Lincoln's companion Allen] Gentry and Lincoln may well have laid eyes on, if not experienced." "One of the features of the flatboat system," recalled Watkins,

> was that a certain boat was tastily fitted up with a stage, with scenery and with other appointments for theatrical exhibitions. This floating theatre was tied up for several months at a time at the Rodney landing during the seasons from the year 1826 to the year 1834, and the company gave performances which were highly enjoyed by the country-folk of the vicinity, and along the river. "Hamlet," "Othello," "Richard III," the melodrama—they hesitated at nothing.[14]

Although this sounds somewhat more respectable than the Shakespeare performances of Mark Twain's King and Duke in *Adventures of Huckleberry Finn*, the plays were very probably stripped-down presentations, perhaps little more than readings. If Lincoln did experience something of this kind, it could have been his introduction to Shakespeare performance.

Lincoln had a number of opportunities to see Shakespeare performed in Springfield, even if, in the words of John Hay, that city combined "the meanness of the North with the barbarism of the South."[15] Hay's scorn aside, Springfield was not entirely without culture, and amateur theatricals are known to have taken place there by the mid-1830s.[16] Paul Angle finds that a "Thespian Society" was organized in November 1836, the year before Lincoln settled in the town: "The first performance, a melodrama called 'The Charcoal Burner,' was given on December 7."[17] The Thespian Society gave at least two more performances, one in January 1837 (of "the last two acts in the tragedy 'Pizarro or the Death of Rolla'") and two in February (of the "entertaining drama of the RENT DAY"),[18] before seemingly disappearing from the record. We also know that at least one touring theater company played in Springfield before 1839, when the town became the capital of Illinois. In February 1838, MacKenzie and Jefferson, also known as the Illinois Theatrical Company, which in 1837 had been the first company to establish itself in Chicago, put on a twelve-day run of plays in the dining room of the American House Hotel that illustrated "the beauties of virtue, and the hatefulness of vice."[19] The only Shakespeare play mentioned in the *Illinois Weekly State Journal* is *Othello*, though it is difficult to tell if the play was actually performed. As the time of the company's departure neared, the *Journal* expressed the hope that "by the time they visit us again, we may have a good theatre built for their reception."[20] The company did indeed return in the summer of 1839, in advance of which we read that "a commodious building is now being erected . . . for the use of the company."[21] Their stay appears to have been short, but they were back in November and planned to remain "during the ensuing session of the Legislature," when they were expected to "add to the variety of entertainments to be presented to our visitors this winter."[22] Again, there is no reference to Shakespeare or to any other of the plays they put on.

We know a bit more about the Illinois Theatrical Company's visit to Springfield from the reminiscences of the famous actor Joseph Jefferson, who, many years after the event, wrote of visiting the Illinois capital as a boy in 1839 with his father and uncle, Joseph Jefferson II and Alexander MacKenzie. The company built a theater—Jefferson describes it as looking like "a large dry-goods box with a roof"[23]—in what had become the capital city, but, in part because of pressure from a religious revival going on at the time, the city fathers did not allow it to open or plays to be put on without the payment of a punishing tax. As Jefferson tells it, a young lawyer heard of their plight and volunteered his services: "He handled the subject with tact, skill, and humor, tracing the history of the drama from the time when Thespis acted in a cart to the stage of today. He illustrated his speech with a number of anecdotes, and kept the council in a roar of laughter; his good humor prevailed, and the exorbitant tax was taken off."[24] After this build up, we are not altogether surprised to discover that the young lawyer was Abraham Lincoln. Though this is another of those stories that sound almost too good to be true (and Jefferson was writing in 1890, fifty years after the events he describes, though he had often told the tale to friends and even to audiences during curtain calls),[25] support for Jefferson's claim can be found in the *Law Practice of Abraham Lincoln* on-line archive, which includes the following entry excerpted from Lincoln's fee book: "Lincoln and Stuart provided unspecified legal services related to notes on the Illinois Theatrical Company. Lincoln received $3.50 and Stuart received $1.50 for their services."[26] No other details are known, but the case was argued in July 1839, which nicely fits Jefferson's account and the announcement in the Springfield newspaper.[27]

Although we do not know if MacKenzie and Jefferson provided Lincoln with a couple of complimentary passes along with his legal fee, he seems to have gone to at least one of the Illinois Theatrical Company performances. Many years later, Sarah Rickard Barret recalled meeting Lincoln when she was around twelve years old and a frequent visitor to the home of her sister and brother-in-law, William Butler, where Lincoln was boarding—and, for a time, perhaps rooming—from 1837 to 1842. "As I grew up," she told William Herndon, "[Lincoln] used to take me to little Entertainments the first was Babes in the woods, he took me to the first Theater that ever played in Springfield, when I arrived at the age of 16 he became more attentive to me"[28]—so attentive, indeed, that he proposed marriage to the young woman. "She rejected the offer because, as she later explained, 'his peculiar manner and his General deportment would not be likely to fascinate a young girl just entering the society world.'"[29] Not all biographers and historians accept the marriage proposal story (there is nothing about it in David Donald's *Lincoln*), but Sarah's account of going with Lincoln to "the first Theater that ever played in Springfield" is quite straightforward and accords well with the known facts.

Unfortunately, Joseph Jefferson does not indicate what the company played during its several-months-long Springfield stay, but we know from other sources that MacKenzie and Jefferson had a large repertoire that at various times included *Hamlet, Othello, Romeo and Juliet, Richard III, Macbeth,* and *Catharine and Petruchio.* When visiting the mining boom town of Galena, Illinois, probably not long before their visit to Springfield, they "presented the classics of Shakespeare and Goldsmith—*Hamlet, Othello, Macbeth, She Stoops to Conquer*—as well as the more commonly produced contemporary European and American melodramas like *Pizzaro* or *The Lady of Lyons*."[30] In the course of their 1839 Chicago season, they presented *Macbeth, Romeo and Juliet, Catharine and Petruchio*, and *Hamlet*, among other plays;[31] playing in Dubuque, Iowa, the previous year, they had performed *Othello* and *Richard III* along with the usual melodramas and comedies. The season in Springfield, in any case, "lasted only slightly longer than the earlier one in Galena and was not as great a success as the company had hoped."[32] Mary Todd did not come to live in Springfield until October 1839 (though she made a brief visit in 1835 and again in the summer of 1837), so she is unlikely to have had any influence, theatrical or otherwise, on Lincoln before then.[33]

What other theater, and in particular Shakespeare productions, Lincoln might have seen in Springfield is an open question; Katherine Helm, presumably relying on the reminiscences of Mary Lincoln's sister, writes that "[Mary] sympathized warmly with Mr. Lincoln in his fondness for the theater, and they rarely missed a good company playing in Springfield."[34] As we have seen, however, "good companies" would have been few and far between in Springfield, at least in the early years of the Lincoln marriage. But by the mid-1850s Shakespeare productions had begun to appear, if sporadically. On February 24 and March 2, 1855, for example, *Othello* was performed by "a talented Dramatic Company from St. Louis and New Orleans Theatres" featuring one Boothroyd Emmett playing the title role on the first occasion (when "the Laughable Farce of a LOAN OF A LOVER" was also presented) and Iago on the second.[35] A surprisingly balanced review of the later staging noted that "Salisbury as Othello . . . outdid himself," though "some portions of the third and fourth acts were overacted." "Mr. Emmett's personification of Iago was superb," however, and "others who appeared did not hinder the principal characters by very bad playing." On March 3 "the tragedy of Richard III was performed with great success" by the same company, and a repeat of the same play was announced for March 13.[36] Yet another performance of *Othello*, with an unknown cast, played on June 11, 1856; coincidentally, Lincoln, who was in Springfield for each of these dates, had delivered a speech condemning slavery the evening before.[37]

Lincoln's best opportunity to see Shakespeare came when the now-forgotten actor Charles Walter Couldock performed for several weeks in Springfield early in 1857. Couldock, an Englishman brought to America by Charlotte Cushman, was known both for his performances of Shakespeare's major roles and as a star of popular drama.[38] "Between 1850 and 1855

"A Long Farewell to All My Greatness." Charles W. Couldock as Cardinal Wolsey. *Folger Shakespeare Library.*

Couldock was leading man in the stock company of Philadelphia's Walnut Street Theatre, appearing in Shakespeare one night (*Othello, Macbeth, King Lear, Hamlet, Henry VIII, As You Like It*, and *Much Ado about Nothing*) and romantic melodramas the next (*The Wife, The Hunchback, The Honeymoon,* and *Louis XI*)."[39] One of his best-known Shakespearean roles was as Wolsey in *Henry VIII*—a portrait of him in that role bears the caption "So farewell to the little good you bear me, farewell, a long farewell to all my greatness,"[40] the first line of a speech Lincoln appears to have known well from a play he counted as among his favorites. In Springfield, Couldock's Shakespearean roles were Hamlet on February 12 and 14, Othello on February 18 and 20, Petruchio (presumably) in *Taming a Shrew* on February 21, and Richard III on February 19 and 25. His repertory also included appearances in *Richelieu* on February 9 and 16, *The Willow Copse* on February 13, and *The Advocate,* which was paired with *Taming a Shrew*, on February 21.

Springfield newspapers greeted Couldock warmly. Announcing his debut the following evening in *Richelieu,* the *Daily Illinois State Journal* informed its readers, "Mr. Couldock is said by critics in the eastern cities, to not be inferior to the world renowned tragedian Edwin Forrest in the character of Richelieu. The citizens of Springfield may never again have an opportunity of revelling in real intellectual enjoyment, let them embrace the present."[41] Reporting on his opening-night performance the next day, the paper color- fully noted, "One of the greatest tragedians now on the American boards, last night represented the character of Cardinal Richelieu, at the Metropolitan, before an interesting crowded house, composed of the beauty and chivalry of the State."[42] The *Daily Illinois State Register* told its readers, "Mr. Couldock has established a lasting popularity with our people [Illinois? America?]. He is truly great in every thing he undertakes. . . . Mr. [Edwin] Forrest has but one rival in the United States, and that is Mr. Couldock."[43] In a follow-up no- tice, the *Register* commented, "Mr. C. can just play Hamlet a little better than any other live man" and promised those going to *Othello* that they would see "this world renowned tragedy performed in a style that you may never again have an opportunity [*sic*]."[44] As it is almost impossible to separate editorial comment from paid advertising or simple boosterism, these testimonials should not be taken entirely at face value.

Lincoln was not available for all of Couldock's performances, however. For one thing, this was the "gay season," as Paul Angle writes, and social events were frequent.[45] In a letter dated February 16, Mrs. Lincoln wrote to her sister Emilie, "Within the last three weeks, there has been a party, almost every night & some two or three grand fetes, are coming off this week."[46] The

Lincolns attended a gala at the governor's mansion on the thirteenth; on that date, Couldock was performing in a favorite of his audience's, *The Willow Copse.* And Lincoln visited Chicago during that period, leaving sometime between February 21 and 26—he was certainly there by the twenty-eighth, when he gave a speech—and not returning until March 4 or 5.[47] If he left on February 21, as he had planned, he could not have seen Couldock in *Taming a Shrew* or the reading of *Macbeth.* But he could have seen *Hamlet* on February 12 or 14, *Othello* on the eighteenth or twentieth, and *Richard III* on the nineteenth. Unfortunately, there is little in the way of specific description of either the acting or the staging of these plays in the local notices. Couldock's supporting casts are scarcely mentioned in the press ("Kate Denin Ryan as Ophelia. Dance . . . Miss Delia Wright"),[48] and at least some of the players would have been drawn from local talent. (When Couldock played in Ohio the previous year, a reviewer commented of his appearance in *Macbeth* that "miserably supported as Mr. Couldock was . . . yet in two acts at least—the 2d and 3d, he rose superior even to these harassing difficulties and disqualifications.")[49] Sets and costumes, likewise, are ignored in the reviews.

If we look elsewhere for evaluations of Couldock's Shakespeare productions, we discover little more in the way of specifics. What reviews there are, almost exclusively of Couldock's acting, range from high praise to withering abuse, neither of which tells us what kind of performer he was. His reading of *Macbeth* was particularly well received. When he gave it in Cleveland soon after appearing in Springfield, the *Plain Dealer* was impressed: "Mr. Couldock's face—changing color with the sentiment of the writer; now pale with terror; then flushed with passions; his eye searching the hearts of men with its deep-fraught thought, which the frame dilates with; quick coming emotion, all conspire to make this 'star' of the Western boards the very first in the constellation."[50] He seems to have been particularly popular in Chicago, where we read, for example, that "a more perfect Othello has never been given on the Chicago stage."[51] A critic in Columbus, Ohio, wrote, "No actor that we have seen since the great Booth, can do more complete justice to this great character [of Richard III]."[52] The *Mobile (Ala.) Evening News* of December 20 and 26, 1855, on the other hand, was not happy with Couldock's Richard—evidently, the actor made of it "a farce . . . and a devilish broad farce at that." The critic went on to suggest that Shakespeare was beyond Couldock's reach and that he would be better off sticking to melodrama.[53] Commenting on several performances in New York in 1860, *Frank Leslie's Illustrated Newspaper* noted, "Of Mr. Couldock's Cardinal Wolsey and Macbeth we cannot speak in terms of praise; he is hard and angular, and jerks out the words of the text with an apparent unconsciousness of their meaning."[54] When Couldock appeared for a run in Washington at Ford's Theatre in November 1862, he did not perform in Shakespeare at all.

In addition to stagings of Shakespeare's plays, Springfield hosted lectures and readings that would feature or at least include Shakespeare. The essayist and poet Ralph Waldo Emerson delivered three lectures there, on January 10, 11, and 12, 1853, and Lincoln probably attended at least one of these.[55] On December 15, 1858, the Library Association announced that "the distinguished lecturer" Reverend Henry Giles would give two lectures, the first of which was to be "Women in Shakespeare."[56] On January 27, 1855, the aforementioned Boothroyd Emmett read from *Othello*; regretfully, "there were few persons present." He read again, this time from *Richard III* on the twenty-ninth, the *Daily Illinois State Journal* noting, "Admission is free, but a collection will be taken to pay the expense of the Hall."[57] Women seem to have been popular as lecturers and readers: on March 17, "Mrs. Macready" gave an evening of readings that included scenes from *Macbeth*, and on July 7, "Miss M. A. Tree" gave "one of her much admired Shakspearian Readings" of *Hamlet*.[58] The February 18, 1854, program, "Shakespeare and Dramatic Olios," might best be described as an in-between entertainment, neither stage production nor reading, in which "the Celebrated Tragedian Mrs. H. L. Clark" gave "Entertainments in appropriate costume, consisting of Scenes from the plays of Shakespeare and other celebrated authors," including two scenes from *Macbeth*; the *Journal* advised its readers to "patronize the chaste entertainments now presented nightly at the Court House."[59] When Couldock read from *Macbeth* during his 1857 run, the *Daily Illinois State Register* asserted that this presented "an opportunity to many persons who do not patronize theatres to hear the immortal bard read by a man capable of doing so."[60] Clearly, one advantage of Shakespeare readings and lectures over stagings, apart from logistics, was that they could be thought to avoid the moral taint associated with actual theater.

The "elocutionist" James Murdoch came to Springfield in 1849 to perform in Friedrich Schiller's *The Robbers* (but not, evidently, in Shakespeare),[61] and, as mentioned in chapter 2, he performed two public readings in Springfield in January 1861, one devoted to *Hamlet* and one that included selections from "Othello and Macbeth, and the historical play of King Henry the Fourth, together with selections from Byron, Scott, Tennyson, [and] T. Buchanan Read" and concluding with "the trial for breach of promise" from *The Pickwick Papers*.[62] The *Hamlet* evening consisted of the "Recitation of the Principal scenes and soliloquies" together with a running commentary.[63] According to the *Daily Illinois State Journal*, "A rich intellectual feast awaits our citizens."[64] Lincoln attended one or both of the lecture-readings[65] and met and conversed with Murdoch—discussing, among other things, the characters of Dickens's Sam Weller and Shakespeare's Falstaff. "His [Lincoln's] clear insight into characterization was apparent in the expression of his conception of the personalities of Falstaff and old Weller, who seemed to be especial favorites with him," Murdoch later recalled. "Speaking of Dickens, he said that his works of fiction were so near the reality that the author seemed to him to have picked up his materials from actual life as he elbowed his way through its crowded thoroughfares, after the manner, in a certain sense, of Shakespeare himself."[66] Commentators have doubted Murdoch's word here, on the grounds that Lincoln, who had once been quoted as saying that he had never read a novel to the end, was unlikely to have read Dickens. But he may simply have been responding to Murdoch's readings.[67] Lincoln would come to know Murdoch better later in Washington, when the actor contributed his talents to the Sanitary Commission and visited the White House on at least one occasion to give patriotic readings.

Lincoln could also have seen Shakespeare in Chicago, a city he visited on a number of occasions from 1847 to 1860. Although the theater scene in Chicago in the 1830s was not notably advanced over what was on offer in Springfield in the same period—the first recorded performance where an admission was charged was in 1833,[68] and it was nearly the end of the decade before Shakespeare began to make regular appearances—by the early 1840s the city had seen a fairly rapid growth in theatrical activity. Beginning in 1847, perhaps even earlier, Lincoln made almost yearly trips to Chicago, initially on legal business and later for politics as well. Orville Browning, a Whig officeholder and close friend from Illinois, records in his diary two visits to the theater in Chicago in July 1857 with Lincoln, when they were both attending circuit court sessions, though in neither case was it to see a Shakespeare play. On the first occasion, they saw the famous comic actor William E. Burton perform one of his signature roles, Timothy Toodles, and the second time they saw Burton as Captain Cuttle in an adaptation of Charles Dickens's *Dombey and Son*.[69] Browning's diary is the best evidence we have that Lincoln attended the theater in Chicago, and it allows us to suppose that he may have done so on other occasions. A less reliable source, Henry C. Whitney, remembered that

> on or about the 23d day of March, 1860, only a few weeks before the sitting of the Chicago Convention, [Lincoln] was at Chicago attending

the United States Court, being then quite a candidate for the Presidency. I had three tickets presented to me for Rumsey & Newcomb's Minstrels, a high-toned troupe, and I asked him if he would like to go to a "nigger show" that night; he assented rapturously; his words were: "of all things I would rather do to-night, that suits me exactly," and I never saw him apparently enjoy himself more than he did at that entertainment.[70]

We know from other sources as well that Lincoln was in Chicago on that date and that he did indeed enjoy minstrel shows; whatever the accuracy of the details, the manner in which Whitney tells the story contributes to his seeming enjoyment at presenting Lincoln as a country bumpkin.

If we look at the Shakespeare productions taking place in Chicago and coordinate that information with Lincoln's visits to the city, we find that he more often than not missed opportunities to see Shakespeare. Lincoln's first recorded trip to Chicago was in 1847, the year that city's first building specifically designed as a theater was constructed and its first dramatic stock company was founded,[71] when, as newly elected congressman, he attended the Rivers and Harbors convention from July 3 or 4 to July 7. Had he visited a month later, he could have seen his future acquaintance James Murdoch in *Hamlet, Romeo and Juliet,* and *Macbeth.*[72] He stayed in Chicago again for a few days in 1848 (October 5 to 7), just missing an extended appearance by Junius Brutus Booth in *Hamlet, Richard III, Macbeth,* and *The Merchant of Venice*; earlier in the year (June 8 to 20), Edwin Forrest had appeared, playing, among other roles, Othello, Hamlet, and Lear. On a visit from July 7 to July 26, 1850, he once again missed the chance to see Murdoch, who played in *Romeo and Juliet* on June 15. No Shakespeare production seems to have been available to Lincoln from December 8 to 14, 1852, when he visited on legal business, but he could have caught a production of *Uncle Tom's Cabin* at Rice's Chicago Theatre on December 13. In 1854, Lincoln may have been in Chicago from February 16 to 18, though this is not certain; he was there on October 27, when he gave an anti-Nebraska speech; Shakespeare, as far as can be determined, was not playing on either occasion. No productions were available on his next trip, which lasted from around July 2 to at least July 14, 1855. He made three trips to Chicago in 1856, at various dates in July (15, 19, and perhaps 26); on August 26 and 28; and on December 9, 10, and 11. In July, he was particularly busy: he combined legal business with politics, making speeches not only in Chicago but also in the Illinois towns of Galena, Dixon, Oregon, and Sterling. Again, the evidence—which is necessarily incomplete—suggests that little Shakespeare was performed on these dates;

he would have just missed an appearance by Charles Walter Couldock in *Hamlet, Macbeth, Othello, Catharine and Petruchio,* and *King Lear* (the run ended on June 22).

The next year, Lincoln was perhaps in Chicago February 21 and 23 and was certainly there on February 28, when he gave a speech to Republicans at Metropolitan Hall; on February 23, he could have seen "the rising sou-brette"[73] Maggie Mitchell, whom he would later see in Washington, in *Satan in Paris* and *The Maid with the Milking Pail.* Lincoln was again in Chicago on March 2 and perhaps 3 (on March 20, James H. Hackett began a run that ended on April 11 and that included performances of both *Henry IV* and *The Merry Wives of Windsor*), and on May 21 and possibly on 22 and 23; the purpose and exact length of this last visit is not known. On the evening of the May 21 he could have chosen from several Shakespeare performances. At the Chicago Theatre, Jean Davenport, a popular English actress who may have been the model for the "infant phenomenon" in Charles Dickens's *Nicholas Nickleby,* was playing Shakespeare's Juliet, one of her most popular roles. J. W. Wallack, whom Lincoln would see in Washington in *Macbeth,* was at North's National Theatre, playing *Othello* on May 19 and *Richard III* on May 21. Lincoln's final 1857 stay was from July 7 to July 18, during which time, as we have seen, he attended the theater on two occasions (on July 8 and July 13) with Orville Browning. He may have attended the theater at other times during this stay, but there does not appear to have been any Shakespeare on offer.

Not surprisingly, Lincoln spent a good deal of time in Chicago in 1858–1860, a period crucial to his political fortunes. In 1858, he visited the city four times: February 15 to 18; March 9, 10, and 11; July 9 to 13; and July 21 to 24; he passed through on October 28. Had he visited in January, he could have seen Charlotte Cushman, one of the most highly praised Shakespearean actors in the country, in *Macbeth, Romeo and Juliet* (she played Romeo), and *Henry VIII* (as Constance); he would see her Lady Macbeth later in Washington. On February 18, he could have seen, once again, a production of *Romeo and Juliet* at McVicker's Theatre, though with an apparently undistinguished cast. During his March and July visits, little in the way of Shakespeare was playing; he missed seeing the up-and-coming Edwin Booth making his Chicago debut in *Hamlet, Othello* (as Iago), *Macbeth,* and *Richard III,* along with several non-Shakespearean roles, playing from the end of May to June 12. Hackett again appeared—"brought out of retirement," not for the first or last time—in Chicago in December 1858 in *Henry IV* and *Merry Wives*; we know from his own testimony that Lincoln did not see Hackett at this or any other time before he became president. In 1859, Lincoln made five trips to

Chicago: February 28 to March 2; June 3 to June 7 or 8 (he was accompanied by his young son, Willie, on this trip); July 20, as well as some possible dates before and after, though he was back in Springfield on July 22; September 29 and 30 (when he shuttled between Chicago and Milwaukee); and November 10 to 12. On none of these visits was Shakespeare available, as far as we can tell (Hackett was performing in Chicago in April; Murdoch played Hamlet on May 9). Lincoln, in any case, was very busy with law cases and speech making and probably would have had little time for the theater. The following year, he visited Chicago March 23 to April 4 (on a big law case); and as president-elect, November 21 to 25 (departing on the morning of the twenty-sixth). Though, as we have seen, he may have gone to a minstrel show on the earlier visit, no Shakespeare was available. Had he gone to the theater as president-elect, some notice would have been taken of it; in any case, Shakespeare was not being played at that time.

In addition to his Chicago visits, Lincoln had opportunities to attend the theater when he traveled east on various occasions before becoming president, though there is scant evidence that he did so. (He was less likely to have gone to the theater, if theater had been available, when he went to Ohio, Wisconsin, Kansas, and elsewhere in the 1850s making political speeches on usually tight schedules.) He did see at least one play while he served in the U.S. Congress for the 1847–1849 term. We know, on the basis of good if indirect evidence, that he and Mary went to see the popular young actress Julia Dean. In a letter to a friend written from Springfield in January 1860, Mary reports on her visit to St. Louis to see several of her cousins for a week. "Whilst there," she writes, "Julia Dean Hayne had a benefit. . . . Ten years ago, about the time of her debut, I saw her in Washington, she has failed greatly since then."[74] The Lincolns left Washington sometime around March 21, 1849; Dean's one- or two-week engagement in that city ended on Saturday, March 24. Although Dean sometimes played Lady Macbeth and other classical roles, her plays on this occasion were *The Italian Wife, The Wrecker's Daughter, The Lady of Lyons, The Lydian Queen,* and *Ion,* for the most part popular, contemporary plays. A newspaper critic, in praising Dean's D.C. run, gives us as well an indication of the marginal state of theater in the nation's capital in the late 1840s: "When we consider the limited size of the stage, the want of appropriate scenery and decorations, and the absence of a large stock company, [Dean's performances] cannot, in our judgment, be excelled."[75] The only other entertainment, apart from bowling,[76] we hear about from the Lincolns themselves was of a musical kind: we know that sometime in early January 1848, the congressman and his wife attended a performance by the Ethiopian Serenaders," a minstrel show, at Carusi's Saloon (in spite of its name, a respectable venue) and that he went alone (Mary had left Washington to visit relatives in Kentucky) to listen to music on the Capitol grounds on the first of July.[77] Junius Brutus Booth played in Washington around April or May of 1848, but we have no evidence that Lincoln saw him. His campaign tour of Massachusetts in September 1848, accompanied by Mary and the children, kept him sufficiently busy with speeches, meetings, and banquets that he would hardly have had time for anything else.[78]

Lincoln was in New York with Mary, ostensibly collecting a legal fee, for more than a week in late July and early August 1857 and was there alone in late February 1860, when he delivered his Cooper Union address and afterward spoke in several New England towns. Once again, however, existing records are silent on what he might have done for entertainment on these occasions. President-elect Lincoln did attend the opera—Giuseppe Verdi's *Un ballo in maschera*—in New York on his preinauguration visit in February 1861, staying only through the first act. The children, according to the *Chicago Tribune*, rather surprisingly went to Laura Keene's theater, which was playing a musical extravaganza, *The Seven Sisters*, described in one source as an "operatic, spectacular, diabolical, musical, terpsichorean, farcical burletta," into which Keene, some ten days earlier, had incorporated a new element, "Extracts from Uncle Sam's Magic Lantern, a series of tableaux bearing on the great tragedy of Secession then rending the republic."[79] *The Seven Sisters*, however, was also something of a "leg show," featuring, according to one theatergoer, "a bevy of beauties, dressed in good, tight-fitting clothes."[80] The patriotic aspect of the program presumably outweighed possible parental concern about the burlesque element, and one assumes that eighteen-year-old Robert, at least, enjoyed himself.[81] Mary and a friend evidently saw the production during the week she famously spent shopping in New York in May 1861.[82]

The Washington, D.C., that Lincoln came to in late February 1861 had "only two shabby theatres" actively putting on plays, both "with reputations for shoddy productions and less-than-refined audiences."[83] The beginnings of theatrical activity can be dated from the removal of the capital from Philadelphia in 1800, and Shakespeare was presented at least once in that year when English-born Thomas Abthorpe Cooper, America's leading actor in the first quarter of the nineteenth century, and his company performed *Romeo and Juliet* in September at the United States (or, alternatively, the National) Theatre, which was located in the Blodgett Hotel.[84] In 1804, what appears to have been the first structure in the city built specifically for putting on plays, the Washington Theatre, opened at Eleventh and C Streets N.W.; it burned down in 1820. A new theater, the Washington City Assembly Rooms, also known as Carusi's Saloon (salon), was constructed at the same site in 1822. Another theater, the Washington, was built in 1821, but it closed in 1836. In the meantime, in 1835 a second National Theatre was built on E Street between Thirteenth and Fourteenth Streets, its present site. Consumed by fire in 1845, it was rebuilt in 1850 as the New National Hall. That structure partly collapsed in 1851; rebuilt, it was renamed once again the National Theatre, only to burn down in 1857 and reopen in 1862 as the New National (also known as Grover's National).[85] Soon considered inadequate, it was refurbished before once again reopening, with much fanfare, on October 6, 1863, with President Lincoln present to witness E. L. Davenport in *Othello*. The other venue that figures prominently in Lincoln's theatergoing was, of course, the one managed by John T. Ford. In 1861, Ford acquired the lease on an abandoned building that had housed the First Baptist Church and used it as a theater. Renovated early in 1862, the building was severely damaged by fire at the end of the year. Ford then constructed a new building that reopened as Ford's New Theatre in August 1863.

In an essay not published until 1909, Leonard Grover, who managed the National Theatre, made much of his association with Lincoln, writing, among other things, "During the four years of his administration, he visited my theater probably more than a hundred times."[86] Grover's claim, often repeated by subsequent biographers (notably, Carl Sandburg), is unsupported by any solid evidence, and the number is in any case highly suspect. It is reasonable to suppose that Grover's memory, fifty-plus years on, played tricks on him. He writes, for example, that Lincoln "often came [to the theater] alone, many times brought his little son Tad, and on special occasions, Mrs. Lincoln" but that, as far as he knew, "he was never accompanied by any other member of his household." Again, this does not really square with the facts: we know, for example, that John Hay, at least, accompanied Lincoln on several occasions, even though Grover specifically writes that neither Hay nor John Nicolay ever went with him.[87] Grover claims, somewhat more convincingly, that he would at times sit in the presidential box and converse with Lincoln:

> Such conversation as took place was always about the theater. As auditor, or spectator, Mr. Lincoln was not exacting. As is well known, he was exceedingly conversant with Shakspere. He enjoyed a classical representation, of which I gave many, . . . but he was satisfied with being

entertained and amused, and to have his mind taken from the sea of troubles which awaited him elsewhere. On one occasion he said to me, "Do you know, Mr. Grover, I really enjoy a minstrel show."[88]

The last comment is supported by a report in the *New York Herald* for February 26, 1863, noting that Lincoln attended Grover's for a performance by Barney Williams, a well-known Irish comedian and blackface minstrel.

Observations of a similar nature come from another source, albeit one close to Grover, his business partner, William E. Sinn. He, too, remembers (his account dates from 1895), though less precisely, that Lincoln "was a frequent visitor at Grover & Sinn's National Theatre."[89] The president, Sinn writes, "was a great admirer of the drama, and was particularly fond of comedy. When a good strong comedian appeared at our house, male or female, you would always find Mr. Lincoln present at the performance, unless sickness or extremely important business prevented his attendance." Again, one has to consider the word "always" as an exaggeration. Sinn also notes that Lincoln paid his own way: "From a business point of view, we were only too glad to have him visit the theatre, because it was a good advertisement, and we would have willingly given him complimentary tickets; but he would firmly decline them, invariably directing his secretary, or the messenger, to pay for the box." Lincoln, evidently, had no interest in going behind the scenes, telling Sinn that he did not want to ruin the theatrical illusion. At other times, however, "When very prominent actors appeared . . . in whom he was specially interested, Mr. Lincoln would invite them into his private box between the acts, and have a chat with them," as when, according to Noah Brooks, he invited John McCullough, who was playing Edgar to Edwin Forrest's Lear, to his box to praise his performance. Sinn also provides an amusing view of Lincoln, looking over the crowded auditorium and exclaiming, "Ah! . . . I guess *this* business will pay."[90]

During the first two years of his presidency, Lincoln, in fact, seldom attended the theater; it was not until 1863 that he began to visit more regularly.[91] According to Lincoln's young journalist friend Noah Brooks, "President Lincoln's theater-going was usually confined to occasions when Shakespeare's plays were enacted; for, although he enjoyed a hearty laugh, he was better pleased with the stately dignity, deep philosophy, and exalted poetry of Shakspere than with anything that was to be found in more modern dramatic writings."[92] Brooks clearly wants to make the martyred president appear as respectable as possible; insofar as Lincoln's theatergoing can be limited to Shakespeare, he can remain above criticism, at least for some commentators.

Shakespeare, here, becomes the "beard" that guarantees respectability. But even Shakespeare could not shield Lincoln from attack. When he went to see Hackett in *Henry IV*, William Stoddard reports,

> There were some persons . . . who criticized the President severely for his heartless wickedness in ever going to the theater, . . . A critic shouts: "There he is! That's all he cares for his poor soldiers." . . . Another party . . . in uniform, was instantly up, declaring vociferously that: "De President haf a right to his music! Put out dot feller! De President ees all right! Let him have his music!" There was a confused racket for a few seconds and then the luckless critic went out of the theater, borne upon the strong arms of several boys in blue who agreed with their German comrade as to the right of Abraham Lincoln to as much theatrical relief as they themselves were.[93]

That Lincoln was murdered while attending the theater would not go unnoticed by some of the ministers who delivered eulogies in the days and weeks after the president's death. Most seem to have resisted the impulse to expand on the topic, though John Wilkes Booth's profession was not ignored: obliquely, at least, Lincoln's theatergoing could be critiqued even if, as time would show, it was more or less happenstance that Booth murdered Lincoln in a theater.

The truth is that Lincoln, like many of his contemporaries, had a taste for melodrama, sentimental performance, minstrelsy, and perhaps even leg shows, if the report is true that he attended a performance of *Mazeppa, the Wild Horse of Tartary*, featuring the notorious "naked lady," Ada Menken.[94] The non-Shakespearean productions Lincoln saw included, notoriously, a performance of a melodrama called *The Marble Heart*, starring John Wilkes Booth. And, of course, it was to a performance of a popular contemporary play, *Our American Cousin*, that Lincoln went on the evening of April 14, 1865. He saw Barney Williams, as Grover notes, and he attended a benefit performance for the wildly popular Maggie Mitchell in *Fanchon, the Cricket* ("in this and other plays," according to Mitchell's *New York Times* obituary, "she appeared often before President Lincoln"[95]—almost certainly another exaggeration). At times, the Lincolns would attend the theater in support of a favorite charity: on January 20, 1864, for example, they went to Grover's National Theatre to see a benefit performance of Tom Taylor's *The Ticket of Leave Man* "in aid of the Ladies' Soldiers' Relief Association"[96] (Taylor, notoriously, also wrote *Our American Cousin*). During his presidency, Lincoln also attended the opera, almost always with his wife, Mary, as well as a variety of other musical performances.

When Lincoln, in February and March 1863, attended a series of Edwin Booth's productions, he, like most playgoers, saw the actor in his non-Shakespearean roles more often than in Shakespeare. The hold Shakespeare maintained on the American stage throughout the nineteenth century began to loosen in the mid-1850s, and by the mid-1870s the popularity of Shakespeare's plays, relative to the works of other playwrights, had been significantly reduced.[97] "In the decades before 1855," one theater historian reports, "Shakespearean performances in all cities of the Northeast easily outnumbered those of any contemporary playwright by three to one. For roughly 20 years after 1855, however, Shakespeare's relative popularity was cut nearly in half."[98] Many of the "popular" roles Edwin Booth played were also played by his father, his brother John Wilkes, Edwin Forrest, E. L. Davenport, and others; they would continue to be popular well into the next century. "When they weren't doing Shakespeare, the great Shakesperean actors of the nineteenth century were thrilling their audiences with romantic heroes and villains of a lesser order . . . which most playgoers thought as moving and fascinating as Hamlet or Iago."[99] Unproduced and unread today, plays like *Richelieu, The Apostate*, and *The Fool's Revenge* were central to the nineteenth-century repertoire, and they frequently exhibited a style (blank verse, or something like it) and tone "directly borrowed from or inspired by the dramatic masters of past ages, especially Shakespeare."[100] "Irrespective of their literary merits," one theater historian has written, in England, where a number of these plays originated, "verse plays of the nineteenth century share a conviction that Shakespeare represents a cultural and, crucially, a national well-spring to which drama must return if it is to renew itself,"[101] a sentiment that carried over to America.

If Shakespeare was becoming less of a draw in the 1860s than he had been in earlier decades, it is also true that in the period from the 1840s to the 1860s, "one can perceive a certain coming-of-age of Shakespeare in the American theatre," both in terms of developing American scholarship and in growing theatrical independence from England.[102] "By 1870," one theater historian has written, "an experienced theatergoer, now accustomed to decorous surroundings, might struggle to recall the bedlam sometimes known in earlier days."[103] The barnstorming manner of a Junius Brutus Booth came to be replaced by the careful, disciplined work of his son Edwin; the rowdy behavior of audiences, especially in the pit (renamed the "parquette"), gave way to gentility and patience, a change reinforced by the banishing of prostitutes and other "unsavory" types from the balcony or the third tier of boxes of the stage auditorium and by the removal of in-house saloons;[104] and the star system, though it remained central to the theatergoing experience, was moderated by a consideration for the overall effect of a theatrical performance, with some care being taken for a harmonious configuration of able supporting casts and elaborate, coherently designed sets and costumes. Although much of this development did not come to fruition until after the Civil War and was always most advanced in New York City, the theater Lincoln saw in the nation's capital exhibited at least some of these tendencies toward greater respectability and sophistication.

By the early 1860s, the staging of plays was becoming more elaborate as audiences began to demand both greater realism and greater splendor. Not coincidentally, this development paralleled advances in stage lighting: "Before mid-century gaslight had replaced the old oil lamps; limelight and arc-light followed."[105] Audiences, simply put, could now see what was on the stage more clearly than ever before, an improvement that would affect acting as well. Scenery, which had been more or less perfunctory at the beginning of the century ("a couple of standard drops [painted canvases across the back of the stage]—one for outdoor scenes and another for interiors—satisfied all usual requirements"),[106] was gradually replaced by three-dimensional sets. The stage nonetheless remained a kind of box, with the scenic view balanced and the various backdrops and flies presenting walls and other architectural features arranged to be perpendicular to the stage proscenium. Little in the way of diagonal or off-center action was evident. As the century developed, sets and costumes for Shakespeare's plays were rendered more and more according to the standards of historical authenticity: as early as 1846, Edmund Kean's son Charles imported a number of his "scenically ornate productions of Shakespeare"[107] to New York—a mixed blessing, however, as these productions came to resemble archeological period reconstructions that had little or nothing to do with Shakespeare's dramaturgy. Nevertheless, Kean influenced actors and producers like Edwin Booth, whose later *Hamlet* stagings took place, somewhat incongruously, in tenth-century Denmark. Although the Shakespeare productions Lincoln saw in Washington were still comparatively modest affairs, theater managers like Leonard Grover and John T. Ford were endeavoring to catch up with developments in New York and London.[108]

Performance style, too, particularly in the playing of Shakespeare, was being transformed, a change commented on by many observers even if its precise nature was seldom clearly defined. By the 1860s, some observers were suggesting that acting was undergoing a significant development for the better. Lincoln's acquaintance, the actor and elocutionist James Murdoch, would recall the acting standard in his youth in the 1830s as the "teapot" style, "which simply meant one hand on the hip, the other extended and moving in curved lines, with a gradual descent to the side." "When the speaker was tired of this," Murdoch adds, "he simply changed his attitude by throwing the weight of the body on the opposite leg and going through the same routine of gesture."[109] Many a nineteenth-century commentator, attempting to define what good acting should be, quoted from Hamlet's direction to the players:

> Do not saw the air too much with your hand . . . but use all gently; for in the very torrent, tempest, and, as I may say, whirlwind of your passion, you must acquire and beget a temperance that may give it smoothness. Oh, it offends me to the soul to hear a robustious periwig-pated fellow tear a passion to totters, to very rags, to split the ears of the groundlings. . . . Suit the action to the word, the word to the action, with this special observance, that you o'erstep not the modesty of nature. (act 3, scene 2, lines 4–18)

This, no doubt, is excellent advice; it was excellent advice in 1600, it was excellent advice in 1800 or 1900, and it is still excellent advice today. (Interestingly, Herndon's description of Lincoln's speaking style alludes to Hamlet's advice: "He did not gesticulate as much with his hands as with his head . . . He never sawed the air nor rent space into tatters and rags as some orators do.")[110] The real question, however, is, What do these precepts mean to their hearers? Would any actor, in 1600 or now, want to "tear a passion to tatters," or "split the ears of the groundlings"? Not, one would think, without good reason. Murdoch believed, "The genuine artist will exhibit in his representations of Shakespeare's characters the great attributes of his master's expression—*simplicity, nature,* and *truth.*"[111] Unfortunately, as theater historian Charles Shattuck has noted, "We do not know what such words as *beautiful* or *natural* or *gentlemanly* or *indecent* meant a century ago, or two centuries ago, to the writers who used or to the readers who then read them."[112] What is natural to one observer is artificial to another, and "simplicity" and "truth" are equally difficult to pin down.

When Hamlet's words, interpreted in various ways, are alluded to in nineteenth-century theatrical criticism and commentary, it is usually to praise a rising new star. Whichever old retiring actor he is replacing was, of course, guilty of the sins Hamlet details. The new darling of the stage is praised for suiting the action to the word and the word to the action, of providing that smoothness Hamlet desires. But in the end, are we any the wiser if we want to determine what really distinguished Edmund Kean from John Philip Kemble, or Edwin Booth from Edwin Forrest? Even when we have the evidence in front of us, on film, can we really distinguish between, say, Laurence Olivier and Kenneth Branagh on the basis of Hamlet's remarks? The elder Booth, whose larger-than-life, barnstorming performances are often cited in theater history, was praised in the following terms by a Washington critic: "He uses no tricks to catch applause, never descends to the rant and mouthing, or even the strut, which always distinguish the inferior tragedian; but seems to remember that kings and heroes can walk and talk like other people. . . . He has the rare art to conceal all art."[113] Another critic called him "one of the finest actors in the world—chaste, natural, and full of deep passion."[114] The Ovidian tag *ars est celare artem* ("it is art to conceal art"), one would think, was the last thing that could be said of Junius Brutus Booth, but there it is. At the same time, a London critic faults Booth for "a vicious propensity to rant."[115] However we wish to define the "natural style" in acting Shakespeare, it was not universally applauded. By 1872, a critic could complain that "while we revolt against the old, stilted school of those days . . . there is no reason why the grand and lofty in acting should be ignored as a delusion and a mockery. . . . How absurd, in fact, is what is called 'the natural mode' of speaking in *Hamlet* and *Macbeth*. It is obviously an incongruity."[116] In his brief treatise *On Actors and the Art of Acting*, the English critic George Henry Lewes rebelled against the "natural school": "When [Charles] Fechter [as Othello] takes out his doorkey to let himself into his house, and, on coming back, relocks the door and pockets the key, the *intention* is doubtless to give an air of reality; the effect is to make us forget the 'noble Moor,' and to think of a sepoy."[117] In attempting to re-create the performances of actors like Forrest and the Booths, of Hackett and Cushman, we are forced to rely on what are often useless generalizations; only occasionally are we given detailed and specific descriptions of a particular actor in a particular role.

Another important development taking place in the theater in the 1850s and 1860s that particularly affected "provincial" cities like Washington, D.C., was the gradual introduction of touring companies: prior to 1860 or so, "the only actor who travelled was the star."[118] What this meant, in practice, was that each city would have so-called stock companies that would support the visiting star actor when he or she came to perform. The companies varied considerably in quality and seldom spent more than a few days or even a few hours rehearsing with the star. Although it may be true that, as one theater historian has noted, "audiences attended the theatre to enjoy the star's performance" and thus "normally forgave shabby scenery or indifferent supporting casts if the star fulfilled their expectations,"[119] it is equally true that a recurring complaint of reviewers centered on the inadequacy of actors in secondary roles. When Edwin Forrest played Othello in New York in 1860, we read that "the play did not suffer so much at the hands of the actors as 'Lear' and 'Hamlet.'"[120] "Generally, when Shakespeare is on the boards," the Washington critic known as Erasmus noted in an 1864 review, "the stock [actors] stand posted and frozen about, like a chorus with their mouths closed in an opera, a mere appendage to the star."[121] When E. L. Davenport played Hamlet in Washington in 1863 (not, evidently, on either of the occasions Lincoln saw him), a reviewer claimed that "Rosecrans [sic—the Union general of that name was much in the news at this time] and Guildenstern did not know their parts, and consequently made a bad mess of it when they appeared."[122]

By the time of Lincoln's presidency, there was a slightly better chance that the original cast of a notable production, or at least the central members of it, would travel with the star or that several stars would travel together. But it was not until sometime after Lincoln's death that a whole company would go on tour, taking their sets and costumes with them. Remarkably, only a few days before Lincoln saw Charlotte Cushman as Lady Macbeth, the *Daily National Republican* reported that the actress was scouting Ford's Theatre as a possible venue for her performance and that "a suitable representative of Macbeth is wanted for that occasion";[123] in the event, she went with Grover's National Theatre, playing with James Wallack and E. L. Davenport, two actors who were already engaged at that theater. And even when the star performer was accompanied by a cast of supporting players, one continues to hear complaints of the unevenness of the acting. Edwin Booth, in particular, was often criticized for his casting choices; a critic of his 1864 *Hamlet* in New York wrote, "The jewel in the center was surrounded by California diamonds, home-made paste, bits of old looking-glass, and Coney Island pebbles—an atrocious conglomerate that would puzzle a geologist to classify."[124] Matters were improving by the years of Lincoln's presidency, but it remained true that a playgoer went to Shakespeare to see the star actor, hoping that the remainder of the cast would not be too much of a distraction.

The Shakespeare Lincoln would see in Washington during his presidency differed in another way from what he might have seen in the 1840s. Shakespeare was at that time as often as not presented as part of a longer program and was often combined with a type of entertainment that in later decades would more and more be thought to detract from the dignity of the Bard. "What would be Shakespeare's astonishment," a newspaper critic lamented in 1842, "to hear from the orchestra immediately after his inimitable dagger scene, the mysterious solemn strains of Yankee Doodle to please the gallery? Or after the mournful death of his Desdemona, a horn pipe or a country dance?"[125] In both the United Kingdom and America, an evening's entertainment at the theater could be so filled as to stretch over some five hours. One night in Dublin, Edwin Forrest "played Act Two of *King Lear*, Act Three of *Macbeth*, Act Two of *Hamlet*, Act Two of *Richard III*, and Act Three of *Othello*"; also on the bill was Emile, a celebrated French dog "acclaimed for his 'extraordinary sagacity.'"[126] As late as the 1860s, programs combined several Shakespeare plays: John Wilkes Booth could play Shylock and Petruchio on the same night,[127] and Edwin Booth, on a night Lincoln saw him, played both Shylock and the title role in a melodrama, *Don Caesar de Bazin*. And it was still necessary, evidently, to alert theatergoers planning to attend E. L. Davenport's *Hamlet* that the "tragedy is of so great a length that it will be impossible to produce a farce this evening."[128] Shakespeare's dignity was no doubt severely strained as well by the fashion of placing child actors in starring roles; in New Orleans, Junius Brutus Booth once "played Richmond to little Louisa Lane's Richard III; Miss Lane was but nine years old at the time."[129] Horses, too, could compete for attention with established Shakespearean actors: "The nobility of the steeds in one production [of *Richard III*], a critic wrote, would cause an audience to judge as a fair trade Richard's cry, 'My kingdom for a horse.'"[130] Though this fad in what was called hippodrama was also dying out by the 1860s, John Wilkes Booth evidently once played in an equestrian *Richard III* in Philadelphia.[131]

Although Lincoln may not have experienced firsthand some of the more egregious indignities Shakespeare's plays suffered at the hands of theatrical entrepreneurs, he was quite aware that the Shakespeare in the theater was not always the Shakespeare he read, which may partly explain why he is several times quoted as saying that he preferred reading the plays to seeing them performed. Charles Lamb, the English essayist, had come to a similar conclusion: "It may seem a paradox," Lamb had written as early as 1811, "but I cannot help being of opinion that the plays of Shakespeare are less calculated for performance on a stage, than those of any other dramatist whatever."[132] Lamb was, in part, reacting to what adapters like Colley Cibber and Nahum Tate had done to Shakespeare's texts, and Lincoln may have been reacting to the same thing. Indeed, Lincoln had decided opinions on how Shakespeare should be performed, even if, according to Francis Carpenter, he once remarked, "It matters not to me whether Shakspeare be well or ill acted; with him the thought suffices."[133] His interest in the opening soliloquy of *Richard*

III was at least as much that of a playgoer as of a reader. "The opening of the play of 'King Richard the Third,'" he supposedly told Carpenter, "seems to me often entirely misapprehended."

> It is quite common for an actor to come upon the stage, and, in a sophomoric style, to begin with a flourish:—

> "Now is the winter of our discontent
> Made glorious summer by this sun of York,
> And all the clouds that lowered upon our house,
> In the deep bosom of the ocean buried!"

> "Now," said he, "this is all wrong. . . . The prologue is the utterance of the most intense bitterness and satire."[134]

Carpenter's comments together with his recollection of what Lincoln said have often been taken at face value, but they present several intriguing puzzles. We might first want to suggest that the language and tone of the quoted remarks are rather more studied, stiff, and pedantic than one might expect from Abraham Lincoln in conversation; Carpenter is no doubt embellishing to some extent.[135] If we nevertheless accept that he is giving the gist of Lincoln's ideas, we might wonder just what Lincoln meant when he said that the error he finds in actors' interpretation is "quite common." Did the actors who played Richard (and virtually all Shakespearean actors did at one time or another) throughout the nineteenth century deliver the opening soliloquy as Lincoln describes it—in a "sophomoric style," and with a "flourish"? What might Lincoln have meant by such a description?

Furthermore, the only version of *Richard III* Lincoln could have seen would have been Colley Cibber's rewriting, in which "Now is the Winter of our Discontent" does not come at the beginning of the play but actually begins scene two, though these are the first words Richard speaks in either version. Cibber's revision, which dates from 1700, is a fairly drastic rewriting of Shakespeare's play that cuts about 1,500 lines, making it more than a third shorter than the original. The 2,156 lines of the adaptation are divided about equally between Cibber and Shakespeare, though 200 of Shakespeare's lines are imported from other plays. "Cibber cut and rearranged extensively in such a way as to give Richard most of the lines most of the time."[136] Lincoln undoubtedly knew that Cibber's *Richard* was not Shakespeare's *Richard*. We have already noted how he in a sense reconstructed the opening of Cibber's version when he read to Hay at the Soldiers' Home. In a speech delivered soon after the president's death, William Kelly tells of a conversation between Lincoln and several visitors to the White House, among whom was the actor John McDonough: "Probably you do not know that the acting plays are not the plays as Shakespeare wrote them," Lincoln reportedly said; "*Richard III*, for instance, begins with passages from *Henry VI*; then you get a portion of *Richard III*; then more of *Henry VI*; and then there is one of the best known soliloquies, which is not Shakespeare's at all, but was written by quite another man—by Colley Cibber, was it not, Mr. McDonough?"[137] Carpenter, who must have know this as well, chose to disregard the Cibber problem in streamlining the account of his conversation with Lincoln.

To the question of how many performances of *Richard III* Lincoln could have seen, we have, as I have argued, little more than negative evidence. Of the three noted British actors who performed Richard in America in the first half of the nineteenth century and whose influence continued well into Lincoln's theatergoing life and beyond—Edmund Kean, George Frederick Cooke, and Junius Brutus Booth—Lincoln could only have seen the last mentioned (Cooke died in 1812; Kean last appeared in America in 1826 and died in 1833), but all three performers so dominated the stage that any actor, major or minor, who subsequently played Richard would be measured according to how much he brought to mind one of the three. Booth, who was particularly famous for his Richard, a role he played from his American debut in 1821 to his death in 1852, evidently made his entrance in a notably low key: Walt Whitman, fifty years on, remembered the effect: "I can . . . see again Booth's quiet entrance from the side, as, with head bent, he slowly and in silence, . . . walks down the stage to the footlights with that peculiar and abstracted gesture, musingly kicking his sword, which he holds off from him by its sash."[138] At other times, Booth imitated Edmund Kean (he had acted with Kean in London), whose performance was the model for many a nineteenth-century Richard. Hackett provides a description of Kean's entrance: "Gloster enters hastily—head low—arms folded." (Hackett, who had closely studied Kean's Richard, may have provided Lincoln with descriptions of various actors in the course of several conversations at the White House.) Another observer provides a less admiring description of Kean's manner: "What does he mean by that 'widdle waddle' gait and that horizontal semicircular swing of the shoulders in which he introduces his Richard to the public[?] . . . Who told Mr. Kean that [Richard] waddled like a duck?"[139] As for the actual delivery of the lines, George Henry Lewes wrote of "the thrilling effect of the rich deep note upon 'buried,' when with the graceful curl of the wrist he indicated how the clouds which lowered round his head were in the deep bosom of the ocean buried."[140]

George Frederick Cooke, on the other hand, who first thrilled American audiences in 1810, "came out of the wings in a 'martial stalk,' expressive of command."[141] "He entered on the right hand of the audience," Cooke's biographer, William Dunlap, observed, "and with a dignified erect deportment walked to the centre of the stage amidst their plaudits. His appearance was picturesque, and proudly noble. His head elevated, his step firm, his eye beaming fire. He returned the salutes of the audience, not as a player to the public, on whom he depended, but as a victorious prince, acknowledging the acclamations of the populace on his return from a successful campaign—as Richard Duke of Gloster, the most valiant branch of the triumphant house of York."[142] Cooke's Richard was notable for delivering the soliloquy as an internal monologue: "You seem, verily, to be listening to a man who is unconscious that you overhear him."[143] "During the first three lines . . . he was without motion, his hands hanging at ease,"[144] Dunlap noted. Nothing in the various accounts of either Booth or Cooke would seem to fit Lincoln's description of a sophomoric style, however we wish to interpret the phrase.

Although accounts of his performances in *Richard III* are meager, the enactments by the great American star Edwin Forrest may have been closer to what Lincoln believed was the wrong way for Richard to make his entrance. The only time we can be certain that Lincoln saw Forrest play Shakespeare was in *King Lear*, but it is not impossible that Lincoln saw him as Richard on one of two occasions when he played in Washington, D.C., during Lincoln's presidency, in April 1862 or in March 1864.[145] Forrest, who had played Richmond to Kean's Richard, might be assumed to have imitated Kean, and at least one description suggests that he was influenced by him to an extent. On Forrest's first entrance, according to a contemporary account, he "burst upon the stage, cloaked and capped, waving his gloves in triumph over the downfall of the house of Lancaster. Not in frowning gutturals or with snarling complaint but merrily came the opening words,—'Now is the winter of our discontent / Made glorious summer by this sun of York.' Gradually as he came to descant upon his own defects and unsuitedness for peace and love, the tone passed from glee to sarcasm, and ended with dissembling and vindictive earnestness."[146] The first part of this description could be interpreted as "sophomoric," and Forrest could be seen as exhibiting something in the nature of a "flourish." According to Charles Shattuck, Forrest may have overplayed the sense of jubilation he brought to the early scenes, "in effect [displacing] Shakespeare's villain with the historical heroic Richard,"[147] an interpretation that Lincoln, on Carpenter's evidence, would not have embraced.

The one actor we certainly know Lincoln saw as Richard was Edwin Booth, on March 10, 1864, a little over a week after his conversation with Carpenter (Lincoln saw Booth as Hamlet on March 2, 1864). Unfortunately, though we know a lot about Booth's Hamlet, only generalities have come down to us concerning his Richard; I have not found any useful descriptions of how he would have delivered "Now is the winter of our discontent." Katherine Goodale, who, as Kitty Malony, played the young Prince of Wales to Booth's Richard in the late 1880s, recalled Booth's entrance: "Limping on, he was a figure of evil sure of itself. He might have been the devil by the cunning triumph in his face."[148] Mention should also be made here of the long-standing tradition that Lincoln saw John Wilkes Booth as Richard. An entry in the National Theatre Web site, for example, reads "April 11, 1863—RICHARD III by William Shakespeare starring John Wilkes Booth in his Washington debut in this role. President Abraham Lincoln was in attendance, sitting in the presidential box."[149] The April 11 entry on the *Lincoln Log*, however, places Lincoln elsewhere: "In evening [*sic*], President Lincoln attends the Washington Theater to watch British burlesque actress Matilda Vining Wood portray 'Pocahontas.' A newspaper reports, 'President Lincoln was present and laughed some.'"[150] It was announced that Booth would play Richard again on November 2, 7, 9, and 13, 1863, but there is no record of Lincoln having attended. As with his brother Edwin, no specific information has come down concerning John Wilkes's delivery of "Now is the winter of our discontent."

Carpenter's account of his White House conversation in the end does not reveal much of Lincoln's view of how the *Richard III* soliloquy should be performed. "Unconsciously assuming the character," Carpenter wrote, "Mr. Lincoln repeated . . . from memory, Richard's soliloquy, rendering it with a degree of force and power that made it seem like a new creation to me." "I could not refrain from laying down my palette and brushes," Carpenter adds, "and applauding heartily, upon his conclusion, saying, at the same time, half in earnest, that I was not sure but that he had made a mistake in the choice of a profession, considerably, as may be imagined, to his amusement."[151] No doubt influenced by Carpenter's comments, James G. Randall thought that Lincoln would have made a "powerful tragic actor."[152] Ronald White goes further: "In an alternative life," he writes, "Lincoln might have enjoyed a career as an actor in the Shakesperean plays he loved."[153] The evidence for this is mixed, however. Early in his political life, Lincoln was often described as an awkward public speaker who, at least when he began, spoke in a high-pitched twang. A number of witnesses remarked on his "thin, high-pitched falsetto voice,"[154] a voice "not musical rather high-keyed and apt to turn into a shrill treble in moments of excitement."[155] Herndon, on the other hand, claimed that as Lincoln proceeded into a speech, his voice "lost in a measure its former acute and shrilling pitch, and mellowed into a harmonious and pleasant sound."[156] Other witnesses commented on Lincoln's ability to project to a large audience. A reporter who heard the 1861 inaugural address wrote that Lincoln "read with a clear, loud, and distinct voice, quite intelligible by at least ten thousand persons below him" and that in taking the oath of office he exhibited "by his manner and gestures the full concurrence of mind and heart with the intent of the words he was repeating."[157] More generally, as a public speaker, according to Herndon, his friend "did not gesticulate as much with his hands as with his head. . . . He never acted for stage effect."[158] The evidence also suggests that Lincoln read and recited slowly, exhibiting "a singular clearness of enunciation and deliberation, duly punctuating every sentence as he uttered it," at least when speaking outdoors.[159]

Several observers remarked on Lincoln's skills as a comic actor as well as his strong sense of drama. A *New York Tribune* reporter commented on Lincoln's "tones, [and] gestures, the kindling eye and the mirth-provoking look [that] defy the reporter's skill."[160] "His power of mimicry," Herndon wrote, "and his manner of recital, were in many respects unique, if not remarkable."[161] Horace White, who reported on the Lincoln-Douglas debates, thought Lincoln an "inimitable story-teller" whose "facial expression was so irresistibly comic that the bystanders generally exploded in laughter."[162] But White also responded to the high drama of which Lincoln was capable. Commenting on the 1854 Peoria speech in which Lincoln several times cites Shakespeare, White describes "the tall, angular form with the long, angular arms, at times bent nearly double with excitement, like a large flail animating two smaller ones, the mobile face wet with perspiration."[163] Herndon, in attempting to describe the effect the famous Bloomington speech had on him, described the fire and energy of Lincoln's speaking style in almost baroque terms: "Enthusiasm unusual to him blazed up; his eyes were aglow with an inspiration; he felt justice; his heart was alive to the right; his sympathies, remarkably deep for him, burst forth." As a lawyer, Herndon writes, his partner "very often resorted to some strange and strategic performance which invariably broke his opponent down" and put the other side "in constant fear of one of his dramatic strokes."[164] Lincoln, clearly, was inspired by both the comic and the tragic muse.

The various witnesses who, in addition to Carpenter, testify to being present when Lincoln read or recited specifically from Shakespeare only occasionally provide something of the flavor and manner of those readings. One of Herndon's informants said that Lincoln "would read with great warmth all funny things—humorous things &c.: Read Shake-spear that way."[165] The syntax is unclear, but the witness presumably means that Lincoln enjoyed reading humorous passages from Shakespeare and read them with appropriate feeling. Isaac Arnold wrote that Lincoln "recited and read works of poetry and eloquence with great simplicity, but with much expression and effect. When visiting the army, or on a journey on a steamer or by rail, as well as when at home, he would take up his copy of Shakespeare and would often read aloud to his companions. He would remark: 'What do you say now to a scene from Hamlet or Macbeth?' And then he would read aloud with the greatest pleasure scene after scene and favorite passages, never seeming to tire of the enjoyment."[166] John Littlefield, as noted in chapter 2, remembered that Lincoln "could recite whole passages from Shakespeare, notably from 'Hamlet,' with wonderful effect."[167] A particularly vivid description was given by Josiah Grinnell, who described Lincoln's enjoyment at repeating a line he had recently heard spoken by Hackett as Falstaff in *Henry IV*: "Mr. Lincoln rose from his chair and stepped out from behind the table, struck an attitude, and raised his hand as if in holy horror, 'Lord, how this world is given to lying.'"[168] Several relatives and acquaintances from his youth commented on Lincoln's skill at mimicry, one remembering that he "would often after returning from church repeat correctly nearly all of the sermon which he had heard mimacing the Style and tone of the old Baptist preachers," a talent that no doubt served him well in the acting out his favorite Shakespearean scenes.[169]

Apart from testifying to the "force and power" of his performance, Carpenter provides no details that would allow us to gauge the effectiveness of Lincoln's acting, only adding that a "Mr. Sinclair," who was also present at the time, "repeatedly said to me that he never heard these choice passages of Shakspeare rendered with more effect by the most famous of modern actors."[170] We can conclude from this that Lincoln had his own idea of how Shakespeare's lines from *Richard III* should be rendered and that he appears to have aligned himself with a strand of performance history that goes back even earlier than the actors who played Richard in America. John Philip Kemble, in the eighteenth century, was "peevish and sarcastic,"[171] and this way of beginning fits in with Lincoln's view that Richard exhibits "intense bitterness and satire." But, of course, there are different ways of expressing these emotions and attitudes. It is not surprising that when, in August 1863, he wrote to Hackett inviting him to the White House, Lincoln indicated that he would like to hear the actor "pronounce the opening speech of Richard the Third."[172] If Hackett, on his first visit or on subsequent occasions, fulfilled Lincoln's wish, no one present, unfortunately, recorded the moment. But whatever the precise details of their conversations, Lincoln's friendship with Hackett would provide him the opportunity to discuss Shakespearean acting with a seasoned practitioner of the craft, even as the actor's anecdotes and comic turns would contribute, at least for a time, to the enrichment of Lincoln's few moments of relaxation and amusement.

Lincoln's Falstaff
James H. Hackett

Lost in the fat Knight's humorous embrace,
The tragic mask forgot to show its face;
And when hereafter Hackett's name we call,
'Twill be as Falstaff, first and best of all.
        William L. Keese, "James H. Hackett"
        The Siamese Twins, and Other Poems

On the evening of March 13, 1863, Abraham Lincoln invited one of his secretaries, William Stoddard, to accompany him to a performance of Shakespeare's *Henry IV, Part 1*, starring James H. Hackett as Sir John Falstaff. "I'm going to the theater," he reportedly told Stoddard, "to see Hackett play Falstaff, and I want you to come with me. I've always wanted to see him in that character."[1] This was almost certainly the first Shakespeare production Lincoln saw since arriving in Washington in February 1861. A week later, he received a copy of a book Hackett had written entitled *Notes and Comments upon Certain Plays and Actors of Shakespeare, with Criticisms and Correspondence*, along with a brief letter from the author which read, in part, "Your Excellency favored me last Friday eveng. 13th inst. by a spontaneous visit to the Washington theatre to witness my personation of the Falstaff of King Henry IV, and I would respectfully ask your acceptance of a volume which I have recently published and the concluding portion of which refers particularly to the remarkable points of that renowned character. . . . I . . . venture to hope that at your . . . leisure you may find therein some agreeable relaxation from your cares of State."[2] Hackett's letter and gift, which initiated further

Frontispiece to Hackett's Notes and Comments on Shakespeare. *Folger Shakespeare Library.*

correspondence as well as face-to-face meetings at the White House, provided Lincoln with an opportunity to comment, however briefly, on his knowledge of and interest in Shakespeare's plays, a topic not otherwise addressed in his writings.

It was not until August 17, however, that Lincoln wrote back, apologizing for the delay:

> Months ago [he begins] I should have acknowledged the receipt of your book, and accompanying kind note; and I now have to beg your pardon for not having done so. For one of my age, I have seen very little of the drama. The first presentation of Falstaff I ever saw was yours here, last winter or spring. Perhaps the best compliment I can pay is to say, as I truly can, I am very anxious to see it again. Some of Shakspeare's plays I have never read; while others I have gone over perhaps as frequently as any unprofessional reader. Among the latter are Lear, Richard Third, Henry Eighth, Hamlet, and especially Macbeth. I think nothing equals Macbeth. It is wonderful. Unlike you gentlemen of the profession, I think the soliloquy in Hamlet commencing "O, my offence is rank" surpasses that commencing "To be, or not to be." But pardon this small attempt at criticism. I should like to hear you pronounce the opening speech of Richard the Third. Will you not soon visit Washington again? If you do please call and let me make your personal acquaintance. Yours truly A. Lincoln.[3]

We can guess from his opening words that Lincoln, like many a recipient of unsolicited books from authors eager for a response, had probably not read Hackett's volume through; he does not, in any case, make direct reference to the book itself, though the letter provides indirect evidence that he was familiar, in a general sense and perhaps in some particulars, with its contents. But several months had now passed, and though the president had a variety of pressing matters vying for his attention, the courtesy of a reply was necessary. It may not be a coincidence that around this time Lincoln was reading Shakespeare at his summer cottage at the Soldiers' Home. The entry in John Hay's diary, discussed in chapter 2, that records the amusing incident of his nodding off listening to the president's reading from *Henry VI* and *Richard III*, is dated August 23.[4]

Hackett wasted little time writing in response: "I thank you cordially for your frank, unaffected & courteous letter of 17th," he wrote on September 4; "I appreciate your friendly invitation to 'call whenever again in Washington' and 'let you make my personal acquaintance'; and shall be very happy to avail myself of it the first opportunity—probably early next Winter."[5] A month later, Hackett again wrote to Lincoln to announce his forthcoming December visit to the nation's capital, which, he claims, "will be my last professional visit to Washington," as he plans to "withdraw entirely from the stage after the coming winter" (a plan he would abandon). He invites the president to attend his performances of "first, the *Falstaff* of *King Henry IV*; next, *Sir Pertinax MacSycophant*, in the comedy called—*The Man of the World*; & immediately after it, *Monsieur Mallet, an exiled general of Napoleon 1st.*, in my popular interlude of '*The Post Office Mistake*'; & upon my last night, the *Falstaff* of the comedy of *The Merry Wives of Windsor*; if it may happen to be convenient & Your Excellency to attend upon each or either one of those three evenings named."[6] Hackett was certainly not shy, suggesting that the president of the United States might want to devote three evenings to his theatrical offerings.

Hackett's unapologetic self-promotion had some justification: though pretty much forgotten today,[7] he was quite well known to his contemporaries, and by the time he wrote to Lincoln he was one of the most popular comic actors in America.[8] Initially going on stage after failing in business, Hackett made an inauspicious debut: "His nervousness, or stage fright . . . so overcame his faculties that he failed to make a favorable impression on the audience."[9] But he recovered and soon found a niche for himself developing and enriching the stock characters of the Yankee and the frontiersman—with names like Solomon Swap, Industrious Doolittle, Major Joe Bunker, Melodious Migrate—in a variety of contemporary plays. "What Hackett first put together, probably working alone on his own material, set a line of comedy that was taken up by a string of native-born actors; when playwrights were available, a line of plays featured a smart, sly country bumpkin who could outsmart and outrun his city cousin. Hackett's penchant for telling Yankee stories—long, complex, and mostly without point—was worked into the format."[10] Perhaps his most memorable performance was as Colonel Nimrod Wildfire, "a role loosely modeled on Davy Crockett and played by [Hackett] for more than twenty years," in a play he had commissioned for himself entitled *The Lion of the West*.[11] Hackett was also an early enactor of Washington Irving's Rip Van Winkle, though in a version different from that later employed more famously by Joseph Jefferson. In all these roles, Hackett "caught much of the flavor of American life—its country types, its city speculators, its military democrats, and its exuberant frontier adventurers."[12] He complemented his American characters by developing a skill in foreign dialect roles, sometimes playing a Yankee and a Frenchman or Irishman as part of a single evening's entertainment.

Hackett's other claim to fame was as one of the earliest of America's native-born Shakespearean actors to achieve a significant reputation.[13] His first forays into Shakespeare were in the nature of gimmicks: he played one of the Dromio twins in *The Comedy of Errors*, precisely imitating a well-known actor who played the other twin.[14] He next acted out a carefully worked-up imitation of the great English actor Edmund Kean in *Richard III*, having seen Kean's performance over a dozen times and having taken copious and detailed notes of virtually every speech pattern and physical movement.[15] But the only Shakespearean role in which Hackett came to excel was Falstaff, which he first played in 1828 in *Henry IV, Part 1*, adding *The Merry Wives of Windsor* in 1838 and *Henry IV, Part 2* in 1841.[16] "For forty years he played Falstaff throughout the country, from Boston to New Orleans, from New York to San Francisco, in almost every American town that had a proper theatre."[17] By 1863, when Lincoln saw him, a reviewer would claim, "Hackett's Falstaff is now the only one on the stage preserving the excellence of the traditionary stage Falstaff."[18] As early as 1840, Hackett was so associated with the role that he was himself imitated: one C. J. Rogers in "his celebrated act of horsemanship . . . imitates Mr. Hackett, as Falstaff . . . in characteristic costume."[19] With rather less success, Hackett briefly essayed tragic or tragically inflected roles, playing Iago, Hamlet, King Lear, and Shylock, as well as his own interpretation of Richard III.[20] But his temperament was not well suited to the tragic note; as he would later remark (apropos of his performance as Hamlet) with an appealing absence of embarrassment, "My habitual love of ease, aversion to extraordinary physical or mental exertion . . . together with a consciousness and dread of painful effects upon my sensitive nervous system . . . combined to discourage my ambition in such pursuit." At the same time that he appears to blame himself for his lack of success, Hackett finds a way to blame the public as well. "I resolved," he tells us, "rather to continue to act easily and quietly and with moderate profit, my former though limited number of *popular* parts, than to embark in a struggle at that time against popular prejudice or stage-precedent of an acknowledged comedian trying to make his *Hamlet* attractive and add that to his repertoire."[21] For all that, Hackett could claim to be one of the first American actors to play Shakespeare with some acceptance in London, reversing the trend—represented by actors like Junius Brutus Booth, the father of Edwin and John Wilkes—of English and Irish actors bringing Shakespeare to America.

Despite his success on the stage, Hackett clearly thought of himself as something more than an actor, as is in part suggested by the volume he sent to Lincoln, which shows him in the role of theater critic and Shakespearean scholar.[22] He wrote to the newspapers on the Shakespeare-authorship controversy (as a firm Stratfordian—Shakespeare was Shakespeare), he several times made plans (evidently not carried out) to produce his own edition of Shakespeare's plays, and he was one of the leading figures (along with Edwin Booth) behind the building of a monument to the Bard in New York's Central Park.[23] Hackett fancied himself a poet as well, publishing a satiric poem in rhymed couplets, "Merchant Princes and Parvenus," in a literary journal.[24] Additionally, drawing on his business experience (however unlucky it had been), he early on went into theater management and even became, for a time, a theatrical agent. Both as manager and as impresario, Hackett appears to have been successful, though, as always in the entertainment business, unforeseen events and personal antipathies could throw off the best-considered business plans: from time to time we find him suing or being sued over matters relating to his theatrical activities. In 1837, for example, he filed suit against the actor George H. Hill to stop him from performing the character Solomon Swap, a role that Hackett claimed as his own.[25] The *Morning Herald*, reporting the story, tartly noted, "The idea of preventing Hill from performing any character he chooses is certainly novel in this country."[26] (The irony here is that Hackett had himself freely borrowed his Yankee characters from an older English actor.) At another time, Hackett, as proprietor of Howard Athenaeum, was himself sued by a double bass player for nonpayment of salary.[27] It was Hackett's particular misfortune, as co-lessee of New York's Astor Opera House, to find himself caught up in the Astor Place Riot (see chapter 1). Though Hackett seems not to have had any involvement in the bloody events of that evening, he and his co-lessee suffered financially: Hackett subsequently petitioned the New York Common Council for reparations of slightly over $5,000.[28] In its obituary of Hackett, the *New York Times* claimed that these events "so disgusted [Hackett] that he threw up his lease."[29]

In all of his various roles—actor, author, or manager—Hackett was an adroit self-promoter, happy to blow his own horn and to use whatever contacts came his way as a means of advancing his career and prestige. When he played *King Lear* in Boston in 1841, he went so far as to take out a self-aggrandizing ad in the newspapers. Writing in the third person, he thanks the audience for its reception of his previous night's benefit performance "notwithstanding 'the pelting of the pitiless storm,' and despite general prejudice, to give their confiding countenance to one reputed only as a Comedian, in his first attempt here to personate one of the greatest and most difficult of

Shakespeare's tragic heroes."[30] Connecting himself to a distant relative, Hackett "did not mind the story getting about . . . that, had he wanted to, he could have assumed the title of Baron Hackett of Hackett's Town in Ireland."[31] Indeed, newspapers began to refer to him as Baron Hackett, with perhaps only a touch of irony.[32] The volume he gave Lincoln exhibits him as, among other things, a shameless name-dropper: going off to England, he tells us, "I carried a special letter of introduction from our eminent statesman, the Hon. Henry Clay." Washington Irving, former president John Quincy Adams ("our venerable friend") and James Fenimore Cooper ("another eminent literary friend"), are among other celebrities Hackett claims intimacy with. In spite of the fame and fortune he had already acquired by the 1860s, his letter and accompanying gift to Lincoln can be seen, at least in part, as a strategic move designed both to enhance the image he had of himself and to further his reputation with his public.

Lincoln's remarks on the soliloquies from Hamlet suggest that he had at least glanced over, even if he had not read, Hackett's *Notes and Comments.* The first part of this rather peculiar collection of widely disparate materials consists of a long essay (nearly fifty pages) on Hamlet's "To be or not to be" soliloquy that purports to defend Shakespeare from Oliver Goldsmith's claim that the famous passage was "a heap of absurdities." It is followed by a section titled "Extracts from my journal of correspondence respecting Hamlet." The "extracts" from Hackett's correspondence include letters on *Hamlet* and other Shakespearean subjects to and from John Quincy Adams, Washington Irving, James Fenimore Cooper, and others, suggesting, as much as anything, the pleasure Hackett took in advertising his acquaintance with the great and near great. Somewhat incongruously, Hackett includes in this section an account of his own attempt at playing Hamlet, a task he was able to achieve, he tells us, by "overcoming my constitutional and habitual love of ease and my aversion to close study or any prolonged physical labor."[33] This is a good example of Hackett's ability to be simultaneously self-inflating and self-deprecating. He does not blush at citing a program note that describes him as "now Universally acknowledged to combine a higher degree of Excellence with Versatility than has been recorded in the annals of the Stage of any individual since the days of Garrick."[34] At the same time, he describes this as a "puff-announcement," to some degree undercutting the fulsomeness of the praise. Perhaps the most valuable parts of Hackett's volume, however, are his "Notes on King Lear" and "Actors of Hamlet" in which Hackett reviews, with sensitivity and good sense, a number of performers he had seen over some forty-plus years of theatergoing.

Between the time Lincoln had responded to the gift of *Notes and Comments* and its accompanying note and had received the author's next letter, Hackett had done something that by all rights should have quickly ended friendly communication between the actor and the president. Without asking permission or giving any intimation of his plan, Hackett had Lincoln's August 17 letter reproduced as a handbill headed "A Letter from President Lincoln to Mr. Hackett" with the added words "Printed not for publication but for private distribution only, and its convenient perusal by personal friends."[35] Now if Lincoln had read well into Hackett's book, he would perhaps have thought twice about writing to him in the first place. For Hackett had done precisely the same thing to John Quincy Adams many years earlier, as he unashamedly recounts in *Notes and Comments*:

> When the . . . letter from Mr. Adams . . . reached my hand at New York
> . . . I caused it to be *lithographed in fac-simile*, . . . and prior to my return
> from England, . . . it had been obtained by the *New York Mirror* . . . and
> published, without regard to the *notice* thereupon—"*lithographed for
> private distribution only.*" The consequence was, Mr. Adams' letter and
> my reply were copied extensively by newspapers throughout the United
> States.[36]

Lincoln, in any case, paid the price for his exercise in literary criticism. "In a vein of patronizing sarcasm," Roy Basler writes, "the *New York Herald* took notice of Hackett's broadside on September 17."[37] One sentence in the *Herald* piece in particular provides a good sense of its general drift: "If Mr. Lincoln had time to dilate upon the subject of his letter and to analyze the plays and passages to which he particularly refers, we would have an article on Shakespere which would doubtless have consigned to merited dust and oblivion the thousands of tomes that have been printed on that subject, and would have been accepted as the standard authority henceforth."[38]

Basler goes on to provide a detailed account of the entire episode, reproducing a column Hackett had clipped from the *Liverpool Post* and subsequently (October 22) sent Lincoln strongly defending the American president, finding that the "simplicity and candor" of Lincoln's letter "are as fresh as new-mown hay." The *Liverpool Post* article, perhaps not incidentally, praises Hackett as well: "Not only is he a brilliant and unctious [*sic*] Falstaff, but a thoroughly estimable man."[39] Hackett also expressed how shocked, shocked he was, as he had been with the Adams letter, at "the unwarrantable liberty taken by certain Newspaper presses" in publishing Lincoln's "kind,

sensible, & unpretending letter," and "more particularly at the Editorial remarks upon & perversion of its subject-matter to antagonistic political purposes, accompanied by satirical abuse in general."[40] Lincoln wrote back two
weeks later, assuring Hackett that he had not taken offense, adding, "My note
to you, I certainly did not expect to see in print; yet I have not been much
shocked by the newspaper comments upon it. These comments constitute a
fair specimen of what has occurred to me through life. I have endured a great
deal of ridicule without much malice; and have received a great deal of kindness, not quite free of ridicule. I am used to it."[41] One would like to think that
if Hackett had not been shamed before receiving this reply, he would have
been afterward. The exchange of letters, at Hackett's request, was published
in the *New York Times* after Lincoln's death, with a prefatory note: "So many
personal friends having heard of, became curious of seeing and perusing Mr.
LINCOLN's letter, that it was in danger of mutilation, and I caused it to be
'printed for private distribution.'"[42]

Historians and commentators on this episode (including John Hay), influenced by the exchange of letters with Hackett and by the *Herald*'s response,
have left the impression that Lincoln was widely ridiculed for his "small attempt at criticism."[43] Seemingly on the basis of little other than the *Herald*
piece, one writer has remarked that "to his contemporaries . . . Mr. Lincoln
did not seem a particularly acute or profound student of Shakespeare."[44]
But this ignores the context; the *Herald* was, throughout much of Lincoln's
presidency, an antiadministration paper.[45] The journalistic reaction, in any
case, was mixed. A number of newspapers—the *New York Times*, for example—reprinted Lincoln's letter without comment. The *Living Age* prefaced
its reprint by simply noting, "From a letter dated August 17th from President Lincoln to Mr. Hackett, the tragedian, we glean the President's critical
opinion upon some of Shakspeare's plays."[46] The *San Francisco Daily Evening
Bulletin* introduced the letter with a swipe at Hackett: "The following private
letter, which has somehow 'got into print'—probably through the vanity of
Mr. Hackett—has been used to throw ridicule on 'Honest Abe.'"[47] The *Chicago Tribune* reprinted a portion of the *Herald* piece, but with only a touch
of satire: "The Falstaff of our stage has been honored with an autograph letter from the American autocrat, just as Shakespeare himself was honored
with an amicable letter from King James the First, and which, we are told,
'that most learned prince and great patron of learning was pleased with his
own hand to write.'"[48] The *New Haven Daily Palladium* is more generous:
"President Lincoln was so pleased with Hackett's Falstaff, last winter, that
he has invited the actor to come and call on him. The President, in his note,

expresses his preference for 'Macbeth' over all of Shakespeare's other plays, and in Hamlet thinks that 'O, my offense is rank,' surpasses the soliloquy 'To be, or not to be,' in which latter point those who look strictly at their ability to understand one or the other the better, will, we believe, agree."[49] All in all, Lincoln's comments were not thought to be particularly eccentric or foolish, at least by those elements of the Northern press not already disposed to be critical of the president.

Antiadministration papers, north and south, unsurprisingly found in Lincoln's letter opportunity for satire and denunciation.[50] After noting Lincoln's preference for *Macbeth* over *Hamlet*, the *Savannah Daily Morning News* suggests that the president's "reappearance in a kilt and that 'Scotch cap and cloak' would no doubt create quite a sensation in theatrical circles."[51] The reference, of course, is to the legend that Lincoln, when passing through Baltimore on his way to his inauguration, was so disguised. One of the bitterest attacks, though evidently reprinted at least in part from a Northern paper, appeared in the *Richmond Sentinel*. The fairly lengthy commentary begins by noting Lincoln's preference for the plays featuring Lear, Richard III, Henry VIII, and Macbeth: "They were fond of blood; so is he—they were tyrannical; so is he."[52] "He particularly admires the play of Macbeth," the writer continues; "we trust he is not unmindful of the hero's fate." A number of passages from *Macbeth* are quoted and applied to the president: "The time may come when the ghosts of murdered men will visit Mr. Lincoln' [*sic*] banquets, and when he, in terror, may exclaim 'Avaunt! and quit my sight! let the earth hide you!'" The *Sentinel* takes note as well of Lincoln's signaling out Claudius's soliloquy from *Hamlet* in preference to "To be or not to be," reproducing the passage in its entirety and adding, "It is not wonderful that this soliloquy has made a deep impression upon the mind of the President." Returning one more time to *Macbeth*, the anonymous author, like his Savannah colleague, cannot resist a reference to Lincoln's change of trains in Baltimore. "Mr. Lincoln's choice of that 'Scotch cap,' by means of which he entered Washington, unharmed, to assume his kingly career, may be traced to his admiration of 'Macbeth'; but though, like the Thane, he succeeded so well in reaching the throne, we hope our king will not imitate his Scotch model in the manner of leaving it." Lincoln is urged, nevertheless, to read *Macbeth* to the end: "There's a moral in this story."[53] The *Mobile Daily Tribune* reproduced comments from "a German paper" in Chicago: "After two years of a bloody, murderous war, while streams of blood are being spilled unnecessarily, while the nation (that is, the people who sent their sons to the field of battle) walk [*sic*] in mourning, . . . Lincoln continues to tell us his stories, and asks actor Hackett to produce

Falstaff before him!"[54] Presumably, neither Lincoln nor Hackett took much notice of these harsh, politically motivated attacks.

Hackett, in any case, was unfazed by the fallout from his faux pas, writing Lincoln again on November 14 to update him on his forthcoming engagement:

> Referring to my letter of 3d Oct. & to your Excellency's courteous observation, dated 2d Nov. inst.,—"I look forward with pleasure to the fulfillment of your promise made in that letter"—I will forthwith try to arrange for the most effective representations practicable of the plays I proposed to get up at Washington the evenings of *Monday, Tuesday & Wednesday—21st 22d & 23d Decr proxo.*; and, inasmuch as your Excellency seems not to foresee any hindrance, I will hope & trust that none may occur to render inconvenient your visits to the theatre upon those particular evenings.[55]

On December 11, Hackett follows up on the previous letter, taking note of Lincoln's recent illness (he had contracted a mild form of smallpox) and adding, "Fearing that, however convalescent after your recent malady, it might not be considered prudent for your Excellency to venture forth & to a theatre upon the evenings hitherto submitted, I have arranged to act at Ford's theatre Washington next week & as follows." Oddly enough, the new dates Hackett now proposes—December 14 through 19—are earlier than the ones he had previously suggested. "Should your Excellency's health & other events permit your personal countenance upon any one of those evening's performances I shall esteem the compliment but if not, shall regret the cause, & endeavor to afford your Excellency some future & convenient opportunity." And Hackett now announces his intention to visit the White House. "I expect to arrive at Willard's hotel, Washington, next Sunday eveng, about six o'clock I shall be inclined to do myself the pleasure of a call about 7 o'clock;—but if it may not happen to be convenient *then* to receive me, Your Excellency will please to let me find at Willard's some intimation of the fact."[56]

True to his expressed intention, repeated in the November 2 letter ("I look forward with pleasure to the fulfillment of the promise made in the former [letter]"), Lincoln, though still recovering from his illness, indeed went to see *Henry IV, Part 1* on December 14.[57] (Hackett did not perform in *Henry IV, Part 2* on his Washington visit.) A few days after that, he saw *The Merry Wives of Windsor.* What did Lincoln see and hear when he attended the theater to enjoy Hackett's Falstaff? Though it is impossible to re-create the precise outlines of what a playgoer would have experienced at Ford's Theatre on this occasion, we can be reasonably certain that, as a reader of Shakespeare, Lincoln would have been bothered by what had been done to the texts of the plays. In addition to the alterations dictated by Victorian delicacy (the word "guts" was replaced by "paunch," "belly," and even "bowels"; swearing was omitted altogether), both *Henry IV* and, to a lesser degree, *The Merry Wives of Windsor* would have suffered from various cuts and alterations, though these are hard to pinpoint given Hackett's fondness for experimentation over the many years he acted in these plays.[58] By the early nineteenth century, in any case, *Henry IV, Part 1* had been shorn of a number of scenes and characters on both the British and American stages.

Shakespeare in his *Henry IV* plays exhibits a skillful balance of historical chronicle and social comedy; nineteenth-century acting editions eliminate much of the history in favor of the purely comic. The so-called Welsh scene (act 3, scene 1) in *Henry IV, Part 1*, for example, was eliminated, as was the play within the play in act 2. And Hackett is known to have sometimes used, in addition to a shortened five-act version, a three-act cutting of the play, which suggests even greater omissions.[59] Lincoln, however, would have almost certainly seen the longer five-act version, since the newspaper advertisements and reviews clearly indicate the presence of Hotspur, a character who does not appear at all in the shortened versions.[60] If Lincoln had come to see *Henry IV* primarily for the history, he would have been disappointed. He came, however, to see Hackett, and he was in any case quite able to translate what appeared to be innocent comic business into a political lesson. Iowa Congressman Josiah Grinnell recalled many years later that he had mentioned to Lincoln having seen him at the theater. "Yes, and they said my coarse laugh was very audible," Lincoln responds. "We had some good war news yesterday, and I was glad to unbend and laugh. The acting was good, and true to the case, according to my experiences, for each fellow tells his own story and smirches his rival."[61] Lincoln quotes Falstaff's line from *Henry IV, Part 1* (act 5, scene 4), but he was no doubt thinking of the earlier scene in which Falstaff, Hal, and their associates are discussing the robbery in which they had participated. Hackett seems to have cut relatively little from *Merry Wives*, a Falstaff play lacking a specific historical context, though he did employ an arrangement of a ballad-opera based on Shakespeare's play, albeit with the songs left out.[62]

Lincoln was sufficiently concerned over the traditional elimination of the play-acting scene from *Henry IV, Part 1* that he questioned Hackett about it when the latter visited him at the White House, as promised, on the evening of December 13, 1863, the night before he saw Hackett's Falstaff for the second time. In his diary, John Hay gave an account of the actor's visit:

Tonight Hackett arrived and spent the evening with the President. The conversation at first took a professional turn, the Tycoon [crossed out] President showing a very intimate knowledge of those plays of Shakespeare where Falstaff figures. He was particularly anxious to know why one of the best scenes in the play that where Falstaff and Prince Hal alternately assume the character of the King is omitted in the representation. Hackett says it is admirable to read but ineffective on stage. That there is generally nothing sufficiently distinctive about the actor who plays Henry to make an imitation striking.[63]

Robert Lincoln also recalled the conversation in a letter he wrote to Hackett in 1871: "I remember you could not convince [my father] of the propriety of cutting out the scene where Falstaff and Prince Hal play King and Prince and lampoon their assumed characters."[64] The conversation with Hackett tells us as much about Lincoln's sensitivity to Shakespeare's art as about the way the plays were presented on the nineteenth-century stage. Lincoln here rightly praises what is not only one of the funniest but also one of the most thematically important scenes in *Henry IV, Part 1*. "This greatest, perhaps, of Shakespeare's comic scenes," the theater historian Arthur Colby Sprague notes, was seldom acted in the eighteenth and early nineteenth centuries.[65] John Russell Brown writes that "awareness of [the scene's] dramatic potential seems to have been a discovery of the mid-twentieth-century theater."[66] Hackett, however, probably makes a valid point: Shakespeare's play had become so much of a showcase for Falstaff that the roles of Prince Hal and of his father, the king, were often neglected by the better actors of the company.[67] Today, it would be unthinkable to cut this scene. Lincoln's questions to Hackett give us further proof that he knew his Shakespeare sufficiently well to challenge contemporary theatrical orthodoxies, and at the same time they suggest a more extensive playgoing experience for Lincoln than the evidence we have can fully confirm.[68]

Like most other theatergoers of his time, Lincoln went to these plays to see Hackett as much as to see Shakespeare; unfortunately, we can only guess at what aspect of Hackett's presentation of Falstaff would have particularly attracted the president. Reconstructing Hackett's performance—or any performance by a nineteenth-century actor—is no simple matter. In attempting to describe and evaluate Hackett's Falstaff, we have essentially three kinds of firsthand information. We know, from Hackett's writings, what his view of Falstaff was, and so, presumably, what he intended to present to his audience; we have many of the reviews and comments by playgoers who recorded their impressions at or near the time of witnessing Hackett's performances; and we have as well the retrospective analyses of theatergoers summarizing impressions some years after originally observing Hackett's Falstaff. In addition, promptbooks, some in manuscript and some printed, are extant that provide hints of stage business Hackett may have used at various times during his long career. To this, one could add passing observations made in contexts unrelated to theatrical matters as such but suggesting the extent of Hackett's fame as an interpreter of Shakespeare's fat knight. A political attack on Franklin Pierce at the time of the 1852 presidential election, for example, equates Pierce's behavior at the Battle of Churubusco with Falstaff's at the Battle of Shrewsbury, the author of the piece adding, "We can almost imagine we can see General Pierce, as we have seen Hackett, in Falstaff, after the fall of Hotspur, peeping cautiously over the field to see if the storm of strife was clearing up."[69] We are given here, unexpectedly, a small piece of stage business of the kind often missing from the accounts of professional reviewers.

What Hackett himself thought of Falstaff can be gleaned both from what he says of his intentions in performing the role and from the few observations he makes on other actors. As far as his own interpretation is concerned, he tells us, "After many years of stage-practice in the *Falstaff* of both parts of *King Henry IV*, and also in that of *The Merry Wives of Windsor*, I think there was not a phase of the character—either as exhibited in his own words, or as relatively indicated by their context—which has escaped my minute observation and very careful consideration before I resorted to histrionic art to embody and represent it to an audience."[70] Interestingly, given the popularity of his interpretation, Hackett's view of Falstaff was moralistic and unsentimental: Falstaff is a coward, and he is no gentleman. This view is certainly traditional enough (Samuel Johnson, in the eighteenth century, had described Falstaff as "a thief and a glutton, a coward and a boaster,")[71] but it goes against the more generous view of the character that many an actor before or since has adopted (even the moralist Johnson goes on to say that Falstaff's "licentiousness is not so offensive but that it may be borne for his mirth.")[72] As a literary character, as distinct from a dramatic one, Falstaff had by the eighteenth century become something of a romantic hero. Typical of the pro-Falstaff forces is Corbyn Morris, who, writing in 1744, "viewed Falstaff as 'entirely an amiable character . . . superior to all other Men.'"[73] And Maurice Morgann, in an influential essay published in 1777, found that

GRAVURE, GEBBIE & CO.

JAMES H. HACKETT AS FALSTAFF.

Henry Fourth. ACT IV SCENE II.

James H. Hackett as Falstaff. Folger Shakespeare Library.

Falstaff was "vigorous, amiable, and courageous."[74] Hackett, however, takes the abusive and deliberately provocative comments of Prince Hal and other characters in the *Henry IV* plays as evidence of Falstaff's character. Here, he is being perversely literal-minded. And in what appears to be the only time he commented on another actor's Falstaff, that of Charles Kemble, he is critical of a performance that sounds very much like his own approach to the role: "[Kemble's Falstaff] was chaste and sensible, but showed no mellowness, nor unctuosity, or rich humor—it was very dry and hard."[75] Ironically, we have here some of the very words employed to critique Hackett in the late 1860s: Hackett's Falstaff, according to one view, "lacked a universal and constant unctuousness. . . . There were hard moments; impressions of dryness."[76]

Firsthand descriptions of Hackett's performance as Falstaff from early in his career are not as useful as one might wish. "There is very little valuable commentary in the American press on Hackett's early performances in the part," one theater historian has noted, "probably because his early critics regarded him only as a purveyor of comic American Originals and did not take him seriously as a Shakespearean."[77] What is perhaps the earliest review of Hackett's Falstaff in *Henry IV, Part 1* (in the *New York Morning Herald*, May 16, 1838) delays any mention of Hackett until the third paragraph, after praising the Hal of James Wallack, the Lady Percy of one Miss Monier, and the Hotspur of Henry Wallack. "Of Hackett's 'Falstaff,'" the reviewer continues, "we are sorry to speak in terms of qualified praise; it wants softness, mellowness, richness." Hackett's voice "does not do for the part. . . . It is a compound of the Cape Cod coaster, the Yankee clock pedlar, the Penobscot lumber dealer, the Bangor land auctioneer, and the Portland pedagogue."[78] The writer, clearly, is using Hackett's Yankee parts against him; whether fairly or not it is impossible to tell. A Washington, D.C., reviewer makes a similar observation: "Either he cannot, or does not, avoid mixing up with the character [of Falstaff] the tones and gestures of a genuine Yankee—his great forte and penchant being in that line."[79] An 1841 review of *The Merry Wives of Windsor* is less than flattering: "We would most respectfully suggest to Mr. Hackett to let the fat man have the use of both his legs, and not to let him figure about with the agility of a premiere danseuse. Had the genuine Falstaff hopped about as Hackett does, no wonder it was said of him, that he larded the lean earth as he went along."[80] By 1860, Hackett's possession of the role is generally acknowledged, though not without qualifications; no actor, of course, could ever please all of the critics, then or now.

The English press was generally more detailed and circumstantial in its comments than the American; at the same time, however, London reviewers were even more likely to find fault. Hackett's performance, the *Times* found, "bears the mark of study. There is, probably, not a gesture, look, or motion, on the part of Mr. Hackett, which has not, in his mind, its meaning and significance. This is, in itself, a commendation. . . . We should say that Mr Hackett looks upon *Falstaff* as a slower and more deliberate person than he is usually considered—less rejoicing in the play of his own fancy, more pre-meditative with his jokes, and more seriously irascible. . . . Should we sum up the whole performance of Mr Hackett, into one formula, we should say, clever but hard." Other London papers were less generous: The *Spectator*'s critic wrote, "Mr Hackett labored amain to make his coarse Yankee notion of Falstaff effective, and the other performers aided him in his buffooneries, and emulated him in his grimaces." The *Post* termed Hackett's performance "a glaring mistake. . . . His only conception of the part was of a swaggering buffoon."[81] "There is probably not a more conscientious actor on the stage," the *Times* critic writes, revisiting Hackett's Falstaff in 1851. "[Hackett] has evidently studied the speeches of the fat knight, whether uttered in *Henry IV* or *The Merry Wives of Windsor*, with a carefulness worthy of a commentator on Sophocles. . . . You approve of the result at which the artist has arrived, but you always see the pains he takes to reach it."[82] We can see here that the very thing Hackett prided himself on—"I have made the character a practical study the greater portion of my professional life"[83]—was perhaps only too evident in his performance.

By the time Lincoln saw him, Hackett was thoroughly established as America's greatest Falstaff. "When he [Hackett], and you, and I, and sixty years have gone, old gentlemen will say to the play-goer of the day, 'I saw Hackett in *Falstaff*, sir. He was the finest "*Sir John*" that ever enacted the character!'"[84] At times, however, it is difficult to determine whether one is reading an actual, disinterested critique or an advertisement planted by a theater manager. The "review" that appeared in the *Daily National Intelligencer* a few days after Lincoln saw Hackett in *Henry IV, Part 1* at Ford's Theatre, for instance, reads like a press release: "Mr. Ford's beautiful New Theatre was crowded to excess on Monday evening on the occasion of the first appearance of that truly eminent artist and genuine Shakspearean expounder James H. Hackett. . . . Mr. Hackett's rendition of this most difficult character is universally recognized and accepted as among the unapproachable excellences of the modern stage."[85] This kind of writing is next to useless as criticism. An 1867 essay in *Harper's Monthly* provides a better sense of the actual performance: "The voice was delightful. The fat laugh chuckling away into silence, or exploding, in irrepressible fun, was inimitable; and in the great scene where he describes the Gadshill fight—'I knew ye, Hal!'—the transition of expression and tone, from the truculent boasting to the pure glee of the audacious lie, was admirable." This appreciation is not all praise, however. "The face not always jolly," the critic writes, "there was a sudden chill and curdle of sympathy with him upon his necessary perception of his own humiliation which is inconsonant with the idea of Falstaff. He seemed superior to himself, as if he were playing a part, and that is fatal."[86] The writer here echoes the English critics of many years earlier.[87]

Lincoln, in any case, found much to enjoy in his evening at the theater, as Stoddard somewhat fancifully reports: "He is enjoying himself. He has forgotten the war. He has forgotten Congress. He is out of politics. He is living in Prince Hal's time."[88] In an earlier account, Stoddard presents a more sober view of Lincoln's reaction. "To my surprise," Stoddard writes, "he appeared even gloomy, although intent upon the play, and it was only a few times during the whole performance that he went so far as to laugh at all, and then not heartily." Stoddard adds that Lincoln seemed "to be studying the character and its rendering critically, as if to ascertain the correctness of his own conception as compared with that of the professional artist."[89] However much he may have enjoyed Hackett's Falstaff, Lincoln was not uncritical. David Homer Bates, in his memoir *Lincoln in the Telegraph Office*, remembering an occasion when Lincoln read passages from Shakespeare aloud, noted that the president "criticized some of Hackett's renderings."[90] One of those "renderings" may be the one mentioned by Hay, who also went with Lincoln to see *Henry IV*. "Hackett was most admirable," Hay writes, adding, "The President criticized Hackett's reading of a passage where Hackett said, 'Mainly *thrust* at me' the President thinking it should read 'mainly thrust at *me*.' I told the Presdt. I tho't he was wrong, that 'mainly' merely meant 'strongly' 'fiercely.'"[91] On one occasion, according to another observer, Lincoln questioned Hackett's understanding of Shakespeare in a conversation with the actor John McDonough.[92] "I want to put some questions to you that I put to Mr. Hackett," Lincoln reportedly said, "for I want to learn something of Shakespeare. I don't get much time to study his writings, and I will tell you frankly that Mr. Hackett's replies on one or two of the points were very unsatisfactory to me; they almost impressed me with a doubt as to whether he studies Shakespeare thoroughly, or only the acting plays."[93] Lincoln once again makes a distinction between Shakespeare's plays as printed literature and the plays as texts for acting; he knew very well that what he saw on the stage was not necessarily the same thing as the plays published for reading.

Though Lincoln would never again see Hackett perform, the correspondence did not entirely cease, as has sometimes been thought, at least from Hackett's side. When Hackett next writes (February 4, 1864), he refers to an earlier letter, now lost, in which he had asked the president's help in allowing for the compassionate discharge from military service of one Oscar D. Hall, the brother-in-law of his son, John. Here we have the first intimation of Hackett's propensity to ask for favors from the president. Lincoln evidently approved the request, via the War Department, and Hackett was fulsome in his thanks:

> For this very prompt, signal & gracious token of yr. Excellency's personal regard & generous confidence in the reliability of my simple representation . . . I pray you to accept my heartiest thanks. . . . Whilst Mr. Hall, his kindred & family connections are ever bound to be grateful to yr Excellency as a humane, potent & noble benefactor, let each of us hope you will accept the assurance of our several & united good-wishes for your future welfare & happiness & of those near & dear to yr. Excellency;—and also, for my humble self particularly, I desire that I may be regarded hereafter by yr. Excellency, as an inexpressibly-obliged friend & an ever dutiful & obedient servant.[94]

We do not have Lincoln's response; in fact, Lincoln does not appear to have written to Hackett at all after his letter of November 2, though it is possible that he communicated with him through one of his secretaries.

Hackett, who did not, as he had earlier hinted, retire from the stage (he was still performing in 1871, the year he died), wrote to Lincoln again on March 14, 1864, inviting him to attend his performances at Ford's Theatre:

> Yr. Excellency may remember that I was very desirous last Decr that you should witness once my "*Sir Pertinax MacSycophant*," (the Politician,) but, that, on the eveng. when it was given, as you mentioned afterwards—"Mrs. Lincoln had previously promised to hear Bayard Taylor[95] at Willard's & bound you to attend also"—Let me now observe that I have arranged to perform next *Monday* the Falstaff of the *Merry Wives of Windsor*—on *Tuesday 15th*, *The Man of the World* with the exiled General of *Napoleon the Great, Monsieur Mallet:*—And, on *Friday 18th*, the great & *most intellectual Falstaff*—viz—that of "*The First Part of King Henry IV.*"[96]

He also invited himself to the White House: "I expect to reach Washington & to do myself the pleasure of an unceremonious call upon your Excellency next Sunday eveng."[97] We learn, from this letter, that Hackett was now cultivating the acquaintance of General Ulysses S. Grant, who, on the very day of Hackett's letter, had received his commission as lieutenant general from Lincoln. Hackett concludes by presenting himself as a loyal supporter of Lincoln's reelection hopes, quoting a political acquaintance known also to Lincoln as saying to him, "'Hackett! You ought to be a personal if not a political friend of Prest. Lincoln, & now that you are about to quit the Stage might by your personal address & popularity help us materially in promoting Mr Lincoln's reëlection'—I rejoined—'Within a few weeks I will make it a point to confer with you confidentially upon that subject.'" Hackett's brief note on March 14, proposing an alternate, more convenient date for Lincoln to catch his performance of Sir Pertinax MacSycophant in *The Man of the World*, confirms the previous evening's visit. Lincoln does not appear to have attended either performance of *The Man of the World*, however; he may not have been as interested in Hackett's other popular characters as he was in Falstaff.

In his next letter, dated July 1, 1864, Hackett alludes to his work on the Central Park Shakespeare Statue Commission: "I mailed to you lately one *Circular*, respecting the projected monument to Shakespeare; but, as you may not have noticed or not have preserved any newspaper-report of the *laying of its Cornerstone on the 23d of April last*, I have prefixed one to another circular, for preservation among your archives & send it herewith."[98] Hackett then provides a flattering report of his experience attending a Union Square "Demonstration of thanks to General Grant," telling Lincoln, "It afforded me great satisfaction to perceive, whenever any allusion to you was distinctly made, by even a political opponent, in his address, that there seemed to prevail among the multitude present so very general a regard & respect; indicating unmistakeably your personal *popularity*." "Accustomed, as I have been, to study the human heart," he continues, "& to try & find, & paint professionally, the mind's construction in the face as well as its motives, I analysed & considered philosophically the *cause* of the effect & concluded it was in the fact that all agreed—'President Lincoln is an *honest* man!' which Pope said is '*the noblest work of God.*'" Hackett, after adding, "Such a trait of character commands universal respect," follows with a personal note alluding to his youthful business difficulties: "When I became a bankrupt merchant of this city [New York] in 1825, I was more ambitious to deserve *that good* name, than I have been to acquire great fame as an actor since." He ends by noting that he has enclosed an article from the *Edinburgh Mercury* in praise of the president.

In retrospect, we can see that Hackett is buttering Lincoln up and preparing the way to ask a larger favor than he had hitherto contemplated. Writing a few weeks later (July 19), Hackett exhibits a duplicity that must have put the president on his guard. After making reference to yet another clipping he is enclosing for Lincoln's edification, he mentions that his disgust at England's hostility toward the Union cause has become so marked that "much as I would have liked in some respects the position, could I have obtained the next *U. S. Consulship to London* . . . I should fear that I could not reconcile it to my outraged national-pride."[99] Hackett is here refusing an appointment that, as far as we know, has not been offered him. Lincoln could have guessed what was coming next. Writing again on August 1, Hackett's animosity toward Great Britain seems to have evaporated, and his interest in being posted to London is now unqualified. He reminds Lincoln of "our tete a tete chat last winter" at which time he had made a passing observation indicating "how very agreeable to me it would be could I obtain the Secretaryship of Legation." "You," Hackett continues, "after a short meditative pause remarked, '*I am glad you have mentioned this!*'"[100] Lincoln's response may have been nothing more than a polite brush-off, but Hackett clearly did not take it as such. "But, my dear Mr. Lincoln!" Hackett continues, "as Hamlet said once to Horatio—'something too much of this!' I leave the subject to time, assured from your past kindness, that, should a convenient opportunity transpire, you will 'know your cue without a prompter,' & fitly *cast* me for a little part in our acting & great national drama." Completely shifting gears, Hackett, who was then sixty-four years old and had been a widower for nearly twenty years, tells Lincoln, half apologizing and half bragging, of his recent marriage to "an unsophisticated country girl, of *25*," adding, "I *know*, of myself, that I have not yet begun to feel any of the physical infirmities common to men at my years; & as Sir Pertinax said, *when he had run away with his second wife from the boarding-school*, 'I am *ready to begin the world again*.'" One might suspect here that this "man of the world" talk would have amused Lincoln and that Hackett knew it.[101]

Hackett writes again the next day, enclosing a clipping that refers to his son John K. Hackett (who was recorder of the City of New York) and recounting a weak joke, which, he fears, he may have already told Lincoln: "There is something said in Shakespeare about 'a *thrice* told tale, vexing the dull ear of a drowsy man.' I feel sure you never heard this from me but '*onest*' before; & contend that if you had, '*twict*,' you still have the advantage of any *listener*, who, if *bored*, cant throw his ears—as you can the enclosed—in the *fire*, unread."[102] There is no reference here to a diplomatic appointment, but a New

Year's letter returns to the subject: "You may remember that, in one of our latest Sunday evening chats last winter, I ventured to say—'I think I could, upon an occasion, obtain from a number of the eldest, most prominent & influential merchants & residents of New York city some signed evidence of their good esteem, confidence & benevolence.'—In November last, about thirty such citizens united & signed, & have furnished me with their application—brief and pertinent, & whereof the following is a verbatim copy." What follows is a petition presenting Hackett as "a suitable person to fill the U.S. Consulate at London, in the event of a vacancy in that office" and signed by, among others, Cornelius Vanderbilt and William B. Astor. Oddly addressing Lincoln in the third person, Hackett warms to the topic. "I did not think it expedient to visit Washington or to mention this subject to the President," he continues, "but, yesterday, hearing casually that—'Mr. Morse, now U.S. Consul at London, for some reason was desirous to return to his home in Maine & had already sent over from London his family,' I am advised to—'go at once!' and I purpose to set out tomorrow & expect to reach Willard's hotel Tuesday morning." Hackett closes, "In the hope of soon exchanging salutations with you personally, I remain, my dear Mr. Lincoln! Your obliged friend & grateful Servant ever."[103] Hackett's "plot" made its way to the newspapers, as he no doubt intended.[104] This is the last extant letter from him to Lincoln.

Hackett did visit Lincoln again, on Sunday, January 8, but this was probably the final time. The evidence for this is a letter Hackett wrote to John Hay, dated January 12, 1865, which includes the line "At the close of our interview last Sunday evening the President had the kindness to make a remark to me . . . ." This would be Sunday, January 8, 1865. Lincoln, according to Hackett, had expressed the wish to see Falstaff once more.[105] He evidently encountered difficulties arranging this visit, writing to his wife on January 3 and again on January 8 to complain of his frustration at being unable to see the president.[106] A story told by a young friend of Lincoln's, the journalist Noah Brooks, may refer to this visit, or possibly to a later one not otherwise recorded.[107] Late one night, according to Brooks, Lincoln, on being told that Hackett was waiting in the anteroom, complained, "'Oh, I can't see him; I can't see him. I was in hopes he had gone away.' Then he added, 'Now, this just illustrates the difficulty of having pleasant friends and acquaintances in this place. . . . Just because we had a little friendly correspondence, such as any two men might have, he wants something. What do you suppose he wants?' I could not guess, and Lincoln added, 'Well, he wants to be consul to London. Oh, dear!'"[108] Whether or not this refers to the January 8 visit, Hackett was not offered the consulship. John Hay, referring to the initial exchange of letters, remarked, "This incident had the usual sequel; the veteran comedian asked for an office, which the president was not able to give him and the pleasant acquaintance ceased."[109]

It is tempting to see the Shakespeare-loving president and the Shakespearean actor as reproducing something of the relationship between the future King Henry V of England and his boon companion Falstaff. Was Hackett, like Falstaff, amusing to have around but, having presumed on an unequal friendship, finally banished from the "royal" presence? The idea is not entirely fanciful. The president clearly enjoyed the actor's visits. Hackett had a well-attested reputation for wit and humor, and in addition to taking pleasure in conversations relating to Shakespeare, Lincoln would have been entertained by Hackett's personality, which included elements of what today we might identify as the stand-up comic—a skill at mimicry (a talent Lincoln shared with him) and a whole catalog of comic characters based on the Yankee types Hackett had acted over his many years of stardom as American's premier comic actor. John Hay found Hackett to be "a very amusing and garrulous talker."[110] A eulogist remarked of Hackett, "He was the very prince of companions, whether at a dinner table, or in a social circle; in a rail-way car or a stage-coach, or a stroll through the streets. He was wise, witty, mirthful, anecdotical." "As a *raconteur*," according to another witness, "he was inimitable."[111] If Lincoln found it necessary to break off the friendship, it was not because Hackett had a corrupting influence on him, as Falstaff had on Prince Hal, but because the actor expected too much from what was ultimately a casual relationship. The break must nonetheless have been painful on Lincoln's side, as the Noah Brooks story suggests. Though no doubt a sentimental exaggeration, one already tinged with nostalgia, there may be something quite true in the tone of an 1872 obituary that claims that Hackett "made a close acquaintanceship with the late President Lincoln, and many were the critical and story-telling bouts which the two had together during the stirring scenes of the war."[112]

As brief as it is, Lincoln's letter to Hackett and the conversations to which it led allows us to trace the outlines of his lifelong engagement with Shakespeare, and at the same time it reveals a generally hidden insight into his literary tastes and critical acumen. Although Lincoln may have preferred reading Shakespeare's plays to seeing them performed, as president he took the opportunities that presented themselves to see and hear Shakespeare on the stage, not only because going to the theater offered him one of the few available means of relaxation but also because he found intellectual pleasure in measuring the readings of the great actors of his time against his own understanding of the texts. Hackett, at least for a time, was central to this process. In the letter referred to above, Robert Lincoln wrote to Hackett, "Although it may be no news to you, I cannot refrain from expressing to you how often I have heard my father speak [?] of the great pleasure he used to derive from your visits to Washington and your discussions with him on [Shakespeare]."[113] Whatever "Falstaff" Hackett's self-aggrandizing habits and other personal foibles, he gave the president some respite from the awful weight of responsibility he endured for nearly every day of his years in the White House, and at the same time, both as actor and as scholar, he served as a sounding board and foil that allowed Lincoln to exercise his critical appreciation of and indulge his love for Shakespeare's plays. Over the two years that remained to him, Lincoln would expand his theatrical horizons and refine his critical acumen as he attended the performances of the other major Shakespearean actors of his time.

President Lincoln and
the Great Shakespeareans

Although it is clearly mistaken to suggest, as some writers have, that Lincoln's attendance at the theater was motivated primarily either by a sense of social and political duty or by a desire to hide from the responsibilities of office (or both), it is nevertheless true that he sometimes combined duty with pleasure.[1] When, for example, Lincoln saw E. L. Davenport in *Othello* on the evening of October 6, 1863, the occasion was the long-anticipated reopening of Leonard Grover's theater, a "great social as well as theatrical event," according to the next day's *Daily National Republican*. "The house was completely filled from floor to ceiling and the performance of the play ... gave the vast audience the greatest satisfaction."[2] Particular note is taken of Lincoln's presence at this performance: "The private boxes were occupied by the President and his family, and Mr. Stoddard, his Private Secretary, members of the Cabinet and other distinguished persons." Although the *National Republican* was consistently and enthusiastically a mouthpiece for the administration, it probably should not be doubted that "the audience found it difficult, between the acts, to repress the enthusiasm that their consciousness of the presence of Mr. Lincoln stirred within them, and once or twice they came near ignoring the drama altogether and turning the affair into an ovation to their President—a proceeding that would have been highly distasteful to him as he came there to see Shakespeare's play, and for nothing else."[3] Another newspaper reported, "The President had intended to remain only an hour, but was so pleased with the play that he stayed it out,"[4] which would suggest that Lincoln felt free, at times, to leave early or arrive late (as he did for *Our American Cousin*).

Similarly, when he attended a performance of *Macbeth* at Grover's on the evening of October 17, 1863, Lincoln was supporting a benefit for the U.S. Sanitary Commission while witnessing one of the most famous and beloved actors of the time, Charlotte Cushman. The Sanitary Commission was the premier private agency providing support to wounded and sick soldiers during the Civil War, and Lincoln did all he could to encourage its crucial work. Cushman, a strong Union supporter, happily lent her talents to raise money for the commission (from September 12 to October 22, she gave five performances in various cities and raised over $8,000),[5] and the combination of her presence and the worthy cause to which she and others were contributing combined to make this evening a social event of note. The *Daily National Republican* reported on October 19 that "Grover's Theatre [on Saturday night] embraced within its walls a larger amount of the intellect gathered in Washington, in official circles and civic life, than is often witnessed." "Many persons who seldom attend the drama—seldom enter Shakspeare's ideal world—were present," the writer adds, "having been attracted somewhat by the unusually powerful cast of the tragedy, but mainly by the noble charity for our soldiers to which they were contributing."[6] Lincoln was accompanied by Mary and Tad and by Secretary of State William Seward and his family, who were friends of Cushman's; Secretary of the Treasury Salmon P. Chase and the British legate, Lord Lyons, among others, were also present.

At the same time, Lincoln undoubtedly went to see productions of Shakespeare not only for pleasure but also to test his own sense of what the plays meant and how they should be performed. For a variety of reasons, he does not appear to have seen a Shakespeare play or even to have gone to the theater more than a handful of times between his arrival in Washington in early 1861 and early 1863. For the first two years of his presidency, presumably, the immediate pressures of his office were such as to demand Lincoln's nearly constant attention. In addition, a period of mourning for their son Willie, who died on February 20, 1862, would have kept the Lincolns away from most kinds of entertainment (although they did attend a concert by opera star Clara Louise Kellogg in May)[7] for some time afterward. (As far as can be determined, it was exactly a year to the day of Willie's funeral, on February 24, 1863, that Lincoln first went to a nonmusical event, to see Barney Williams, an Irish comic and blackface minstrel.)[8] From March 13, 1863, to November 16, 1864, Lincoln went to at least ten productions of eight of Shakespeare's plays. The plays he saw were those that, for the most part, provided star vehicles for the famous actors of the time: Edwin Booth (Lincoln saw him most frequently) in *Hamlet, Richard III, The Merchant of Venice,* and *Catharine and Petruchio* (David Garrick's version of *The Taming of the Shrew*); Edwin Forrest in *King Lear*; Charlotte Cushman and James Wallack in *Macbeth*; E. L. Davenport in *Hamlet* and *Othello*; and, of course, James H. Hackett as Falstaff in *Henry IV Part 1* and *The Merry Wives of Windsor*. None of these is particularly surprising: these were, with the possible exception of *Merry Wives*, the most popular Shakespeare plays on the nineteenth-century stage.[9] It is not possible, given the paucity of evidence, to re-create exactly what Lincoln would have seen and heard when he attended these Shakespeare productions at Grover's and Ford's theaters, but we can make some reasonable assumptions based on evidence gathered from newspaper reviews, biographies and memoirs of actors, and some eyewitness accounts as to the general shape and manner in which Shakespeare was presented to mid-nineteenth-century audiences, particularly on New York stages. In a few instances, too, we have valuable evidence of Lincoln's own reaction to what he experienced in the theater at a particular performance.

The first Shakespeare production Lincoln attended soon after seeing Hackett in *Henry IV* was E. L. Davenport's *Hamlet*, on March 25, 1863. He had been invited (and provided with free tickets) by theater manager Leonard Grover. "No public announcement will be made," Grover wrote Lincoln. "It is purely to be the instrument to confer a pleasure to meritorious Artist [*sic*] and true Union lover—and at the same time I hope, to minister in some slight degree to your Excellency's gratification, that this offer is made."[10] The American-born Davenport was a well-liked performer, though the evidence suggests that his Hamlet was not particularly exciting. "Mind, grace, force, variety, and occasional flashes of fire were characteristic of Davenport's acting," the critic William Winter wrote, but, he added, "it was deficient in soul."[11] The *New York Herald* found that "Mr. Davenport's delivery lacked spirit."[12] Another critic wrote that his Hamlet "wears that woe-begone, depressed look which is seen in Roman Catholic ecclesiastical students, whose young hearts and souls are chained down in irons, and he seems half stupefied with the load which weighs upon his mind."[13] On the other hand, a Philadelphia critic, lamenting the naturalism infecting American acting, praises Davenport in general terms for his expressiveness: "If he has a passionate passage to recite, he does not talk of it as though he were speaking of a comfortable dinner of pork and beans. Rage with him is not cooled off by a superhuman stoicism. It is real demonstrative and perceptible passion."[14] "His Hamlet," a *New York Times* obituary writer wrote, "though a trifle cold, was by many held to be the most perfect portrayal of the Danish Prince ever witnessed on the American stage."[15] A brief review of one of Davenport's appearances in Washington, though not one of the times Lincoln saw him, is positive in a general sense: "His most excellent performance of Hamlet was enjoyed by all those in the large audience who are capable of appreciating Shakespeare's poetry, philosophy, and delineations of human passions."[16] Clara Morris, who acted with him, wrote, "He always seemed to me a *Hamlet* cut in crystal—so clear and pure, so cold and hard he was."[17] These comments may not be damning with faint praise, but they do suggest a performer who fails to catch fire.

Of the Davenport *Hamlet* production overall, we have little in the way of specifics; as usual, the star is all anyone wants to talk about. The day Lincoln saw him, a newspaper merely noted, "Mr. Davenport is well known to all in his great impersonation of this character as being without a rival, while Mr. Wallack is equally great as the 'Ghost of Hamlet's Father.' The characters are all very strongly cast."[18] In a surprisingly detailed review of an 1855 performance in New York, one bit of stage business is noted: while watching the King's response to the "mousetrap" play, "Mr. Davenport makes Hamlet in the eagerness of his analysis crawl stealthily almost to the King's face to read still more closely and revel in the evidence of his guilt. This rendering was highly applauded by the audience"—though not, as he makes clear, by the reviewer.[19] When, some years later, Davenport played Hamlet in San Francisco, the *Daily Evening Bulletin* commented, "[The] fine scene of the King at his devotions was omitted, and thus one clue to the delay of Hamlet's purpose was lost."[20] Although the chances are good that the scene, including Claudius's soliloquy beginning "O, my offense is rank," which we know Lincoln particularly admired, was missing on the two occasions he saw Davenport's *Hamlet* as well, a newspaper notice on October 10, 1863, anticipating that evening's performance, notes, "Mr. Bokee enacts the part of the King of Denmark; and, according to President Lincoln, he has the best soliloquy in the piece." Citing Lincoln's letter to Hackett, the writer adds, "We shall see how Mr. Bokee will deliver this to-night."[21] Unfortunately, we do not know if Mr. Bokee did, in fact, deliver Claudius's soliloquy on that or any other occasion. Lincoln must have been impressed by Davenport's performance (or perhaps he had missed parts of the earlier production), as he saw it again the following year (on November 15, 1864).

When Davenport's *Othello*, with Lincoln in attendance, opened Grover's new theater on October 6, 1863, the reviewers seemed more interested in what was happening in the audience than they were in the activity onstage. We learn, for example, that there were few women present, "partly, we suppose, because Othello is not a favorite play with the ladies, who do not like to see one of their sex unjustly smothered with a pillow, and partly because the gentlemen feared to trust their wives, daughters, and sweethearts in a new building until its strength had been thoroughly tested." The refurbished theater was particularly noted, mention being made of new scenery and curtains; "the proscenium, and all the scenic accessories, are capitally done. There is a harmony about the whole which is seldom found in modern theatres."[22] As for the production itself, the reporter's observations are quite general and perhaps a bit lukewarm: "The actors last night did their best, and Othello was performed excellently well." Both Davenport (Othello) and James Wallack (Iago) "rendered their parts intelligently, and with all the enthusiasm tempered with enlightened judgment that characterizes their acting in general." The actress playing Desdemona "looked lovely . . . and acted the part in its true spirit," while the actress playing Emilia "was perhaps a little too deliberate in rendering some portions of the last act, but on the whole her part was well performed."[23] According to William O. Stoddard, Lincoln "did not lose a word or motion of Mr. Davenport, who played his part exceedingly well, and conversed between the acts with, for him, a very near approach to excitement."[24] If we want more specifics regarding the production Lincoln witnessed, however, the evidence is slim.

A few clues regarding Davenport's interpretation of Othello can be gathered from a surprisingly detailed, substantially negative review in the *New York Daily Tribune* of an 1855 performance. From the outset, the reviewer was disappointed in the actor's overall manner: "When Mr. Davenport appears we are at once struck with his incapability to personate the character. . . . Every movement should speak of the fiery Arab, and a feeling of sympathy seize and hold the heart." Davenport, however, "enters with a stealthy pace and more with the air of some lugubrious Eastern dervish." The overall impression is of an actor too cool, too gentlemanly to enact the fire and passion Othello exhibits: "No effort of art can picture a big child of nature like the Moor if the natural power of the actor is too limited." On a more positive note, we read that the "startling transition of the weak noble man from relentless jealousy to tender confidence is surrounded in Mr. Davenport's rendering with much of poesy, and kindles the sympathy of the audience."[25] When Davenport played Othello with Wallack in Brooklyn in 1861, the *Herald* review, presumably written by a different critic, was more generous though less revealing: "The Othello of Mr. Davenport is another of those careful and finished studies which place him in the foremost rank of the representatives of the Shaksperian drama. Graceful, dignified and forcible, he is never obliged to resort to rant to give effect to the more striking passages of the text." And even Iago gets noticed: "Mr. J. W. Wallack's Iago is a light, pleasant sort of villain, without any of that depth of malice which we are accustomed to attribute to the character."[26] Whether or not this is a good thing, the reviewer does not say.

Regardless of the precise form the October 6 production of Davenport's *Othello* took, for Lincoln, as for many in the audience, the play itself, with its climactic scene of a black man murdering a white woman, however well or ill presented, would have presented a complex knot of implications. *Othello*, unlike *Richard III* and *King Lear*, was not produced in drastically rewritten form in the eighteenth and nineteenth centuries, although Lincoln would have seen the play cut to remove "improprieties" and vulgarities of different kinds: among other things, the word "whore" was not spoken and Othello's epileptic fit and his striking of Desdemona were eliminated, though in some productions he was allowed to strike her with the letter. As late as 1881, in a review of John McCullough's Othello in London, one reviewer noted that American audiences could not endure the sight of a "coloured gentleman" striking a white woman.[27] The characters of Bianca and the Clown, Desdemona's "Willow" song, and probably the whole of the so-called brothel scene (act 4, scene 2) were also dropped. Beyond these kinds of alterations, productions of the play in the nineteenth century often presented the title character in a way that downplayed or eliminated the suggestion of a Negro or "African" Othello. Quite apart from the fact that the role was played by (and had been written for) Caucasian actors (the African American actor Ira Aldridge only acted Othello abroad; James Hewlett, the first black American known to have played Shakespeare, acted Othello with an all-black company),[28] makeup, costuming, and textual revisions often reinforced the idea that the "Moor" was an Arab.

But if Shakespeare is somewhat vague concerning the precise nature of Othello's origins and ethnicity, the text is clear enough that to other characters in the play, the Moor is black; as Sylvan Barnet notes, "to call him tawny or golden or bronzed, or to conceive of him as something of an Arab chieftain, is to go against the text of the play."[29] Even though nineteenth-century acting editions sometimes cut up to 1,000 lines, phrases like "a measure to the health of black Othello" and "Haply for I am black" remain in the promptbooks and presumably on the stage. "For most antebellum southern performances," one historian writes, "no explicit evidence about Othello's makeup survives . . . [but] however bronzed the makeup or oriental the costuming, [nineteenth-century] audiences saw an African, a blackamoor Othello."[30] We can also point to the various parodies of *Othello*, beginning in England in the 1830s—such as *Othello Travestie* (1833)—although in America these parodies mainly date from the immediate post–Civil War era. A number of them rely for their humor, such as it is, on the fact of Othello being a "nigger" ("Otello" is "a Nigger good as a white man, and a little gooderer," from *Rice's Grand Shakespearian Burlesque*).[31] (In an essay on *Othello* published in 1869, Mary Preston, who sympathized with the defeated Confederacy, concluded her commentary by writing "Othello *was* a *white* man!")[32] When Davenport played Othello in New York in 1855, the reviewer, in the course of delineating the positive aspects of the performance, makes a suggestive allusion to Othello's color: "You almost see every cunning arrow [of Iago's] cleave the air, steal through the dark skin and rest and rankle in the rich, luxuriant Arab heart."[33] How dark the skin, it is not now possible to tell.

Whatever the precise hue of Othello's skin in various productions, historians of the American theater are divided on the question of how nineteenth-century audiences might have responded to the implications of the marriage between Othello and Desdemona. English essayist Charles Lamb, who did not believe Shakespeare's plays benefited from being performed, wrote that as much as we may accept Desdemona's love for Othello in the reading, on stage there is "something extremely revolting in the courtship and wedded caresses of Othello and Desdemona."[34] John Quincy Adams, in spite of his hatred of slavery, notoriously found Desdemona's "fondling with Othello . . . disgusting," something Lincoln could very well have known from Hackett's *Notes and Comments*, in which Adams's observations are reproduced. (Hackett, in a note, appears to modify, if not entirely reject, Adams's racist assumptions.) "The great moral lesson of the tragedy of *Othello* is," Adams wrote, "that black and white blood cannot be intermingled in marriage without a gross outrage upon the law of Nature; and that, in such violations, Nature will vindicate her laws."[35] It might seem reasonable, given views likes these, that "by the nineteenth century, when the barbarities of 'the peculiar institution' of slavery had peaked in the Western world, audiences could no longer tolerate nor would directors depict the 'monstrous' sexual relationship of black males and white females on the stage."[36] Certainly, lines about the "old black ram tupping your white ewe" or "making the beast with two backs" were cut from performance. That the play could be seen as subversive, especially in the South, is indicated by the Charleston, South Carolina, city council's refusal of a license for a performance of *Othello* in 1807. "The council's objection to the play was that it 'contained sentiments incompatible with the real interests of this country.'" The theater manager tried to comply, evidently without effect, with the objections, stating that the play had been "revised, corrected, and (I may add) adapted to Carolina, . . . so that no sentiment remains, which could be distorted or interpreted into a meaning inimical to the true interests of the community."[37] Nevertheless, in spite of this sort of perceived danger, *Othello* "was performed frequently on all southern stages up to the Civil War, its popularity being only slightly less than that of *Richard III*, *Macbeth*, and *Hamlet*."[38] Whether or not Othello is seen as black or tawny, for anyone who has actually read Shakespeare's play, as we can reasonably assume Lincoln had (he several times alludes to it), the racial issue, and the specific "problem" of miscegenation, must have been an inescapable aspect of the performance.[39]

Othello is not mentioned in the letter to Hackett as one of the plays Lincoln had studied with care, but as we have seen, *Macbeth* comes in for particular praise: "It is wonderful." In witnessing Charlotte Cushman in his favorite play, Lincoln would necessarily have seen a production more centered on Lady Macbeth than on the title character. A masculine-looking woman, Cushman excelled in both female and male roles: she played Romeo to great acclaim, and she was successful both as Queen Katherine and as Cardinal Wolsey in *Henry VIII*. But she was *the* Lady Macbeth of her generation virtually from her debut in 1835 (at the age of nineteen) in New Orleans to her retirement in 1874. In her interpretation, Lady Macbeth was "the dominant goading force in an essentially masculine play, hands clutching a pair of daggers, eyes blazing an obsessed ambition, chin set firm to the task ahead, overriding completely Macbeth's own moral doubts."[40] Under the circumstances, Macbeth would no doubt have seemed a secondary role. Much of the audience that evening, it can be assumed, was at the theater to see and hear Charlotte Cushman, who at this point in her life and career occupied a special and nearly unique position in American cultural life; along with Edwin Forrest and the up-and-coming Edwin Booth, she was considered the finest tragic actor of her time. But she was more than a great star: to William Winter, writing long after her death, she was "a noble interpreter of the noble minds of the past, and thus she helped to educate the men and women of her time,—to ennoble them in mood, to strengthen them in duty, to lift them in hope of immortality."[41] Though Winter was given to flights of rhetorical fancy, his comments here are very much congruent with the kind of praise Cushman often inspired. She was friends with artists, writers, and politicians: when she came to Washington in the 1860s, she usually stayed at the home of Secretary of State Seward. It was Seward who, in July 1861, introduced her to Lincoln, at which time "Lincoln told her that *Macbeth* was his favorite play, and that he hoped some day to see her in the role of Lady Macbeth."[42]

She later reported to Seward, "I was so completely taken up with [President Lincoln] and his humour that I forgot my mission and came away."[43] (She evidently had hoped that Lincoln could appoint the son of a friend to West Point.) She and Lincoln met again at the White House on October 11, 1863, less than a week before the *Macbeth* performance.[44] That the two of them discussed *Macbeth* is not improbable, but their conversation was not recorded.

We have little evidence of how *Macbeth* was staged and performed on the evening of Lincoln's attendance. As one theater historian notes, there were so many adaptations of *Macbeth* in the nineteenth century that it is "challenging to isolate which version of the play would have been seen by a particular audience."[45] In a prompter's copy of *Macbeth* used by Cushman in Baltimore in 1858, the comic character of the Porter was cut (a few of his lines were given to another character), the murder of Lady Macduff's children took place offstage, and the England scene (act 4, scene 3) was shortened. The so-called Hecate scenes (act 3, scene 5; act 4, scene 1), on the other hand, were not only staged but also filled out with lines from Thomas Middleton's play *The Witch*.[46] We would not learn any of this, however, from the Washington newspapers, which were, as usual, maddeningly vague and capricious. "We do not feel called upon to go into a criticism or analysis of the acting on the occasion," the *Daily National Republican* tells us, adding, "All the principal performers are well known, their qualities appreciated, and their reputations well established."[47] The performers referred to, in addition to Cushman, were James Wallack as Macbeth and E. L. Davenport as Macduff; like Davenport, Wallack was a popular, experienced actor; *Macbeth* thus had something of an all-star cast. Davenport and Wallack were then acting at Grover's theaters, where they had been playing their repertoire of Shakespearean and non-Shakespearean plays since September 28, first at the Washington and then at the newly reopened National. It was probably Grover's willingness to provide these male leads that encouraged Cushman to choose Grover's theater over Ford's (a venue she had earlier considered)[48] for the benefit.

The last-minute casting, combined with the fact that only one performance was given, might suggest that this *Macbeth* was unlikely to have the kind of unity, coherence, and attention to detail we would today expect of a major Shakespeare production. But Cushman had acted with both men on numerous occasions (Davenport had played Mercutio to her Romeo) and had played Lady Macbeth opposite both Wallack and Davenport; furthermore, she had performed the play as recently as September 12 in Brooklyn, with Edwin Booth as Macbeth. Davenport and Wallack, for their part, had appeared in *Macbeth* at Grover's less than a week earlier (with, of course, a different Lady Macbeth). For that occasion, the *Daily National Republican* predicted on the day of the performance that "Macbeth will be rendered at this elegant temple of the drama this evening in a style never before attempted in this Metropolis. This thrilling tragedy will be presented with all the new and correct costumes and music of the period, weapons, armor, etc.,"[49] the same accoutrements that, we can assume, would be in evidence for the Cushman performance. Nevertheless, there would have been very little time for rehearsal in this instance, given that Cushman was still considering Ford's Theatre as late as October 10; Grover announced the event on the fourteenth.

To get a better sense of the qualities that made Cushman's Lady Macbeth so compelling, we need to look at accounts written of her earlier appearances in the role. The overwhelming impression is one of unusual force and power. A Philadelphia critic praises her "graphic and highly intellectual performance," finding that her "personation of the character is distinguished by all that masculine strength of purpose, bold, remorseless spirit, and firm, unfaltering pursuit of an ambitious end, which enters into our conception of Lady Macbeth."[50] A review of her performance in Cleveland from 1857 provides some detail. Cushman is described as of "tall figure, rather harsh features and a voice to correspond, her first appearance [giving] little promise of her correct rendering of Lady Macbeth's character, who, with all her crimes, was yet a woman and not a fiend." "In the murder scene," the reviewer adds, "she has wrought her spirits up to her share in the deed, but startles with fear at every sound. . . . Only those who watched attentively the expressive play of her features during every moment of her stay on the stage could fully appreciate the thorough manner in which every minute shade of character was represented."[51]

Not all commentators were charmed by Cushman, however. James Murdoch, who acted with her in New Orleans early in her career, while acknowledging that "her understanding was never at fault; it was keen and penetrating," nevertheless found that "that glow of feeling which springs from the centre of emotional elements was not a prominent constituent of her organization." "She was," he added, "intensely prosaic, definitely practical, and hence her perfect identity with what may be termed the materialism of Lady Macbeth."[52] George Vandenhoff, another of her Macbeths, believed her "too animal" and felt she was wanting in "intellectual confidence," relying too much on "physical energy." "As one sees her large clenched hand and muscular arm threatening him, in alarming proximity," Vandenhoff remembered, "one feels that if other arguments fail with her husband, she will have recourse to blows."[53] Edwin Booth, who played with her in Brooklyn on September 12

Charlotte Cushman as Lady Macbeth. Folger Shakespeare Library.

and on other occasions, would recall in later years that as they plotted to kill King Duncan, he longed to say to her, "Why don't *you* kill him? *You're a great deal bigger than I am!*"[54] Even if she intimidated her leading men to a greater or lesser extent, most theatergoers were impressed by Cushman. Commenting on her first Lady Macbeth, the *New York Times* obituary writer noted that from the outset of her career, "She made the people understand the character that Shakespeare drew; she was neither stilted, nor mock-heroic, nor monotonous, but so fiercely, so vividly natural that the spectators were afraid of her as they would have been of a pantheress let loose."[55]

The newspaper reviewers had little of note to say about the specifics of the Cushman-Wallack-Davenport *Macbeth* that Lincoln attended, but several eyewitnesses who saw the production that evening wrote down their impressions. Benjamin Brown French, the New Hampshire politician who was commissioner of public buildings, unhelpfully wrote that Cushman was "perfect." "She always is," he added. "I think her the greatest actress living. In the sleep walking scene she was great."[56] Somewhat more useful are the comments of Annie Fields: "Charlotte Cushman played Lady Macbeth for the benefit of the Sanitary Commission to a large audience. Her reading of the letter when she first appears is of one of her finest points. She moves her feet execrably and succeeds in developing all the devilish nature in the part, but discovers no beauty. . . . Charlotte in the sleeping scene was fine—that deep-drawn breath of sleep is thrilling."[57]

Neither diarist had much good to say of Wallack, however. French notes that the play was "well done, but, as Macbeth himself would say, 'It were well it were done quickly.' I never saw a character so 'long drawn out' as Wallack's Macbeth was last night. The curtain rose at about 8 & 20′ and fell for the last time at 20′ before 12! At least an hour longer than it should have taken."[58] (Elsewhere in his diary, French writes, "I would never see a female upon the stage in male attire, could I avoid it.")[59] Fields, after praising the "intelligence" and "clarity" of Cushman's delivery, adds, "It would be impossible to say this of the man who played Macbeth, who talked of 'encarnardine,' and 'heat-oppre*st* brain,' for oppre*s̀*ed, besides innumerable other faults and failures, which he mouthed too much for me to discover."[60] When Wallack and Davenport had played *Macbeth* the previous March, the *Daily National Republican* had reported, "The part of Macbeth . . . was enacted by J. W. Wallack with his usual fire and energy. Macduff was finely done by Mr. E. L. Davenport, and the closing scene between these two artists produced an effect rarely witnessed."[61] Reviewing Wallack's Macbeth a decade earlier, a Boston reviewer wrote, "[Wallack's] make-up was a picture; his conception and execution the finest we have witnessed for many a day. His rendering of the part showed he had devoted long and serious research to it."[62] When he played in Mobile in 1858, one newspaper complained that he "mouthed his words and over-acted."[63] More generally, "descriptions of Wallack's acting suggest . . . that the element of calculation in his art was not always concealed, and that his dignity was the result of effort, something he took care to preserve."[64] Wallack, in any case, was essentially a comic actor, and Macbeth was never a part for which he was particularly noted.[65]

Although in most instances we can only guess at what Lincoln thought of any particular playgoing experience, we are fortunate to have an eyewitness account of his response to at least one scene in the October 17 *Macbeth*. On October 21, the *Chicago Tribune* printed a letter from the Washington correspondent of the *Springfield Republican*: "I had the pleasure on Monday night of seeing Macbeth rendered upon the stage by Mr. Wallack and Mr. Davenport [oddly, Cushman is not mentioned], and also of seeing Mr. Lincoln present at the time with his little 'Tad' (Thaddeus Lincoln) with him. It is Mr. Lincoln's favorite play [the letter to Hackett had recently been published], and one could not repress a certain curiosity to know (though he is familiar with them as he is with stump-speaking, doubtless) how certain passages would strike him." The writer then quotes an exchange from act 4, scene 3 of *Macbeth*, where Malcolm and Macduff lament the ills that have fallen on Scotland under Macbeth's usurping rule; among the quoted lines are these:

> Each new morn
> New widows howl, new orphans cry; new sorrows
> Strike heaven on the face that it resounds
> As if it felt with Scotland and yelled out
> Like syllable of dolour.

"Mr. Lincoln leaned back in his chair in the shade after this sentence was pronounced," the writer tells us, "and for a long time wore a sad, sober face, as if suddenly his thoughts had wandered from the play-room far away to where his great armies contest with the rebellion a vast empire."[66] It would not be surprising if Lincoln's thoughts had taken him to immediate concerns. Earlier in the day, he had signed a proclamation calling for 300,000 volunteers, asking for "cheerful and effective aid to the measures thus adopted, with a view to reinforce our victorious armies now in the field and bring our needful military operations to a prosperous end, thus closing forever the fountains of sedition and civil war."[67] And several days earlier, a battle had taken place at Bristoe Station, Virginia, which resulted in nearly 2,000 casualties on both sides; though a nominal Union victory, General George Meade, as at Gettysburg, had failed to follow up on his advantage.[68] "On October 17 the most solemn of the play's associations might have been thoughts of death, of fate, of last moments—of all that art could be a ground for," Alexander Nemerov writes.[69] But of course, at no time during his presidency were such thoughts likely to be far from Lincoln's consciousness.

In watching Cushman's performance as Lady Macbeth, did Lincoln have occasion to think of his ambitious, sometimes domineering, though also loving and supportive wife? Whether or not he ever referred to her as "my dearest partner of greatness," as several writers have claimed,[70] historians and commentators have occasionally seen Mary's interest in political matters and her powerful personality as sufficient grounds for an analogy between the first lady and Lady Macbeth.[71] Jean Baker writes, "The record is full of those who remembered Lincoln's saying that his wife expected him to be President, to which idea he responded with bemused astonishment, at least until November 6, 1860."[72] We know that Lincoln was himself ambitious, and we know that Mary was ambitious for him; her sister called her "the most ambitious woman I ever knew."[73] When Lincoln learned of his election, according to one source, "he hurried home and woke his wife, saying, 'Mary! Mary! we are elected!'"[74] "This frank expression," Michael Burlingame comments, "might be interpreted as evidence of a marriage rooted, like the Macbeths', in 'mutual ambition,'"[75] but whether we can claim that Lincoln would ever have compared himself and his wife to Macbeth and his lady is quite another matter. It is probably just happenstance that Adam Badeau, Ulysses S. Grant's aide and Edwin Booth's friend, alluded to *Macbeth* when commenting that Mary, as "the unfortunate partner of [her husband's] elevation and unwitting cause of many of his miseries," had "eaten on the insane root that takes the reason prisoner."[76] As Catherine Clinton rightly notes, "Idle speculation on the First Couple became popular during the nineteenth century, and continues to fascinate well into the twenty-first."[77] But if dark musings affected the Lincolns' pleasure as they watched the play, it did not prevent them from cheering Cushman's performance.[78]

For all her popularity, Cushman was considered a bit old-fashioned by the time Lincoln saw her ("Miss Cushman belongs to the old school of acting, and the admirers of the modern school might take exception to her redundant action and violent gesticulation; but all must admit its exceeding effectiveness," one critic wrote in 1857).[79] Edwin Booth, on the other hand, was the up-and-coming new star, and Lincoln must have been aware of the actor's growing fame; he attended no fewer than seven of Booth's productions, Shakespearean and non-Shakespearean, at Grover's New National Theatre in the three weeks from February 19 to March 10, 1864. The acting family to which Edwin Booth belonged exemplifies the movement and development of the American theater and in particular of Shakespearean acting over the course of the nineteenth century. The father, Junius Brutus Booth, was an exemplar of the larger-than-life barnstorming star-actor of the first half of the century. John Wilkes, more like his father (whom he had probably never seen act) than was Edwin, continued the tradition and at the same time translated it, with his extraordinary good looks, into a romantic, matinee-idol popularity. Edwin, a close witness to his father's performances, refined and intellectualized the older man's style into something like the psychological naturalism that became prominent in the last years of the century. Notoriously, Edwin, John Wilkes, and a third brother, Junius Jr., appeared together in a benefit performance of *Julius Caesar* in New York on November 25, 1864, helping raise money for the Shakespeare statue that now stands in Central Park; Edwin and Junius were Brutus and Cassius, and Lincoln's assassin played Mark Antony.[80] Lincoln, as we have suggested, may have seen the senior Booth; he saw Edwin perform a good part of his repertoire;[81] and he saw John Wilkes at least once.

Given the institutional status Edwin Booth had acquired by the time of his death in 1891, it would be possible to see him as some kind of Victorian waxwork, sober, respectable, and rather dull. He exists for us primarily in a series of photographs, paintings, and statues, with only a brief, scratchy recording made late in his life to give us any sense of his vocal qualities,[82] and the praise he received from contemporary admirers takes on a note of embarrassingly fulsome hero worship that it is difficult for us to connect with. In fact, however, Booth achieved respectability long after living the life of a scrappy survivor, a youthful libertine who inherited some of his father's weakness for alcohol. Though he had been acting since his early youth, when he traveled with Booth senior in the West, and then later, after his father's death, toured as far away as Australia with a company headed by Laura Keene, it was not until an engagement in Boston in 1857 that he emerged as a genuine star, playing ten roles, four of them Shakespearean (what would become his signature Shakespearean role, Hamlet, was played only once in two weeks). His New York debut the same year was not particularly successful; being well-received in Boston was no guarantee of approval in America's center of theatrical activity. It was not until the 1860–1861 season that Booth began to improve his critical and popular standing in New York. After appearances in

England, in Manchester, Liverpool, and London, he returned to New York for the 1862–1863 season. By the time Lincoln saw him, in February and March of 1864, his position as America's premier Shakespearean actor had become established. He was being referred to, at least in ads, as "the eminent tragedian, Edwin Booth."[83] Soon after his appearance in Washington, he played Hamlet at the Winter Garden Theatre in New York, commencing on November 26 for an unprecedented 100 consecutive performances, a record that would not be broken until John Barrymore played Hamlet for 101 performances in 1922.

Booth's Washington, D.C., engagement began on February 15, with *Hamlet*. Lincoln did not attend, probably because he was already committed to a benefit at the Capitol for the Sanitary Commission featuring James Murdoch, the elocutionist and actor he had met in Springfield. The remainder of Booth's run, which lasted until March 12, included most of what would become his signature roles: Othello (February 16) and Iago (March 3); Shylock in *The Merchant of Venice* (February 17 and 26); Richelieu in the play of that name (February 18 and March 4); Edward Mortimer in *The Iron Chest*, which played on a double bill with *Katharine and Petruchio* (as Booth titled his own version of David Garrick's adaptation of *The Taming of the Shrew*), with Booth as Petruchio (February 19); Richard III (February 20, March 5, and March 10); the title role in *Don Caesar de Bazin* on a double bill with *The Merchant of Venice* (February 26) and on a double bill with *The Apostate*, in which Booth played Pescara (March 12); the title role in *Ruy Blas* (February 22, 23, and 24 and March 1); Brutus, in the play of that name by John Howard Payne (February 25); Macbeth (February 27 and March 9); Sir Giles Overreach in *A New Way to Pay Old Debts* (February 29); Hamlet again (March 2 and March 11); and Bertuccio in *The Fool's Revenge* (March 8). Of these performances, Lincoln saw *Hamlet, Richard III, Katharine and Petruchio,* and *The Merchant of Venice,* as well as *The Iron Chest, Richelieu, Brutus, Don Caesar de Bazin,* and *The Fool's Revenge.* Somewhat surprisingly, given his interest in the play, he evidently did not see Booth's Macbeth (on February 27 there was a reception at the White House, and on March 9, among other activities, Lincoln commissioned Ulysses S. Grant as lieutenant general and later consulted with General William T. Sherman). He also missed one of Booth's favorite Shakespearean roles, Iago.

Booth's non-Shakespearean repertoire is a seemingly haphazard mix of old and new, of tragedy, melodrama, and comedy. Only *A New Way to Pay Old Debts*, written by Shakespeare's younger contemporary Philip Massinger, dates from the pre-Restoration era, and it was the only play from that time, apart from Shakespeare, to have a continuing life on stage throughout the nineteenth century. The villainous central character, Sir Giles Overreach, was evidently irresistible to actors and audiences alike. Edward Bulwer-Lytton's *Richelieu* and John Howard Payne's *Brutus* were pseudo-Shakespearean in tone and style. The former had been written for William Charles Macready, but Booth adopted the role and made the French cardinal one of his and his audiences' favorite parts. Payne's play, written for Edmund Kean and first performed in 1818, tells the story of Lucius Junius Brutus, an ancestor of Shakespeare's Brutus and the founder of the Roman Republic.[84] Booth had acted the role of Titus, Brutus's son, with his father. *The Fool's Revenge* was adapted by Tom Taylor (of *Our American Cousin* fame) from Victor Hugo's *Le Roi s'amuse* (whose plot was also used by Verdi for his opera *Rigoletto*). *Don Caesar de Bazin*, by Dumanoir and Adolphe d'Ennery, was based on a character from another work by Hugo, *Ruy Blas*, a play in which Booth also acted. *The Iron Chest*, written near the end of the eighteenth century by George Colman the Younger, was based on William Godwin's novel *The Adventures of Caleb Williams*; like *A New Way to Pay Old Debts*, the play features a larger-than-life melodramatic villain, Sir Edmund Mortimer, a magnet for actors of the era. David Garrick's *Catharine and Petruchio*, published in 1756, was based on Shakespeare's *Taming of the Shrew* but was significantly altered from the original. Shakespeare's text was cut, adapted, or supplemented, and the whole was shortened to three quick acts; this "travesty held the stage for a hundred years, and more, in America as well as in England."[85] Booth almost always performed *Catharine and Petruchio* either as an afterpiece or as part of a double bill, as it was on February 19, when he paired it with *The Iron Chest*.

Theater manager Leonard Grover made much of Lincoln's evident interest in Booth's month-long engagement. He wrote twice to the president inviting him to see Booth play Shylock and Don Caesar, on the first occasion offering him "a double Private Box" and adding, "Your favorable answer will be taken as a great compliment to the artist, as well as an additional honor to / Yours loyally / Leonard Grover." He followed this up with a confirming note claiming that the roles were selected by Booth "with a view almost entirely to the invitation sent you today."[86] An announcement appeared in the *Daily National Republican* stating that the evening's double bill was selected by Booth "with reference to the visit by President Lincoln and Secretary Seward, who have engaged boxes for this evening, and will be present during the performance."[87] For Booth's March 2 performance as Hamlet, Grover's newspaper ad reads "To-morrow night, HAMLET, by request of the President of the United States," and a separate item on the same page announces "the special presidential visit" to Grover's "when, by previous arrangement with the President and Mrs. Lincoln, Mr. Booth will give his splendid rendition of Shakspeare's 'Hamlet.'"[88] However much some of this sounds like Grover's puffery, Booth was certainly aware of Lincoln's interest both in him and in Shakespeare, and he undoubtedly did his best to accommodate the president's wishes and schedule.

Much of what we know of Edwin Booth as actor and producer derives from the voluminous writings of William Winter, who, however, was not altogether disinterested, he and Booth having been close friends for a number of years. Winter's writing, furthermore, tends to be both florid and highly subjective; not entirely without reason, H. L. Mencken called him "the greatest bad critic who ever lived."[89] It is hard to know, for instance, what to make of Winter's observation that "Booth's Richelieu was a noble and touching image of righteous power protecting innocent weakness; and no person who saw it, with appreciation, could help being exalted in magnanimity of spirit and moral worth." "People were made better for seeing Booth in Richelieu,"[90] he adds. Nonetheless, Winter was at times a careful observer, and his closeness to Booth offers insights not otherwise available. Writing of his performance as Hamlet, for example, Winter tells us that Booth "possessed the princely mind, the gloomy temperament, the introspective propensity, the contemplative disposition, the moody manner, and the slender, nervous physique that are appropriate to the character of *Hamlet*."[91] Commenting on Booth's temperament in general, Winter records a conversation on a topic Booth seldom alluded to: his brother's murder of Lincoln. "All my life I have thought of dreadful things that might happen to me," Booth remarked, "and I believed there was no horror that I had not imagined, but I never dreamed of such a dreadful thing as *that*."[92] It is telling that with the characteristic egotism of an actor, Booth should see the tragedy of Lincoln's death as something dreadful that happened to *him*.

We know more about Booth's Hamlet than we do about any of his other roles (or, indeed, about any nineteenth-century actor's performance in any role), but our most detailed knowledge comes primarily from witnesses who saw Booth's New York productions, early and, mostly, late, and these cannot be readily transposed to a performance in Washington or any other "provincial" city. Booth did not travel with his sets and costumes (apart from his personal collection) until after the Civil War, when the ever-expanding peacetime railroads made the transportation of elaborate theatrical productions possible. For his Washington engagement, Booth, in *Hamlet* as well as in all the other productions, would have been supported by casts drawn from

Edwin Booth as Hamlet. Folger Shakespeare Library.

Grover's stock company, and his productions would have been mounted with the theater's own collection of scenery. When Booth appeared in *Hamlet* at the Winter Garden in 1864–1865, a playgoer was struck by the evocative theatricality of the setting:

> As the curtain rose on the lonely sentinels pacing their beat before the castle, a wind seemed to blow across from the northern sea with premonition of death. There was terror in the tale of the night watchers shivering under the black skies. It was a relief when the scene shifted and the warm light glowed on the crimson audience chamber and the rich dresses of the court.[93]

Lincoln would probably not have seen anything so grand or evocative. Nor can we reconstruct the text Booth would have used on this occasion with any certainty. Alluding primarily to 1870 and later, but probably reflecting a development that had been going on for some time, Winter takes note of at least some of the cuts and rearrangements of the play. "Booth's arrangement of 'Hamlet' was designed to clarify obscurity and rectify error, and it was made with the reverence of a loving disciple." What cuts there were "were made with a view to accelerate movement, eliminate description, and avoid repetition," as well as to remove "offensive words and passages."[94] Charles Shattuck, who has carefully studied the promptbooks and acting editions of Booth's Hamlet, is far less sanguine; noting that "Booth did not honor the text of the play quite as we would expect of a serious producer in our own time," he finds that of the nearly 4,000 lines of Shakespeare's text, Booth cut over 1,000.[95] Act 4, which includes Ophelia's mad scenes and Fortinbras, was severely cut: "All of scenes 1, 4, and 6," and "only portions of scenes 3, 5, and 7—330 lines out of a total of 662."[96] Again, however, at least some of Shattuck's sources relate to 1870 and later.

One question that we would like an answer to is, Did Lincoln see and hear Claudius deliver the soliloquy "O, my offense is rank" that he so much valued? Here the evidence is inconclusive. For one thing, the so-called prayer scene (act 3, scene 3), though less than 100 lines long, is actually made up of distinct actions and business, any part of which might be cut. The crucial elements are three: Claudius's soliloquy, revealing that he has indeed killed his brother; his silent prayer and concluding spoken couplet; and Hamlet's appearance and soliloquy during which he contemplates, and decides against, killing the king at prayer. It would seem that it was the last part that aroused the greatest objections. Thomas Hamner, an eighteenth-century editor, thought Hamlet's words "so inhuman, so unworthy of a hero, that I wish our poet had omitted it."[97] David Garrick cut this soliloquy, a choice followed by many other actors. We know that Booth at times included at least part of act 3, scene 3, and at other times not. The scene was restored for Booth's first New York Hamlet in 1860, to the discomfiture of the *New York Times* reviewer:

> The tragedy, as produced last evening, was noticeable for sundry restorations of the text, one of which at least was questionable. That scene in which the King retires to prayer, in his closet, where he is seen kneeling before the altar by Hamlet, and where the latter is almost disposed to kill him as he kneels, has been a stranger to the stage since the time of GARRICK. Why restore it? It offends the sense of propriety of many people, and does not add anything to the grand features of the play.[98]

The Winter Garden production during the 1861–1862 season saw "copious restorations of the original text,"[99] Shattuck writes, and this included the two central elements of the prayer scene, which were also used in the 100-nights *Hamlet* in New York in 1864–1865.

Shattuck claims that "the [prayer] scene was never omitted, even when Booth gave up his own portion of it, being necessary as a 'carpenters' scene,'" which could be played in front of the curtain while the carpenters were putting up new scenery.[100] This, however, seems to contradict comments made at other points in his discussion, as when he writes that by 1870 Booth had restored the King's prayer and speech, suggesting that before that date the scene had been cut. In an annotated copy of the 1869 edition of Booth's *Hamlet* edited by William Winter and employed as a promptbook, Claudius's speech is marked for deletion and crossed out in ink. The printed text notes of Hamlet's subsequent lines, "The following speech is sometimes omitted." The speech is then crossed out in ink line by line.[101] Under the circumstances, it seems unlikely that Booth included the scene during his Washington appearance. In any case, no review makes mention of it. Curiously, as late as 1880, a London critic was faulting Booth's inclusion of the "long-drawn scene, so frequently omitted, of Claudius's tardy but prayerful remorse."[102] We do know that Booth valued the role: he invited the great Italian star Tommaso Salvini to play Claudius to his Hamlet, but Salvini preferred to play the Ghost. Booth even suggested, in a letter to his acting and producing partner Lawrence Barrett, that he might at some point like to play the role himself:

"I am studying *Claudius* in 'Hamlet,' & would like to try my hand at it some day.... The neglected King is a part not to be despised.... I consider it a very difficult part to portray properly."[103] Written by an actor who had played with many a Claudius over the years, these comments suggest the general inadequacy with which the part was traditionally performed.

As for Booth's interpretation of Hamlet, a role he played over a period of thirty-eight years (from 1853 to 1891), frequently revising and refining his approach along the way, we may be fairly certain that by the early 1860s the broad outlines of his performance were essentially set. Hamlet, for Booth, was very much the gentleman and scholar, thoughtful, kind, sensitive—almost, as Booth himself recognized, effeminate. To Mary Isabella Stone, Booth looked "every inch the noble Prince and true-born gentleman; strong, pure, and refined, in soul and senses." Seeing Booth was "like beholding some magnificent Greek statue suddenly endowed with life and motion, sense and speech, with soul, and moreover with the intellect and education of the 19th century!"[104] One important observer, Adam Badeau, who was also Booth's admirer and for a time close friend, connected Booth's interpretation to his feelings toward his father:

> His greatest scenes in this tragedy were those with the ghost, and when Booth addressed the shade, and exclaimed:
>
> I'll call thee Hamlet,
> King, *Father*, royal Dane,
>
> there was a pathos in the word "father" which those who ever heard him utter it must recall. He dropped on one knee as he spoke it, and bowed his head, not in terror, but in awe and love, and tender memory of the past; he had a feeling that he was actually in the presence of that weird shade whom he had known on earth, and he was not afraid.[105]

According to Winter, Booth, like William Charles Macready, "and, indeed, the majority of actors, held the opinion that the 'madness' of Hamlet is assumed."[106] Observers stressed the nobility, rationality, and gentleness of Booth's interpretation, and Booth himself made reference to Goethe's romantic view that in *Hamlet* Shakespeare set out to portray the effect of "a heavy deed placed on a soul which is not adequate to cope with it."[107]

Though newspaper reviews of Booth's *Hamlet* are frequently unhelpful—"in the presence of genius so thrilling and art so potent and delicate, one feels the pen of criticism should rest"[108]—they do at times contribute telling observations. Writing of a performance in New York a few months after Lincoln had seen him, the New York Times reviewer thought Booth's Hamlet "bold and picturesque in its physical outlines, as the youth and personal presence of Mr. Booth justify; and intellectually well defined, yet coquettish in its rapid and delicate transition from one mood to another."[109] An 1870 review in the Times found that Booth was physically and temperamentally suited for the role: "His spare and almost attenuated frame, his thoughtful, and, indeed, habitually mournful expression; his hollow, low-pitched voice; his splendid dark eye; his jetty, disheveled locks, and a certain morbidness that is suffused by his whole look and bearing, carry conviction to the mass of beholders that in him they see as near an approach to the Hamlet of SHAKESPEARE." At the same time, it noted, "There is a want of fire and *electricity* in the great test scenes of Mr. BOOTH's Hamlet which is inconsistent with the requirements of the part and with the artist's own reputation."[110] Of the specific Washington performance Lincoln saw, the reviewer for the Daily National Intelligencer, who called himself Erasmus, provides more generalized praise. "Edwin Booth is a young man," he writes, "but a matured actor. Unquestionably inheriting genius from his father, he tutors, subdues, and directs it within the rules of art. . . . He proved himself to be *the* Hamlet of our stage—i.e., judged by the critical opinion which we have adopted of the character. His conception of the part was markedly correct, and was executed—in so far that it made apparent the wonderful subtlety of thought, sentiment, and passion which belongs to the creation." Erasmus was rather less impressed by the supporting cast: "Ophelia was 'fair.' Polonius was respectable. Laertes seemed inclined to 'cry' rather than weep. The Ghost was well. The Queen not bad."[111]

Of the other Shakespeare productions and performances Lincoln saw during Booth's run at Grover's, the evidence is scanty. Erasmus, for instance, writes that he has no space to be specific on Booth's various roles, but says that anyone who has good taste and knowledge of drama and poetry "will not be disappointed in the delight and instruction which he will receive from the Tennyson of our stage, Edwin Booth."[112] What little is known of Booth's performance as Petruchio in his adaptation of David Garrick's version of The Taming of the Shrew would indicate that he had great fun in the role and that audiences generally enjoyed his comic performances. He played Petruchio as a sincere lover rather than as a mercenary; at the same time, like many an actor before and after him, he "applied the whip freely, racing about the stage to beat one servant or another."[113] A playgoer in 1887 admiringly wrote of Booth, "His is a Petruchio indeed to tame a shrew and one we can understand." Some critics, she notes, complain of the actor "as offering too coarse a rendering," but "if the coarseness of Petruchio's behavior jars on the over-refined sensibilities of some auditors, it is not Mr. Booth's fault."[114]

The evidence we have of Booth's interpretation of Shylock suggests that it was seldom the same from performance to performance. One critic remembered, "I have seen him play Shylock, sometimes as a fierce money-catching old-clothes dealer of Jewry; sometimes as a majestic Hebrew financier and lawgiver; sometimes, at his full maturity, in what I suppose to be the just mean between the two extremes: and the Jew was terrible, vital, convincing, in every aspect."[115] Winter's view of Booth's Shylock is narrower:

> He was a Jew, but more particularly he was a man; and while he hated
> his enemy for being a Christian, he hated him more for being just
> and benevolent in his dealings—the foe of usury and the friend of
> misfortune. In Shylock's envenomed hostility toward Antonio, Booth
> indicated something of Iago's loathing for Cassio: "There is a daily
> beauty in his life, that makes me ugly." That ideal of the part is simple,
> direct, and effective.[116]

In an 1861 performance in New York, Booth was praised for presenting Shylock as proud and dignified. He makes "his final exit—not in the usual fashion of an enraged clothesman, but as became a man of Shylock's mental power, with pride unimpaired, though foiled, and a seeming self-reliance through every misfortune."[117] One theatergoer, writing in 1869, found Booth's performance "uneven, both overstrained and lacking emotion; yet in parts startlingly fine. Though it bore traces of profound study, one could never escape the belief that the actor had not fully possessed himself of the part—as if each day modified his conception—as if he groped for his thought."[118] It is difficult to reconcile these various observations, except to say that Booth could not quite decide on a single, balanced interpretation of the role until late in his career.

Apart from the specifics of Booth's performance, we can be fairly certain that Lincoln saw a *Merchant of Venice* that ended at the conclusion of act 4, finishing with the defeat of Shylock rather than with the harmony that concludes Shakespeare's play. Writing to his daughter from Chicago in 1887, Booth comments on the lukewarm reception to *The Merchant of Venice*: "The attendance fell off one-half, a perfect 'slump,' owing, I presume, to the fact that for many years the play has been cut down to *Shylock's* scenes and has always been given with another piece, which, of course, has weakened its effectiveness; but I think it will soon become known as one of our strongest plays."[119] The fact remains, however, that in London in 1881, Booth was still doing a *Merchant of Venice* that, in spite of standing alone on the bill, concluded with act 4.[120] Lincoln did indeed see *Merchant* with "another piece," *Don Caesar de Bazin*, and the inevitable truncation of Shakespeare's play might in part explain the frequently noted comment reported by Noah Brooks, who writes of accompanying Lincoln to Booth's performance. "And as we went home," Brooks reports, "[Lincoln] said, 'It was a good performance, but I had a thousand times rather read it at home, if it were not for Booth's playing. A farce, or a comedy, is best played; a tragedy is best read at home.'"[121] The play, of course, is a comedy and has been so categorized since at least the 1623 First Folio, but Lincoln's observation is not as odd as it first appears. Without the fifth act, *The Merchant of Venice*, especially as Booth appears to have performed the role of Shylock, becomes a tragedy, albeit one that, as Lincoln sensed, had been inadequately represented on the stage. As a reader of the plays, Lincoln was clearly frustrated at the high-handed manner in which theatrical practitioners handled Shakespeare's texts.

Booth's *Richard III* still adhered to Colley Cibber's text (see chapter 3), though a decade later Booth experimented with staging Shakespeare's original: "Did I tell you that I intended to restore Shakspere's 'Richard' in lieu of Cibber's patchwork drama? If not, I'll tell you now that I have acted it several times to the satisfaction of even adverse critics, who, while abusing me, declare the restoration a success. I shall endeavor to give it a good cast in New York, in order to make it run, and thus educate the ignorant, who suppose Cibber's bosh to be Shakspere's tragedy."[122] Winter claims that even when Booth played Cibber's adaptation, "he made him finer than Cibber's text warrants—because he got the light from Shakespeare to illumine that version."[123] Though some critics thought that Edwin's Richard was "little more than his fading memory of his father's performance,"[124] the evidence suggests that he made Richard more human and less of a monster than had many of his predecessors. An 1878 review, while suggesting that this was a relatively recent interpretation, notes that the traditional stage Richard "is a creature of rant and fustian. . . . That Mr. Booth has restored Richard to the ranks of humanity, may perhaps, years hence, be one of the many things that will be remembered of him as an artist."[125] Lucia Calhoun, on the other hand, wondered if Booth had gone a bit too far in the direction of humanizing Richard: "After the play, when one analyzes the performance, [one] finds . . . Richard to have been dashed with a human gentleness and pity to which the

Edwin Booth as Richard III. Folger Shakespeare Library.

crook-backed tyrant of Shakespeare has no claim."[126] Another critic, who missed Richard's "scoffing, sardonic humorous mockery," thought that the "passion and malice were allowed too much scope" in Booth's interpretation.[127]

William Winter, who comments extensively but whose generalities tell us very little of value, claims, "All the details of [Booth's] performance of *Richard* were subordinated to the central design of embodying a man beneath whose bright, plausible, handsome, alluring exterior sleeps a hellish tempest of passion, a smouldering flame of malevolence, a fountain of deadly purpose."[128] "Lightning perception, prompt resolve, cynical hypocrisy, remorseless ambition, and indomitable will were all denoted in his conception," another critic remembers.[129] As for physical details, Winter writes, "There was no distortion, whether of limp, or hump, or costume, or elocution"[130] in Booth's performance, though portraits suggests the presence of at least a slight hump. As far as the production as a whole, as one theater historian has noted, "there are few available descriptions of Booth's interpretation of specific elements of the text [of *Richard III*], and few references to the settings."[131] As noted in chapter 3, we have little sense of how Booth interpreted the "Now is the winter of our discontent" soliloquy that particularly interested Lincoln.

If, in witnessing the acting of Edwin Booth, Lincoln understood that he was present at a significant sea change in the American theater and in the performance of Shakespeare's plays, the point would be more clearly brought home to him when, only a month after the Booth run, Edwin Forrest began an extended engagement (March 22 to May 6) at Ford's Theatre. Lincoln saw Forrest in *King Lear* and in at least one non-Shakespearean role, Spartacus in *The Gladiator*. (Some sources add *Richard III*, but the evidence for this is slight.)[132] Forrest, whose grand, outsized, muscular style had made him a favorite of the Jacksonian era, had been a star since the 1820s. Though now well past his prime, he was an institution: patriot, chauvinist, democrat, he was the first native-born actor to achieve something like international stardom; his majestic physique and larger-than-life demeanor made him particularly popular with working-class audiences. He had been symbolically, if not physically, at the center of the events leading to the Astor Place Riot (see chapter 1), and he continued to represent, for many theatergoers, a specifically American muscular heroism, even as his body was gradually betraying him. Comparing him to the "effete" English tragedian Macready, the *Spirit of the Times* said that his acting "was as directly opposed to the creamy smoothness and prancing propriety of Macready's art as Walt Whitman's virile lines are opposed to the dainty and supersensuous dialectics of Mr. Tennyson."[133] But while those who embraced his style of acting were unreserved in their praise, those who did not were often scathing. Lincoln's friend Orville Browning thought him a "miserable actor";[134] a Chicago critic wrote that anything "more unnatural, spasmodic, and absurd than Mr. Forrest's interpretation of deep emotion could not be imagined."[135] George Curtis, in an essay in *Harper's New Monthly Magazine*, could not believe "human beings, under any conceivable circumstances, should ever talk or act as they are represented in the Forrest drama."[136] As early as 1847, when Forrest was the undisputed star of the American stage, the *New York Courier and Inquirer*, an anti-Democratic paper, found that Forrest's "gentlemen are not such as Shakespeare drew; they are great roaring boys that cry like fat babies, and puff and blow like sledge men."[137] Class interests as well as aesthetics governed much of the discourse around Edwin Forrest.

Though well past his prime in 1864, Forrest continued to draw audiences for his King Lear, the most successful of his Shakespearean roles, as he did for several of his "popular" roles such as Metamora, Jack Cade, and Spartacus. He had first played the old king in 1826, at the age of twenty; he last played him at the age of sixty-six. Commenting on an 1862 New York appearance, a critic writes, "Of all the Shakesperian characters that he personates Lear is generally allowed to be the one in which he can be seen to the most striking advantage." Acknowledging that theatergoers might no longer be sympathetic to his particular talents, the critic adds, "Popular opinion has always regarded [Forrest's Lear] as one of the grandest performances ever beheld upon the stage—quite sufficient, of itself, to stamp Mr. FORREST the foremost actor of his generation."[138] Forrest was known for the sheer power and forcefulness he brought to the role: "It was his towering rage in the storm scene that critics liked best, not the moments of pathos later on."[139] Beyond this, audiences were impressed by the physical realism he brought to the portrayal of Lear's madness. He prepared for the role by visiting asylums and hospitals, as well as nursing homes. One critic wrote, "We never saw madness so perfectly portrayed. It is true to nature—painfully so."[140] Perhaps the most detailed description of Lear as Forrest played him came from the unsympathetic pen of James H. Hackett in the volume he had presented to Lincoln the previous year. Hackett writes, "[Forrest's] pathos is whining and wants intensity, and seems to spring more from a cool head than a warm heart." Citing phrases from Hamlet's advice to the players, he notes, "*Lear's* occasional bursts of anger certainly require of an actor earnest and forcible expression, in order to realize fully to an audience *Lear's* outraged sensibility; but anger which can find words should, at the same time, acquire a comparative temperance,

Edwin Forrest as King Lear. Folger Shakespeare Library.

to give it smoothness."[141] If Lincoln read Hackett's comments, he would, perhaps, have been predisposed to regard Forrest's Lear with a wary eye.

In spite of his age and infirmities, according to most accounts Forrest continued to play Lear with only slightly diminished vigor. When, at his prime, he played Lear in London in 1845, one reviewer noted, "Although, from Mr. Forrest's personal appearance, one would with difficulty imagine him capable of looking the old man, four score and upwards, all the attributes of age and feebleness, the palsied head and tottering walk, are admirably assumed, and are never lost sight of throughout the performance."[142] Twenty years on, these attributes were perhaps easier to come by. Of an 1868 performance, a New York reviewer could write that the audience "seemed to enjoy Mr. Forrest's peculiar and unquestionably strong rendering of *Lear* as years ago. . . . In fact his vigor of mind and body seem wonderfully preserved, and enable him to still present a *King Lear* of far more force of character than Shakespeare ever embodied in his play."[143] The following year, a Cincinnati critic could find in Forrest's Lear "no abatement of that terrible power, whose manifestations have thrilled so many thousands in days gone by; no flaw in that sonorous voice, whose majestic tones, like those of the great bell of St. Paul's, seem fitted to sound the knell of departed kings."[144] John Hay, when he was chargé d'affaires in Vienna in 1867, saw a production of *King Lear* at the Burg Theatre and was reminded of an earlier theatergoing experience: "I remembered Forrest's storms and tempests of passion—often overdone, sometimes in bad taste, but always full of wonderful spirit and inexhaustible physical energy."[145] The chorus was not unanimous, however. At a Hartford performance in 1865, where Forrest was acting in both *King Lear* and *Richelieu*, a captious critic complained, "If any of the audience are so lucky as to get near enough to him to hear what he says, perhaps they will be delighted with his elocution. We have tried several times to accomplish this, but never could make out anything from him but—chow, chow."[146] This, however, may not refer so much to the actor's diminishing powers as to the critic's view of how stage speech should be rendered.

Of the *King Lear* Lincoln saw on the evening of April 8 at Ford's Theatre, we have few detailed impressions. What is evidently a puff paragraph in the *Daily National Intelligencer* reports, "The largest audience of the season, densely crowding every portion of this vast Theatre almost to suffocation, witnessed Edwin Forrest's truly great and thrilling performance of King Lear last evening, and never have we seen this sublime effort of the immortal Shakespere so admirably rendered throughout. . . . The play was handsomely 'mounted' and so great was its success that it will be repeated on

Monday evening."[147] Reviewing the production a few days later, Erasmus unfortunately devotes the greater part of his column to arguing, as had Charles Lamb and others, that *King Lear* cannot be acted: "Lear and the pitiless storm into which the Great Dramatist drives him are the only fit representatives of each other. . . . Theatrical rumblings and pyrotechnics are not so impotent to counterfeit the 'dread clamors' of Heaven as is the conceit of the actor powerless to present the majestic agony of Lear." That said, "Mr. Forrest makes the best picture of Lear perhaps on any stage." "Allowing a fair margin for the idiosyncrasies of this actor," Erasmus tells us,

> we must say that his elocution in Lear has a rhythm in accord with the Poet's grand lyre. . . . In the vehement and philosophical passages he is successful, and so with all that belongs to the mere dramatic development. The tender passion with which he renders the advent of the old King's returning reason, and the consummate skill with which he paints the clouded sunset of Lear's stormy life and unbinds him from the rack of this rough world, still clinging to Cordelia, who has "gone before"—these indeed are precious stones in Forrest's diadem.[148]

The review is limited to commenting on Forrest; Erasmus has nothing to say of either the supporting cast or the physical aspects of the production.

Aside from professional reviews, we have at least two firsthand accounts by observers who shared box seats with the president and his family that evening. Auguste Laugel, a young French historian, engineer, and diarist, left a vivid description of the experience:

> In the evening, with Mr. and Mrs. Lincoln and [radical Republican senator] Charles Sumner, we went to the theatre direct from the White House. There was no private entrance to the proscenium boxes, and we had to pass behind the spectators in the galleries. The double box we occupied was very spacious, but so plainly furnished that they had not taken the trouble to cover with velvet or cloth the front planking, but had just tacked some red velvet on the rail. The play was "King Lear," with Forrest in the leading role. His part was fairly well rendered, but with too much exaggeration. The rest of the troupe was wretched.[149]

Laugel's comment on Forrest might be regarded as a Frenchman's view of performance style; as we have seen, however, American critics could also find Forrest too much. As for the "wretched" supporting cast, Laugel is in accord with many a commentator of the time. In the 1869 review cited earlier, the critic, after praising Forrest, goes on to complain of an "awkward squad who repeated some part of the words set down for them in the minor characters."[150] Laugel does not comment on other aspects of the mise-en-scène; the Cincinnati reviewer, not so reticent, notes "preposterous costumes that seemed to have been recovered from some chiffonier's pouch—wretched scenery and effects—and all the other abominations, 'the very least, a death to nature.'"[151] It is possible, of course, that the Forrest production in the nation's capital in 1864 was better mounted than the one in Cincinnati in 1869. In his advertising, John T. Ford claimed that the Forrest production had been made "at a very heavy expense, and in addition to the great combination [that is, the cast] the plays will be produced with new scenery, costumes, etc.," words that probably should not be taken too seriously.

Laugel also notes Lincoln's attentive response to the play: "He seemed extremely familiar with Shakspere, and in several places remarked on the changes made in performance."[152] We do not know what those changes were, though we do know that Forrest was no longer using, apart from some details, Nahum Tate's version, which ends with Lear alive and Cordelia married to Edgar; the reviews from this period make it clear that Cordelia and Lear do not survive. But *King Lear*, long and complex as it is, would as a matter of course have been significantly cut, perhaps by as much as a third. Even in a shortened form, the play would have been a challenge for young Tad, as Laugel suggests: "[The president's] boy of eleven was beside him, and the father often clasped him very tenderly, as the child leaned his head upon his shoulder; and when the little fellow, as he often did, asked for explanations, Lincoln invariably made answer, 'My child, it is in the play.'" Laugel concludes his account by recording Lincoln's response to the death of the villain, Edmund. "When the traitor was thrust through with a sword, Lincoln said: 'I have only one reproach to make of Shakspere's heroes—that they make long speeches when they are killed.'"[153] Lincoln's comment, if Laugel has recorded it correctly, is somewhat surprising, given that Edmund is not a hero and does not really have a long speech after he is mortally wounded. Shakespeare gives him some twenty lines, but these are broken up into dialogue, with no segment longer than five lines long (in Tate's version, Edmund speaks even less). Even as a general observation, Lincoln is here mistaken. None of Shakespeare's tragic heroes have long speeches "when they are killed," though Othello speaks at some length in anticipation of his suicide. Only Hamlet has several, fairly brief speeches after he has been wounded with a poisoned foil.

Though Noah Brooks is not mentioned in Laugel's narrative, he was evidently present as well that evening and later remembered that Lincoln "appeared to be more impressed by the acting of John McCullough, in the role of Edgar, than with the great tragedian's appearance as the mad king."[154] Lincoln invited McCullough to visit his box between acts, "and when the young actor was brought to the door, clad in his fantastic garb of rags and straw, Mr. Lincoln warmly, and yet with diffidence, praised the performance of the scene in which he had just appeared."[155] "Genial" John McCullough was still relatively early in his career and had not yet distanced himself from his mentor, Forrest, with whom he played second leads in Shakespearean and other plays from 1861 to 1866. What Lincoln would have appreciated, no doubt, were the qualities often commented on by friends and critics: a handsome build, finely modeled head, and rich, powerful voice, together with his "great-hearted generosity, his manly sweetness, his simple dignity, and his deep sincerity—all of them qualities which characterized the character when off the stage."[156] Today, when the role of Edgar tends to be played by quirky or self-effacing actors, it may seem odd that Forrest would have allowed the role to be played by an actor so much like himself in both physical bearing and style, or that the qualities McCullough was praised for would have served him particularly well as Edgar. Here, however, we may be seeing the influence of Tate, whose version of the play presents Edgar as far more of a romantic hero than does Shakespeare's (an 1860 Forrest acting edition retains the scene invented by Tate where Edgar rescues Cordelia from a gang of ruffians).[157] Ironically, it would be left to McCullough, when he himself played Lear, to purge the text from the last vestiges of Nahum Tate.[158] Lincoln was sufficiently impressed by the two stars that he evidently saw them again on January 31, 1865, in *The Gladiator*, a play written for Forrest in which he played Spartacus, one of his most popular roles.[159]

Apart from E. L. Davenport's *Hamlet*, which he went to see for a second time in November 1864, Forrest's *King Lear* appears to have been the last Shakespeare production Lincoln witnessed. In scarcely more than a year, he had seen virtually all the great (Forrest, Booth, Cushman, Hackett) and near great (Davenport, Wallack, McCullough) Shakespearean stars of his time. No American president before and few since would have wanted or indeed been able to see so much Shakespeare in four years in the nation's capital. Lincoln's playgoing embraced the shift from the "popular" Shakespeare represented by Forrest to the more "high-brow" Shakespeare represented by Booth. In this context, it is of interest that he was drawn to McCullough, who, one theater historian has noted, "serves as an intriguing transitional figure, artistically but not chronologically, between the unrefined muscularity of Forrest and the intellectual gentility of Booth."[160] What Lincoln would not have seen, we can be fairly certain, is anything like a fully integrated theatrical event, a production uniting Shakespeare's (restored) text, actors, sets, lighting, costumes, and other elements into a harmonious whole. A beginning in that direction would be made by Edwin Booth when, in 1870, he was able to mount productions in his own theater in New York. Even with Booth, however, the various aspects of the production were not completely brought together by a fully thought-out interpretive strategy: "directors' Shakespeare," as such productions came to be known, was still a long way off.

If, as has sometimes been claimed on the basis of the conversation reported by Noah Brooks, Lincoln preferred reading to seeing Shakespeare's plays, his choice would be understandable when we consider how the plays were often treated on the nineteenth-century stage. As Douglas Wilson notes, "Lincoln was a reader in an age when a rising tide of literacy . . . [was] helping to create a mass audience for literature. . . . Interest [in Shakespeare's plays] was shifting from the playwright to the poet, from the play to the poem."[161] Lincoln was able to read Shakespeare's plays in carefully prepared editions, but in the theater he had to endure Colley Cibber's *Richard III, King Lear* with remnants of Nahum Tate, *Hamlet* missing his favorite passages, *The Merchant of Venice* without the fifth act, and *The Merry Wives of Windsor* with musical interludes. At the same time, however, he would have enjoyed reasonably undisturbed and unpolluted versions of *Henry IV, Othello,* and *Macbeth.* "Eventually," Wilson notes, "the massive influx of new readers, of whom Lincoln was a celebrated example, would help pressure the theatrical profession to play Shakespeare and abandon the adaptations."[162] Had he lived even a decade longer, Lincoln would have had the chance to see *Richard III* and *King Lear* restored and productions of *Hamlet* in which he would have had a much better chance of hearing Claudius lament "O, my offense is rank." Ironically, the deranged act of a Shakespearean actor would prevent him from ever having that opportunity.

In an 1859 satirical essay, Artemus Ward (Charles Farrar Browne), one of Lincoln's favorite contemporary writers, riffs in his inimitable style on the distance between the immortal Shakespeare and the melodrama at the center of his tragic works. "I manetane that wax figgers is more elevatin than awl the plays ever wroten," Ward begins.

Take Shakespeer for instunse. Peple think heze grate things, but I kontend heze quite the reverse to the kontrary. . . . Thare's Mrs. Mackbeth—sheze a nise kind of woomon to have round ain't she, a puttin old Mack, her husband, up to slayin Dunkan with a cheeze knife, while heze payin a frendly visit to their house. O its hily morral, I spoze, when she larfs wildly and sez, "gin me the daggurs—Ile let his bowels out," or wurds to that effeck—I say, this is awl, strickly, propper I spoze?[163]

Whether or not Lincoln ever read this particular piece of satire, one can imagine him chuckling over it. He came of age at a time when Shakespeare's plays were becoming central to American popular culture and simultaneously beginning to be recognized as the prime representative of high culture, and his own fascination with Shakespeare combined an attraction to melodrama with a sensitivity to and appreciation for poetic expression. Ward's humorous observations reflect the tension between these impulses, undercutting and at the same time acknowledging the cultural significance of one of Shakespeare's most popular plays. As did many of his contemporaries, Lincoln first became acquainted with Shakespeare through schoolbook extracts and "purple passages" to be read and studied for their oratorical and ethical value; he graduated to reading the plays, at least those that most appealed to him—the histories and tragedies. He would have heard and read, and himself came to employ, Shakespeare passages and allusions in oratory and political argument, and as president he was exposed to relatively sophisticated Shakespeare productions in the theaters of the nation's capital. In his Shakespearean "journey," if it may be so called, Lincoln's interests and activities moved parallel with Shakespeare's integration into the texture of America's cultural life; posthumously, Lincoln would himself become a notably visible embodiment of that transformation.

Epilogue

Lincoln, Shakespeare, and the Brothers Booth

"We have supped full of horrors."
Benjamin Brown French, diary entry, April 15, 1865.

No Shakespeare productions were playing in Washington on the evening of April 14, 1865. There is no certainty that Lincoln would have gone even if one had been available or that by doing so he would have avoided the assassin's bullet. The theatrical pickings for that evening were unusually meager. Apart from *Our American Cousin* at Ford's Theatre, the Lincolns could have seen *Aladdin and the Wonderful Lamp* together with a "Magnificent Pyrotechnic Display" in honor of the "Anniversary of Sumter's Fall" and "the Celebration of its Glorious Recapture" at Grover's (where they sent their son Tad); the Washington Theatre was dark in anticipation of Sam Sharpley's Minstrels, Brass Band, and Burlesque Opera Troupe, set to open on the seventeenth. Lincoln, we know, at times went to the theater simply for rest and refuge. James Grant Wilson recalled being with him at the theater in March 1865. "When the curtain fell after the first act," Wilson writes, "I said, 'Mr. President, you are not apparently interested in the play.' 'Oh, no, Colonel,' he replied; 'I have not come for the play, but for the rest. I am being hounded to death by office-seekers, who pursue me early and late, and it is simply to get two or three hours' relief that I am here.'"[1] (The "play," on this occasion, appears to have been Mozart's *The Magic Flute*, perhaps Mrs. Lincoln's choice.) If Lincoln was looking for relaxation on that fatal Good Friday, Laura Keene in Tom Taylor's extremely popular comedy certainly fit the bill. It was probably also a search for light entertainment that had led Lincoln, on an evening late in 1863, to attend a performance by John Wilkes Booth at Ford's Theatre in the popular melodrama *The Marble Heart*. Though it may be surprising that Lincoln would have seen this play in preference to the Shakespeare plays—*Hamlet, Richard III*, or *Romeo and Juliet*—that Booth was acting in that same week, it is not really possible to speculate on the reasons behind his choice without knowing much more than we do about the president's work schedule, social calendar, and the various other demands on his time.[2]

John Wilkes Booth was at that time an up-and-coming actor of considerable though uneven talent, blessed with the charisma and energy of a matinee idol, although Walt Whitman, who had seen and admired the elder Booth, thought that John Wilkes's acting was "about as much like his father's, as the wax bust of Henry Clay . . . is like the genuine orator in the Capitol, when his best electricity was flashing alive in him and out of him."[3] By 1863, John was probably as popular, at least in the South, as his brother Edwin, and he was particularly successful in contemporary plays like *The Marble Heart*. A story long in circulation reports that, upon being "told of the President's appreciation of his acting, Wilkes curtly replied that he would have preferred the applause of a Negro."[4] Mary Clay, the daughter of Kentucky abolitionist Cassius Clay, who was evidently present at the performance Lincoln attended, recalled many years later that "twice Booth in uttering disagreeable threats in the play came very near and put his finger close to Mr. Lincoln's face; when he came a third time I was impressed by it, and said, 'Mr. Lincoln, he looks as if he meant that for you.' 'Well,' he said, 'he does look pretty sharp at me, doesn't he?'"[5] Booth's biographer, Michael Kauffman, however, writes, "Later accounts [of Lincoln witnessing Booth's performance] would mention angry glares and insulting comments, but there was none of that. . . . The president did not come to see [Booth] again."[6] Hay alone saw Booth in *Romeo and Juliet* two nights later, and he was not impressed by either performance, writing that Booth was "more tame than otherwise" in *The Marble Heart* and that the actor playing Mercutio "took all the honors away" from Booth's Romeo.[7] Contrary to what has often been reported, Lincoln does not appear to have seen John Wilkes Booth in *Richard III* or any other Shakespeare play.

Shakespeare was on the minds of many as they tried to find ways to frame the tragedy that John Wilkes Booth had inflicted on the nation. Benjamin Brown French was not the only one to find a line from *Macbeth* particularly apropos: Fanny Seward, too, responded to the terrible, near fatal stabbings of her father and brother that she had witnessed by writing in her diary, "'I have supped full on horrors,' rang over & over in my mind. . . . Blood, blood, my thoughts seemed drenched in it—I seemed to breathe its sickening odor."[8]

On the afternoon of Lincoln's death, the *Daily National Republican* told its readers, quoting from *Macbeth*, "Confusion now hath made his masterpiece! / Most sacrilegious murder hath broke ope / The Lord's anointed temple."[9] An account of the funeral procession a few days later noted that "on the front of the Paymaster's office, adjoining Grover's Theatre were the following words from *Julius Caesar*: 'His life was gentle, and the elements so mix'd in him that nature might stand up and say to all the world: This was a man,'"[10] and the same quotation appeared alongside "a fine large engraving of the President" on a building used by a theatrical company in Portland, Maine.[11] As Lincoln's funeral train retraced in reverse a good part of the 1861 journey from Springfield, signs on businesses and private homes along the way included passages from Shakespeare. In New York City, a "miniature monument" to Lincoln bore various inscriptions, including one from *Hamlet* ("Good night! and flights of angels sing thee to thy rest"), one from *Antony and Cleopatra* ("There's a great spirit gone"), and the "His life was gentle" passage from *Julius Caesar*, which also appeared on a banner in Albany.[12] A store window in New York City even had a passage from *King John* ("All murders past do stand excused in this"), which, however, was misidentified as coming from *Macbeth*.[13]

Given Lincoln's particular affection for *Macbeth*, it is poignantly apropos that eulogists of various stripes would turn to the murder of Duncan as a pertinent analogy to the assassination of a president recently victorious in a bloody civil war.[14] From the pulpits of New York to England's *West Surrey Times*, from a sermon by the Reverend Pliny White of Brattleboro, Vermont, to a eulogy by Governor John A. Andrew of Massachusetts, lines from the following passage were hard to avoid:

> [He] hath borne his faculties so meek, hath been
> So clear in his great office, that his virtues
> Will plead like angels, trumpet-tongued against
> The deep damnation of his taking-off.
> And pity, like a naked new-born babe
> Striding the blast, or heaven's cherubim horsed,
> Upon the sightless couriers of the air,
> Shall blow the horrid deed in every eye,
> That tears shall drown the wind.
> (*Macbeth*, act 1, scene 7)

As Richard Wightman Fox notes, these words "became the virtually official slogan of the mourning period."[15] The caption for *The Martyr of Liberty*, a

THE MARTYR OF LIBERTY

Hath borne his faculties so meek ; has been
So clear in his great office ; that his virtues
Shall plead, trumped-tongued, against
The deep damnation of his taking off."

The Martyr of Liberty—Lincoln and Macbeth. *Folger Shakespeare Library.*

fanciful engraving of the assassination, includes lines from the same passage, and a one-page handbill simply headed ABRAHAM LINCOLN and clearly published very soon after the assassination features three quotations from *Macbeth*: one from the above-quoted lines; one that cites the "treason has done his worst" lines from act 3, scene 2; and one that strings together and paraphrases several passages from the play, suggesting that the search for the conspirators was still hot:

> Let's briefly put on manly readiness,
> And question this most bloody piece of woe [*sic*]
> To know it further—ill deeds are seldom slow
> Nor single—Dread horrors still abound—
> Our country—it weeps, it bleeds; and each new day
> A gash is added to her wounds.[16]

No longer compared to Macbeth, Lincoln had become Duncan, the victim of a completely ignoble assassin ("Lincoln is in his grave; / After life's fitful fever, he sleeps well.")[17] The spiritual aura that Shakespeare provided the brutally murdered king of Scotland was readily transferred to the martyred president.

One post-assassination eulogist, after quoting from the "faculties so meek" passage from *Macbeth*, finds appropriate lines from *King John* to condemn the assassin: "Beyond the infinite and boundless reach / Of mercy, if thou didst this deed of death."[18] Mourning and revenge were closely associated, at least in the early sermons, and Shakespeare could do service for both.[19] The perpetrator of this "deed of death," John Wilkes Booth, as he escaped his pursuers through the swamps, rivers, and farms of eastern Maryland, found moments to record his feelings in a small pocket diary, and he too, as one might expect from an actor, made allusions to Shakespeare. In one entry, he wrote of having done "what Brutus was honored for."[20] This, of course, need not be a specifically Shakespearean allusion, but the association is inevitable. A bit later, he made another indirect but likely *Julius Caesar* allusion, writing of what he saw as "a country groaned beneath this tyranny," which echoes Cassius complaining of Rome "groaning underneath this age's yoke" (act 1, scene 2). He may also have been thinking of Brutus ("No, Cassius, no: think not, thou noble Roman, / That ever Brutus will go bound to Rome; / He bears too great a mind"; act 5, scene 1) when he wrote, "I have too great a soul to die like a criminal." Even before the assassination, if we can trust the memory of his friend John Mathews, Booth, in his never delivered and no longer extant letter to the *National Intelligencer*, cited *Julius Caesar*:

Oh that we could come by Caesar's spirit,
and not dismember Caesar!
But, alas!
Caesar must bleed for it.[21]

The surprisingly regretful tone of this quotation seems out of tune with the force of Booth's revengeful language elsewhere, but the purpose of the document, as Booth wrote in his diary, was to clear his name, and he no doubt saw himself or wanted to be seen as the noble Brutus, doing what he had to do. An undoubted allusion, this time to *Macbeth*, occurs in his second, and final, diary entry: "'I must fight the course' 'Tis all that's left to me."[22] Soon after this, Booth wrote a proud, bitter letter to Dr. Richard Stewart (he actually wrote two letters, the first of which was not sent), who had provided him and his companion David Harold a meal but had refused to shelter them. "It is not the substance, but the way in which kindness is extended that makes one happy in the acceptance thereof," Booth wrote; "the sauce to meat is ceremony. Meeting were bare without it." The final two sentences, which appear in both versions of the letter, are a direct allusion to *Macbeth* (act 3, scene 4).

Although the name of Booth is forever associated with Abraham Lincoln as a consequence of John Wilkes's mad act, the assassin's extended acting family not only touched Lincoln in other ways but can be seen as well to represent the tensions and tragic divisions of Civil War America. Residents of a border state (the elder Booth, soon after arriving from England, settled his family in Maryland), they were split among divergent allegiances: John Wilkes and to a lesser extent his sister Asia were Southern sympathizers; Edwin, apolitical for much of his youth, was a firm Lincoln and Union supporter;[23] and a third son, Junius Jr., who spent most of his antebellum adulthood in San Francisco away from the political storms, was jailed for a time in the aftermath of the assassination. (The three brothers acted together only once in a single performance of *Julius Caesar* at New York's Winter Garden Theatre, a fund-raiser for a Shakespeare statue to be erected Central Park.) Edwin Booth indirectly touched Lincoln's life when he saved the president's son, Robert, from falling between the platform and the tracks at a railroad station in New Jersey.[24] That Lincoln was murdered by John Wilkes Booth made it certain that not only the Booths but actors in general would be victimized in the search for scapegoats in the days following Lincoln's death. A minister in Philadelphia, for example, fulminated in vivid language against "these dens of pollution, these synagogues of Satan" that "collect in and around them, the concentrated abomination of all immorality and crime."[25] A group of actors

John Wilkes Booth, Edwin Booth, and Junius Brutus Booth Jr. in Julius Caesar. *John Hay Library, Brown University.*

in New York found it expedient to pass a resolution "renewing our expressions of loyalty and devotion to the government under which we live,"[26] and in Washington, a similar resolution noted, "The Histrionic profession especially has cause for heart-felt mourning in the awful sacrifice of Mr. Lincoln, the good and kindly man of liberal mind, who, through genial patronage, was refining and popularizing the dramatic art."[27]

In the immediate shock of the assassination, Edwin Booth at once decided to retire from the stage. But he soon changed his mind, returning to the Winter Garden Theatre with *Hamlet* on January 3, 1866. Although there was some controversy over his decision, most theatergoers welcomed him back. He would never again appear in Washington, though he acted in Baltimore (special trains brought theatergoers from the capital) and toured the South on a number of occasions over the succeeding decades. He even revived *Julius Caesar*, though not until 1871, playing Brutus, Cassius, and Antony on different occasions. A final echo of the assassination links Lincoln, Shakespeare, and Booth. On the evening of April 23, 1879, Edwin Booth was appearing at Chicago's McVicker's Theatre in *Richard II*, a play only infrequently seen in the nineteenth-century theater, when a would-be assassin fired two pistol shots toward the stage. No one was hurt, but the dramatic incident was a vivid reminder of the tragic association between the name of Booth and the murder of Abraham Lincoln, even if the press coverage did not emphasize the connection.[28] *Richard II*, like *Julius Caesar*, features a political murder, and it may be that Mark Gray, the would-be assassin, was motivated by the awareness that Booth was appearing in what could be considered an assassination play, even if, in this case, he was playing the victim. Gray, who was clearly unbalanced and would be declared insane, did not himself make the connection; he was evidently a stage-struck young man seeking publicity, and it is probably not coincidental that the date of the assassination attempt was the traditional anniversary of Shakespeare's birth.[29] Edwin Booth lived on to 1891, the most honored and celebrated actor in American theater history.[30]

NOTES

PREFACE

1 *Young Mr. Lincoln*, directed by John Ford (Twentieth-Century Fox, 1939).

2 Dale Carnegie, *Lincoln, the Unknown* (New York: Century, 1932), 28–29.

3 Adam Braver, *Mr. Lincoln's Wars: A Novel in Thirteen Stories* (New York: William Morrow, 2003), 303.

4 John Drinkwater, *Abraham Lincoln: A Play* (Boston: Houghton Mifflin, 1919), 44.

5 *Abraham Lincoln, Studio One*, Columbia Broadcasting System, May 26, 1952, archive.org/details/StudioOneAbrahamLincoln.

6 Robert E. Sherwood, *Abe Lincoln in Illinois: A Play in Twelve Scenes* (New York: Charles Scribner's Sons, 1939), 56.

7 Delmore Schwartz, "Lincoln," in *Screeno: Stories and Poems* (New Directions Publishing, 2004), 117–118, 118.

8 Irving Stone, *Love Is Eternal: A Novel about Mary Todd Lincoln and Abraham Lincoln* (Garden City, N.Y.: Doubleday, 1954), 242.

9 Gore Vidal, *Lincoln: A Novel* (New York: Random House, 1984), 382.

10 Ibid., 327.

11 Tony Kushner and Doris Kearns Goodwin, *Lincoln: The Screenplay* (New York: Theatre Communications Group, 2012), 117, 65, 115, 11. In a review of the film, David Bromwich writes, "Kushner's Lincoln drops quotations from Shakespeare like chocolate-covered dinner treats." "How Close to Lincoln," *New York Review of Books*, January 10, 2013.

CHAPTER 1. ABRAHAM LINCOLN AND AMERICA'S SHAKESPEARE

1 Robert C. Bray, *Reading with Lincoln* (Carbondale: Southern Illinois University Press, 2010), 82.

2 Russel B. Nye, foreword to *Lincoln-Lore: Lincoln in the Popular Mind*, by Ray B. Browne (Bowling Green, Ohio: Popular Press, 1974), 4.

3 One of the earliest studies of Lincoln's interest in Shakespeare is Robert N. Reeves, "Abraham Lincoln's Knowledge of Shakespeare," *California and Overland Monthly*, April 1904, 333–342. See also, in addition to works cited below, Robert Berkelman, "Lincoln's Interest in Shakespeare," *Shakespeare Quarterly* 2, no. 4 (October 1951): 303–312, and Stephen Dickey, "Lincoln and Shakespeare," in *Shakespeare in American Life*, Folger Shakespeare Library, http://www.shakespeareinamericanlife.org.

4 Walt Whitman, quoted in Allen Thorndike Rice, *Reminiscences of Abraham Lincoln by Distinguished Men of His Time* (New York: Harper and Brothers, 1909), 473.

5 Samuel Smiles, *Self-Help: With Illustrations of Character and Conduct* (New York: Ticknor and Fields, 1861), 24, 253.

6 F. B. Carpenter, *Six Months at the White House with Abraham Lincoln: The Story of a Picture* (New York: Hurd and Houghton, 1866), 150.

7 Roy P. Basler, *A Touchstone for Greatness: Essays, Addresses, and Occasional Pieces about Abraham Lincoln* (Westport, Conn.: Greenwood Press, 1973), 226.

8 John Drinkwater, *Lincoln, the World Emancipator* (Boston: Houghton Mifflin, 1920), 116.

9 Louis Marder, *His Exits and His Entrances: The Story of Shakespeare's Reputation* (Philadelphia: J. B. Lippincott, 1963), 297.

10 Esther Cloudman Dunn, *Shakespeare in America* (New York: Macmillan, 1939), 147.

11 Gregory Clark and S. Michael Halloran, *Oratorical Culture in Nineteenth-Century America: Transformations in the Theory and Practice of Rhetoric* (Carbondale: Southern Illinois University Press, 1993), 148.

12 David Herbert Donald, *Lincoln* (New York: Simon and Schuster, 1995), 80.

13 Shirley Samuels, ed., introduction to *The Cambridge Companion to Abraham Lincoln* (Cambridge: Cambridge University Press, 2012), 3.

14 "President, accompanied by Mrs. Lincoln and party, attends recitation from Shakespeare at private residence near Chain Bridge." *Journal*, Samuel P. Heintzelman Papers, Library of Congress, Washington, D.C.; *The Lincoln Log: A Daily Chronology of the Life of Abraham Lincoln*, http://www.thelincolnlog.org/Home .aspx (hereafter *Lincoln Log*), June 4, 1863.

15 Noah Brooks, "Glimpses of Lincoln in War Time," *Century Magazine*, January 1895, 457–467, 464.

16 Leonard Grover, "Lincoln's Interest in the Theater," *Century Magazine*, April 1909, 943–950; 944.

17 Alden T. Vaughan and Virginia Mason Vaughan, *Shakespeare in America* (Oxford: Oxford University Press, 2012), 192. By midcentury, James Shapiro writes, "Shakespeare's works were widely known, a cultural touchstone that transcended region and class." Shapiro, ed., *Shakespeare in America: An Anthology from the Revolution to Now* (New York: Library of America, 2013), xix.

18 Alexis de Tocqueville, *Democracy in America* (1835, 1840), trans. Arthur Goldhammer (New York: Library of America, 2004), 538.

19 Frances Milton Trollope, *Domestic Manners of the Americans*, 2nd ed., 2 vols. (London: Whittaker, Treacher, 1832), 1: 127.

20 Alfred Van Rensselaer Westfall, *American Shakespearean Criticism, 1607–1865* (New York: H. W. Wilson, 1939), 221.

21 Ron Chernow, *Washington: A Life* (New York: Penguin Press, 2010), 126. Barbara Mowat notes that although "it is likely that Washington enjoyed Shakespeare's plays in performance and perhaps even read them with pleasure," little supporting evidence exists, "and [there is] certainly no indication of what, if anything, he found in Shakespeare to admire." Mowat, "The Founders and the Bard," *Yale Review* 97 (2009): 1–18, 1.

22 Tocqueville's comments can even be thought to allude, unknowingly but uncannily, to the most famous log cabin of all, that in which Lincoln was born: in early December 1831, the Ohio River froze and the French traveler was briefly stuck in Westport, Kentucky, about 90 miles from Lincoln's birthplace.

23 *Massachusetts Spy*, August 11–14, 1770, cited in Dunn, *Shakespeare in America*, 108.

24 Lawrence W. Levine, *Highbrow/Lowbrow: The Emergence of Cultural Hierarchy in America* (Cambridge, Mass.: Harvard University Press, 1988), 15–16.

25 James Henry Hackett, *Notes and Comments upon Certain Plays and Actors of Shakespeare with Criticisms and Correspondence* (New York: Carleton, 1863), 191–249.

26 Gary Taylor, *Reinventing Shakespeare: A Cultural History, from the Restoration to the Present* (New York: Weidenfeld and Nicolson, 1989), 196–197.

27 Frances N. Teague, *Shakespeare and the American Popular Stage* (Cambridge: Cambridge University Press, 2006), 13–16.

28 Vaughan, *Shakespeare in America*, 15.

29 Levine, *Highbrow/Lowbrow*, 4.

30 Ibid., 9.

31 Fergus M. Bordewich, *America's Great Debate: Henry Clay, Stephen A. Douglas, and the Compromise That Preserved the Union* (New York: Simon and Schuster, 2012), 3.

32 Ibid., 124, 270, 297, 304.

33 Henry Clay, quoted in Daniel Walker Howe, *What Hath God Wrought: The Transformation of America, 1815–1848* (New York: Oxford University Press, 2007), 339.

34 John F. Marszalek, *The Petticoat Affair: Manners, Mutiny, and Sex in Andrew Jackson's White House* (New York: Free Press, 1997), 191.

35 Even a reporter for the *Clinton (Ill.) Central Transcript* could cite from *Henry VIII* (act 3, scene 2) in writing of Lincoln's return to his home after a speech-making tour in 1859: "He comes back to us after electrifying Ohio, with all his *blushing honors thick upon him*; yet the poorest and plainest amongst our people, fears not to approach, and never fails to receive a hearty welcome from him" (my emphasis; *Lincoln Log*, October 5, 1859).

36 References to and quotations from Shakespeare are to the *New Cambridge Shakespeare*, ed. Philip Brockbank and Brian Gibbons (Cambridge: Cambridge University Press, 1984–2012), unless otherwise indicated. When Shakespeare is quoted by another author, however, I have kept the source version.

37 Henry Hubbard, *Speech of Mr. Hubbard, of New Hampshire, on the Resolution of Mr. Ewing for Rescinding the Treasury Order, Delivered in the Senate, December, 1836* (Washington, D.C.: Blair and Rives, 1837), 17.

38 Thomas Jefferson, *The Works of Thomas Jefferson*, coll. and ed. Paul Leicester Ford, 12 vols. (New York: G. P. Putnam's Sons, 1904), 11: 96.

39 Robert Barnwell Rhett: "Had South Carolina been invaded, upon the first gleam of the bayonet along our mountain passes, he would have seen and known what

the chivalry of the South really was, not in bloodless tropes and metaphors, but in the stern realities of the tented field." *Congressional Globe*, 25th Cong., 1st Sess., vol. 5 (1837), 153.

40 Quoted in John S. C. Abbott, *The History of the Civil War in America: Comprising a Full and Impartial Account of the Origin and Progress of the Rebellion* (New York: H. Bill, 1863), 121.

41 David Ross Locke, *The Nasby Papers Letters and Sermons Containing the Views on the Topics of the Day, of Petroleum V. Nasby [Pseud.]* (Indianapolis, Ind.: C. O. Perrine, 1864), 9.

42 John C. Briggs has made the connection between Shakespeare and the Hayne-Webster debate in "Steeped in Shakespeare," *Claremont Review of Books* 9, no. 1 (Winter 2008–2009), http://www.claremont.org/article/steeped-in-shakespeare/#.VNvqgi4rnLV.

43 Robert Hayne, quoted in *Orations of American Orators, Including Biographical and Critical Sketches* (New York: Colonial Press, 1900), 93; further quotations cited by page number in the text.

44 Quoted in J. C. Clark, "The Case of Marigny D'Auterive," in *Register of Debates in Congress*, vol. 4 (Washington, D.C.: Gales and Seaton, 1828), 916–918; cited in Ayanna Thompson's "What Is a 'Weyward' *Macbeth*?," in *Weyward Macbeth: Intersections of Race and Performance*, ed. Scott L. Newstok and Ayanna Thompson (Basingstoke, U.K.: Palgrave Macmillan, 2010), 3–10, 4–5.

45 Horace Mann, *Slavery: Letters and Speeches* (Boston: B. B. Mussey, 1851), 547.

46 *Washington Globe* for July 26, 1831, cited in Marszalek, *Petticoat Affair*, 181.

47 Daniel Webster, *The Great Speeches and Orations of Daniel Webster, with an Essay on Daniel Webster as a Master of English Style, by Edwin P. Whipple* (Boston: Little, Brown, 1879), 230–231.

48 Ibid., 231.

49 Lynn H. Parsons, *The Birth of Modern Politics: Andrew Jackson, John Quincy Adams, and the Election of 1828* (Oxford: Oxford University Press, 2009), 160.

50 Many of the Lincoln cartoons, including most of the ones mentioned in the text, are reproduced in Gary L. Bunker, *From Rail-Splitter to Icon: Lincoln's Image in Illustrated Periodicals, 1860–1865* (Kent, Ohio: Kent State University Press, 2001). For a useful overview of Lincoln caricature in general, see Harold Holzer, *Lincoln Seen and Heard* (Lawrence: University Press of Kansas, 2000), 103–127.

51 President-elect Lincoln also features in a November 3, 1860, cartoon in which he is shown using a sword to separate the "Siamese twins" Buchanan and newspaper publisher James Gordon Bennett with the comment "Don't be scared, my boys, Tis as easy as lying," a fairly commonplace allusion to *Hamlet*.

52 The question of how dark Othello should be, discussed in chapter 5, is here answered "very black."

53 Harold Holzer mentions the oddity of a gravedigger portrayed in the negative stereotype of an Irish immigrant in a pro–Democratic Party cartoon. See Holzer, G. S. Boritt, and Mark E. Neely, *The Lincoln Image: Abraham Lincoln and the Popular Print* (New York: Scribner Press, 1984), 133.

54 Bunker, *Rail-Splitter to Icon*, 3.

55 William S. Walsh, *Abraham Lincoln and the London Punch; Cartoons, Comments and Poems, Published in the London Charivari, during the American Civil War (1861–1865)* (New York: Moffat, Yard, 1909), 28. "Brother Jonathan," a precursor to Uncle Sam as a visual representation of Yankee America, was often drawn as a tall, thin man dressed in a formal coat, striped pants, and, at times, a stovepipe hat.

56 Bunker, *Rail-Splitter to Icon*, 179. See the reproduction on the same page.

57 Fred Kaplan, *Lincoln: The Biography of a Writer* (New York: HarperCollins, 2008), 133.

58 Justin G. Turner, Linda Levitt Turner, and Mary Todd Lincoln, *Mary Todd Lincoln: Her Life and Letters* (New York: Alfred A. Knopf, 1972), 27. The line Mary cites has sometimes been assigned to *Richard II*. See Douglas L. Wilson, "Prospects for 'Lincoln 2.5,'" *Journal of American History* 96, no. 2 (2009): 459–461, 461.

59 John Hay, *Inside Lincoln's White House: The Complete Civil War Diary of John Hay*, ed. Michael Burlingame and John R. T. Ettlinger (Carbondale: Southern Illinois University Press, 1999), 17, entry for May 4, 1861.

60 John Hay, *At Lincoln's Side: John Hay's Civil War Correspondence and Selected Writings*, ed. Michael Burlingame (Carbondale: Southern Illinois University Press, 2000), 49.

61 Hay to Nora Perry, May 20, 1859, cited in Hay, *Inside Lincoln's White House*, xii.

62 Hay, *At Lincoln's Side*, 111.

63 Ibid, 159.

64 Kim C. Sturgess, *Shakespeare and the American Nation* (Cambridge: Cambridge University Press, 2004), 4.

65 Cited in Vaughan and Vaughan, *Shakespeare in America*, 62.

66 Westfall, *American Shakespearean Criticism*, 151.

67 Charles King Newcomb, *The Journals of Charles King Newcomb*, ed. Judith Kennedy Johnson (Providence, R.I.: Brown University, 1946), 108.

68 *New-York Daily Tribune*, May 19, 1855.

69 James Edward Murdoch, an elocutionist known to Lincoln, would come to write, in an 1880 memoir, that "the *people* followed Forrest, and loved him, while those who claimed to be the elite admired and applauded Macready." Murdoch and J. Bunting, *The Stage; or, Recollections of Actors and Acting from an Experience of Fifty Years* (Philadelphia: J. M. Stoddart, 1880), 295.

70 For a full account of this event and its significance, see Nigel Cliff, *The Shakespeare Riots: Revenge, Drama, and Death in Nineteenth-Century America* (New York: Random House, 2007). For an older but still useful study, see Richard Moody, *The Astor Place Riot* (Bloomington: Indiana University Press, 1958).

71 Lincoln very probably saw and heard Emerson lecture in Springfield in 1853 or 1856, and he hosted the famous author some years later at the White House. He is supposed by some to have read Whitman's *Leaves of Grass*, but even if he did not (this is still debated), he probably remembered the man who regularly took off his hat to him as he made his way to and from his summer retreat at the Soldiers' Home: "We have got so that we exchange bows," Whitman wrote in his

journal, "and very cordial ones." Walt Whitman, *Complete Poetry and Collected Prose* (New York: Literary Classics of the United States, 1982), 733.

72 Ralph Waldo Emerson, *The Collected Works of Ralph Waldo Emerson*, ed. Robert Ernest Spiller et al., 10 vols. (Cambridge, Mass.: Belknap Press, 1971–2013), 4: 120.

73 Whitman, *Complete Poetry and Collected Prose*, 1151.

74 Herman Melville, cited in Shapiro, *Shakespeare in America*, 131.

75 Gail Kern Paster, "Preface," in *Shakespeare in American Life*, by Virginia Mason Vaughan and Alden T. Vaughan (Washington, D.C.: Folger Shakespeare Library, 2007), 7.

CHAPTER 2. LINCOLN READS SHAKESPEARE

1 John Hay, *Inside Lincoln's White House: The Complete Civil War Diary of John Hay*, ed. Michael Burlingame and John R. T. Ettlinger (Carbondale: Southern Illinois University Press, 1999), 75–76.

2 In addition to the references cited below, see two early essays: Robert N. Reeves, "Abraham Lincoln's Knowledge of Shakespeare," *California and Overland Monthly*, April 1904, 333–342; and R. Gerald McMurtry, "Lincoln Knew Shakespeare," *Indiana Magazine of History*, December 1935, 266–277.

3 Daniel Kilham Dodge, *Abraham Lincoln: The Evolution of His Literary Style* (Champaign and Urbana [Ill.]: University Press, 1900), 19.

4 Daniel Kilham Dodge, *Abraham Lincoln, Master of Words* (New York: D. Appleton, 1924), 47.

5 For useful guides to the reliability of witnesses to Lincoln's quoted words, see *Recollected Words of Abraham Lincoln*, comp. and ed. Don E. Fehrenbacher and Virginia Fehrenbacher (Stanford: Stanford University Press, 1996), passim. Robert Bray provides a careful analysis of the various claims that have been made for Lincoln's reading in "What Abraham Lincoln Read—An Evaluative and Annotated List," *Journal of the Abraham Lincoln Association*, Summer 2007, http.www .historycooperative.org/journals/jala/28.2/bray.html.

6 "Speech in U.S. House of Representatives on the Presidential Question," July 27, 1848, in *The Collected Works of Abraham Lincoln*, ed. Roy Prentice Basler, 11 vols. (New Brunswick, N.J.: Rutgers University Press, 1953), 1: 515. Hereafter cited as *CW*. An 1841 tragedy is entitled *Regulus: The Noblest Roman of Them All*.

7 Letter to Elizabeth Caldwell Browning, in *CW* 1: 118.

8 Autograph letter to Jesse Lynch, Washington, March 1, 1848, Shapell Manuscript Collection, SMF 414 (this letter is not included in *Collected Works*).

9 *CW* 7: 394.

10 *CW* 1: 367–370, dated [February 25?] 1846.

11 Speech to the Northwestern River and Harbor Convention, July 6, 1847, in *St. Louis Missouri Daily Republican*, July 12, 1847, http://www.papersofabraham lincoln.org (this speech is not included in *Collected Works*). Stephen Douglas, debating Lincoln in 1858, also used the phrase: "all united as a band of brothers" (*CW* 3: 293).

12 For a number of rather more marginal examples of Shakespearean allusions in

Lincoln's works, see John Channing Briggs, *Lincoln's Speeches Reconsidered* (Baltimore: Johns Hopkins University Press, 2005), 48–50, 72, 104, 131, 156, 282.

13 Cited in Michael Burlingame, *Abraham Lincoln: A Life*, print edition, 2 vols. (Baltimore: Johns Hopkins University Press, 2008), 1: 134. Not all historians agree that Lincoln wrote these letters; Basler did not include them in the *Collected Works*.

14 *CW* 2: 384.

15 Lincoln to Captain James M. Cutts, October 16, 1863, in *CW* 6: 538. See also Hay, *Inside Lincoln's White House*, xvii–xviii. Cutts, who was a brother-in-law of Stephen A. Douglas, went on to be the only person in U.S. military history to be awarded the Medal of Honor for meritorious service in three different campaigns. See Ronald C. White, *A. Lincoln: A Biography* (New York: Random House, 2009), 653.

16 Lincoln originally wrote the word "so" before "bear it" and changed "opposer" to "opposed," which would suggest that he was carefully copying. See Abraham Lincoln to James M. Cutts, Jr., Monday, October 26, 1863 (Cutts's court martial), Abraham Lincoln Papers, series 1, General Correspondence, 1833–1916, Library of Congress, http://memory.loc.gov/cgi-bin/query/r?ammem/mal:@field(DO-CID+@lit(d2749600)).

17 What Dodge actually wrote was that the speech contains "more quotations than any other speech except that at Bloomington two years later" (Dodge, *Abraham Lincoln: The Evolution of His Literary Style*, 45). The Bloomington speech is the famous "lost speech," a reconstruction of which by Henry C. Whitney is now almost wholly discredited. It is worth noting that Whitney's reconstruction includes at least two Shakespeare allusions (identified by Dodge), one from *Hamlet* ("I believe it was Shakespeare who said, 'Where the offence lies, there let the axe fall'") and one from *The Merchant of Venice* ("We grant a fugitive slave law because it is so 'nominated in the bond'; because our fathers so stipulated— had to—and we are bound to carry out this agreement"). Henry Clay Whitney, *Abraham Lincoln's Lost Speech, May 29, 1856. A Souvenir of the Eleventh Annual Lincoln Dinner of the Republican Club of the City of New York, at the Waldorf, February 12, 1897* (New York: Printed for the Committee, 1897), 39, 32.

18 "He wrote it out for publication in full over a week's issues of the *Illinois State Journal*, so that it would be widely read throughout the state." David Herbert Donald, *Lincoln* (New York: Simon and Schuster, 1995), 178.

19 "Speech at Peoria, Illinois," October 16, 1854, in *CW* 2: 270.

20 It does appear in John Bartlett's *The Shakespeare Phrase Book* (Boston: Little, Brown, 1881), 677.

21 *CW* 2: 276.

22 Donald, *Lincoln*, 177.

23 Lewis E. Lehrman, *Lincoln at Peoria: The Turning Point. Getting Right with the Declaration of Independence* (Mechanicsburg, Pa.: Stackpole Books, 2008), xvii.

24 Cited in ibid., 44.

25 Abraham Lincoln to James H. Hackett, in *CW* 6: 392–393.

26 "On the American Stage the play of 'King Henry VIII' has not been, at any time,

especially popular." William Winter, *Shakespeare on the Stage*, first series (New York: Moffat, Yard, 1911), 537.

27 *CW* 6: 393.

28 William Henry Herndon and Jesse William Weik, *Herndon's Lincoln*, ed. Douglas L. Wilson and Rodney O. Davis, Knox College Lincoln Studies Center series ([Galesburg, Ill.]: Knox College Lincoln Studies Center, 2006), xvii.

29 Eric Foner, *The Fiery Trial: Abraham Lincoln and American Slavery* (New York: W. W. Norton, 2010), xvi.

30 Consistency, however, may itself be suspect, as David C. Mearns suggests: "The memories of these 'clouds of witnesses' were, in some instances, almost suspiciously unanimous, as though in leisure moments they had coached one another." Mearns, "Mr. Lincoln and the Books He Read," in *Three Presidents and Their Books*, by Arthur Eugene Bestor, David C. Mearns, and Jonathan Daniels (Urbana: University of Illinois Press, 1955), 45–88, 46.

31 In Douglas L. Wilson et al., *Herndon's Informants: Letters, Interviews, and Statements about Abraham Lincoln* (Urbana: University of Illinois Press, 1998), 229; further quotations cited by page number in the text.

32 Milton Hay, John Hay's uncle, who worked in Lincoln's law office in 1839–1840, recalled many years later that "Burns and Shakespeare were [Lincoln's] favorites" and that he read Burns with a Scotch accent. Walter B. Stevens, *A Reporter's Lincoln*, edited by Michael Burlingame (Lincoln: University of Nebraska Press, 1998), 280n2.

33 "As far as Lincoln's remembered utterances and extant writings are concerned, *no such person as Jack Kelso ever existed.*" Robert Bray, *Reading with Lincoln* (Carbondale: Southern Illinois University Press, 2010), 91. But for evidence that Kelso was remembered by relatives, see the online version of Michael Burlingame's *Abraham Lincoln: A Life*, http://www.knox.edu/about-knox/lincoln-studies-center/burlingame-abraham-lincoln-a-life, chap. 3, p. 228, nn. ccxxi, ccxxii.

34 Herndon and Weik, *Herndon's Lincoln*, 199.

35 Ibid., 200.

36 Ibid., 354.

37 John Hay to William Henry Herndon, September 5, 1866, in Wilson et al., *Herndon's Informants*, 332.

38 Roy Basler, *A Touchstone for Greatness; Essays, Addresses, and Occasional Pieces about Abraham Lincoln* (Westport, Conn.: Greenwood Press, 1973), 206.

39 "Sally Bush Lincoln is supposed to have brought from Kentucky . . . *Lessons in Elocution*. . . . There was a copy of the book in the Bush family, for on May 27, 1806, Isaac Bush purchased at the Bleakley and Mongomery store in Elizabethtown, 'Dictionary, Scott's Lessons in Elocution and Introduction.'" Louis Austin Warren, *Lincoln's Youth: Indiana Years, Seven to Twenty-One, 1816–1830* (New York: Appleton, Century, Crofts, 1959), 76.

40 "In this state of things, while Ann's mind was tortured by suspense and disappointment [over her missing fiancé], Mr. Lincoln went to her father's house to board. Here he first learned to read Shakespeare and Burns. Can we doubt

whose memory made their poems precious during those last few months of his life, in which he was once heard to say, 'My heart lies buried in the grave of that girl?'" C. H. Dall, "Pioneering," *Atlantic Monthly*, April 1867, 403–416, 410. Joshua Shenk writes that Dall, a journalist, was "friendly with Herndon." Shenk, *Lincoln's Melancholy: How Depression Challenged a President and Fueled His Greatness* (Boston: Houghton Mifflin, 2005), 224.

41 Wilson et al., *Herndon's Informants*, 519.

42 "The copy of Shakespeare which Lincoln owned while living in Springfield, and which contains his autograph on the title page, is preserved in the Folger Shakespeare Library in Washington, D.C" (Basler, *Touchstone for Greatness*, 207).

43 Georgianna Ziegler, e-mail message to author, September 29, 2009. The edition is "William Shakespeare, The Dramatic Works . . . from the text of . . . Steevens and Malone, with a life of the poet, by Charles Symmons . . . and a glossary. New York: James Conner. Sold by Collins & Hannay, et al., 1835."

44 Alfred Van Rensselaer Westfall, *American Shakespearean Criticism, 1607–1865* (New York: H. W. Wilson, 1939), 77.

45 Lincoln owned a six-volume illustrated edition of Shakespeare (*The Plays of William Shakspeare. From the Corrected Text of Johnson and Steevens. Embellished with Plates . . .* [London: J. Stockdale, 1807]) given to him sometime in 1864 and later donated to Harvard University. (See William Slade file, J. G. Randall Papers, box 10, Library of Congress.) Clearly intended as a presentation copy, it lacks any explanatory materials. This was the edition Lincoln read from when returning from City Point, Virginia, on the *River Queen* on April 9, 1865, according to Lincoln's daughter-in-law Mary Harlan Lincoln, who was present.

46 Cited in Mearns, "Mr. Lincoln and the Books He Read," 50. Cf. Wilson et al., *Herndon's Informants*, 101, where we learn that Lincoln borrowed Weems from Josiah Crawford; the volume "got dam[aged] by being Wet," and Lincoln had to work off the cost of replacing it.

47 Westfall, *American Shakespearean Criticism*, 97. According to Paul Angle, "in the prosperous year 1856 a weekly wage of $10.00 was considered good pay for a workman" in Springfield. Angle, "*Here I Have Lived*": *A History of Lincoln's Springfield, 1821–1865* (Springfield, Ill.: Abraham Lincoln Association, 1935), 173.

48 See Michael Winship, "Uncle Tom's Cabin: History of the Book in the 19th-Century United States," http://utc.iath.virginia.edu/interpret/exhibits/winship/winship.html.

49 *The Plays of William Shakspeare: Complete in One Volume; Accurately Printed from the Text of Isaac Reed* (Boston: Charles Williams, 1813).

50 *The Dramatic Works of William Shakespeare: With the Corrections and Illustrations of Dr. Johnson, G. Steevens, and Others. Revised by Isaac Reed, Esq.* (New York: Henry Durell, 1817). See Andrew Murphy, *Shakespeare in Print: A History and Chronology of Shakespeare Publishing* (Cambridge: Cambridge University Press, 2003), 149. The supposed "Lincoln Copy" of Shakespeare in the Folger is a one-volume reprint of this edition.

51 Ralph L. Rusk, *The Literature of the Middle Western Frontier*, 2 vols. (New York: Columbia University Press, 1925), 2: 6.

52 "The Presidential Progress. Scenes at the Astor House," *New York Herald*, February 20, 1861.

53 Catherine M. Parisian, *The First White House Library: A History and Annotated Catalog* (University Park, Pa.: Published by the Pennsylvania State University Press for the Bibliographical Society of America and the National First Ladies' Library, 2010), 292.

54 William Shakespeare, *The Dramatic Works of William Shakespeare*, 8 vols. (Boston: Phillips, Samson, vols. 1–7, 1849; vol. 8, 1853). See Parisian, *First White House Library*, 292, for a full bibliographic description.

55 "Neither was this an empty boast, for up to that time no edition could compare with it in elegance." Jane Sherzer, "American Editions of Shakespeare: 1753–1866," *PMLA* 22, no. 4 (1907): 633–696, 660.

56 Murphy, *Shakespeare in Print*, 150.

57 The "Advertisement" was printed in the first and all subsequent editions. It is cited here from volume 1 of the 1836 edition: *The Dramatic Works of William Shakespeare; with a Life of the Poet, and Notes, Original and Selected* (Boston: Hilliard, Gray, 1836), as it appears on Google Books, http://books.google.com/.

58 "There is a very poor set of Waverly—also Shakespeare in house library, so I replaced each with a fine new edition—I presume, with your usual kindness, you are willing to leave such things to my judgment." Mary Lincoln to Benjamin Brown French, July 26, 1862, in Justin G. Turner, Linda Levitt Turner, and Mary Todd Lincoln, *Mary Todd Lincoln: Her Life and Letters* (New York: Alfred A. Knopf, 1972), 129. See also Harry E. Pratt, *The Personal Finances of Abraham Lincoln* (Springfield, Ill.: Abraham Lincoln Association, 1943), 180.

59 The set is in the Lincoln Financial Foundation Collection, Allen County Public Library, Fort Wayne, Indiana. It can be downloaded from http://lincolncollection.org/search/results/item/?q=Phillips+Samson+Shakespeare&item=35043. The bibliographic description notes, "Holograph inscription in ink on prelim. leaves, vols. 4-6, 8: Robert. T. Lincoln, 1862; holograph inscription in ink on prelim. leaf, vol. 7: Robert. T. Lincoln, Nov. 6th, 1862." A blank page at the beginning of volume 1 is inscribed "Robert T. Lincoln / from his Mother / Nov 6th, 1862." See https://archive.org/stream/dramaticworksofw01inshak#page/n3/mode/2up.

60 Parisian, *First White House Library*, 144.

61 Douglas L. Wilson, *Lincoln's Sword: The Presidency and the Power of Words* (New York: Alfred A. Knopf, 2006), 144–145.

62 Herbert Joseph Edwards and John Erskine Hankins, *Lincoln the Writer: The Development of His Literary Style* ([Orono]: University of Maine, 1962), 61.

63 Kenneth Cmiel, *Democratic Eloquence: The Fight over Popular Speech in Nineteenth-Century America* (New York: William Morrow, 1990), 117.

64 Wilson, *Lincoln's Sword*, 174.

65 James Russell Lowell, "Marlowe," *Harper's New Monthly Magazine*, July 1892, 194–203, 196.

66 Robert Alter, *Pen of Iron: American Prose and the King James Bible* (Princeton: Princeton University Press, 2010), 12–13.

67 Ibid.

68 See Orville Vernon Burton, "The Gettysburg Address Revisited," in *1863: Lincoln's Pivotal Year*, ed. Harold Holzer and Sara Vaughn Gabbard (Carbondale and Edwardsville: Southern Illinois University Press, 2013), 137–155, 143.

69 Jaques Barzun, "Lincoln the Writer," in *On Writing, Editing, and Publishing: Essays, Explicative and Hortatory* (Chicago: University of Chicago Press, 1986), 65.

70 *CW* 3: 86.

71 Final verse of Carl Sandburg's "The People, Yes," in *The Lincoln Anthology: Great Writers on His Life and Legacy from 1860 to Now*, ed. Harold Holzer (New York: Library of America, 2009), 518.

72 Garry Wills discusses the rhetorical aspects of Lincoln's speech in *Lincoln at Gettysburg: The Words That Remade America* (New York: Simon and Schuster, 1992), 59–62.

73 David James Harkness and R. Gerald McMurtry, *Lincoln's Favorite Poets* (Knoxville: University of Tennessee Press, 1959), 33. As Robert Bray notes, "Their book is highly assertive about what poetry Lincoln read and admired, yet more often than not the authors provide no sources for their claims" (Bray, "What Abraham Lincoln Read"). The evidence for Merwin's close friendship with Lincoln comes almost entirely from his own testimony. Robert Lincoln many years later described Merwin as "a very good, well meaning man, [who] could not be at all depended upon for his statements." Robert Todd Lincoln, *A Portrait of Abraham Lincoln in Letters by His Oldest Son*, ed. Paul M. Angle with the assistance of Richard G. Case (Chicago: Chicago Historical Society, 1968), 73.

74 Harkness and McMurtry, *Lincoln's Favorite Poets*, 33.

75 Charles Woodward Stearns, *The Shakspeare Treasury of Wisdom and Knowledge* (New York: G. P. Putnam and Son, 1869), 350.

76 Harkness and McMurtry, *Lincoln's Favorite Poets*, 34. See Ralph Waldo Emerson, *The Collected Works of Ralph Waldo Emerson*, ed. Robert Ernest Spiller et al., 10 vols. (Cambridge, Mass.: Belknap Press, 1971–2013), 4: 120.

77 Harkness and McMurtry, *Lincoln's Favorite Poets*, 34. Ibid.

78 Victor Hugo, *William Shakespeare*, trans. Melville B. Anderson (Chicago: A. C. McClurg, 1887), 217.

79 Harkness and McMurtry, *Lincoln's Favorite Poets*, 34.

80 In Editor's Drawer, *Harper's New Monthly Magazine*, February 1866, 400–408, 405. The ultimate source for this incident is Albert B. Chandler, who was a War Department telegrapher. The story continues with Lincoln saying, "I departed, and did not think of pictures again until that evening I was gratified and flattered at the cry of newsboys who had gone to vending the pictures "Eres yer last picter of Old Abe! He'll look better when he gets his *hair* combed!'" Le Grand Cannon, writing to Herndon in 1889, claims that he heard this anecdote from Lincoln himself, though his version does not have the *Hamlet* allusion (Wilson et al., *Herndon's Informants*, 680; and Lincoln, *Recollected Words*, 92).

81 Schuyler Colfax, *Life and Principles of Abraham Lincoln* (Philadelphia: J. B. Rodgers, printer, 1865), 14.

82 A very similar sentiment is uttered by Hal's father, Henry IV, in his "uneasy lies the head that wears the crown" soliloquy in *Henry IV, Part 2*, act 3, scene 1.

83 *CW* 5: 518.

84 "He was a man, take him for all in all," is in the 1856 edition of John Bartlett's *A Collection of Familiar Quotations: With Complete Indices of Authors and Subjects* (Cambridge[, Mass.]: John Bartlett, 1855, 1856). The phrase "in a current broad and deep," from the "Speech on the Sub-Treasury" (*CW* 1: 178) may be an unconscious echo of Lady Macbeth's "those honors deep and broad" (act 1, scene 6), but the wording is not really distinctive.

85 Lincoln, *Recollected Words*, 241–242.

86 For Capps, see Stevens, *A Reporter's Lincoln*, 139, cited from the *St. Louis Globe Democrat*, February 14, 1909, magazine section, 3.

87 Abraham Lincoln to Mrs. Orville Browning, April 1, 1838, in *CW* 1: 119.

88 James M. Scovel, "Personal Recollections of Abraham Lincoln," *Overland Monthly*, November 1891, 500. Scovel himself several times quotes from *Hamlet* later in the essay, describing Lincoln as a man "of imagination all compact."

89 Lincoln, *Recollected Words*, 394.

90 Egbert L. Viele, "A Trip with Lincoln, Chase and Stanton," *Scribner's Monthly*, October 1878, 813–823, 813.

91 Robert Bray, citing an interview of Viele by William A. Crofutt, September 23, 1885, clipping collection, Lincoln Museum, Fort Wayne, Indiana (Bray, "What Abraham Lincoln Read").

92 Luther Emerson Robinson, *Abraham Lincoln as a Man of Letters* (Chicago: Rilly and Britton, 1918), 206.

93 Bray, "What Abraham Lincoln Read."

94 In William Hayes Ward, ed., *Abraham Lincoln: Tributes from His Associates, Reminiscences of Soldiers, Statesmen and Citizens* (New York: T. Y. Crowell, 1895), 116–124, 119–120.

95 Statement of George W. Minier to Herndon, April 10, 1882. "This statement may have been borrowed from Osborn H. Oldroyd, *The Lincoln Memorial: Album Immortelles*" (Herndon and Weik, *Herndon's Lincoln*, 453n9).

96 James Grant Wilson, "Recollections of Lincoln," *Putnam's Monthly*, February 1909, 515–529, 517. Of Wilson, Don E. Fehrenbacher and Virginia Fehrenbacher write, "There may be as much invention as remembrance in his recollected words of Lincoln" (in Lincoln, *Recollected Words*, 503).

97 As his widow later recounted, Lincoln had proposed, "[in] the last week of his precious life, that at the expiration of his second term, we would visit Europe" (Mary Todd Lincoln to James Smith, December 17, 1866, in Turner and Turner, *Mary Todd Lincoln*, 400).

98 Simon Wolf, *The Presidents I Have Known from 1860–1918* (Washington, D.C.: Press of B. S. Adams, 1918), 7.

99 Even John Hay, however, is not above criticism as a witness: "Hay's wartime diary . . . is a rich source of informal remarks by Lincoln, although its lengthier passages in particular raise some questions about the part that literary creativity

played in his reproduction of the President's words" (Don Fehrenbacher and Virginia Fehrenbacher, in Lincoln, *Recollected Words*, 203).

100 John Hay, *At Lincoln's Side: John Hay's Civil War Correspondence and Selected Writings*, ed. Michael Burlingame (Carbondale: Southern Illinois University Press, 2000), 137.

101 Hay supposedly told the story to Elihu Root, who related it to the sculptor James R. Fraser, who in turn is cited in an unpublished manuscript by diplomat William L. Slade (William Slade file, J. G. Randall Papers, box 10, Library of Congress) (Hay, *At Lincoln's Side*, 345–346n).

102 Hay, *At Lincoln's Side*, 138. This story was first published by Hay in the *Century* in 1890.

103 In another version, the book becomes *Don Quixote*. See Talcott Williams, "Lincoln the Reader," *American Review of Reviews* 61 (January–June 1920), 193–198, 196.

104 Herndon and Weik, *Herndon's Lincoln*, 264n. Cf. *Hamlet*, act 5, scene 2.

105 James H. Hackett to Abraham Lincoln, August 17, 1863, in *CW* 6: 392–393.

106 "Recollections of One Who Studied Law with Lincoln," in Ward, *Abraham Lincoln*, 200–206, 203.

107 Fehrenbachers, in Lincoln, *Recollected Words*, 79. In one of the stories Carpenter may be retelling secondhand, Lincoln says to a group of visitors, "In 'these days of villany,' as Shakspeare says, . . . " to which he adds, "I believe, however, it is old 'Jack Falstaff' who talks about 'villany,' though of course Shakspeare is responsible." F. B. Carpenter, *Six Months at the White House with Abraham Lincoln: The Story of a Picture* (New York: Hurd and Houghton, 1866), 162.

108 Carpenter, *Six Months at the White House*, 49–50, 51.

109 Harold Holzer, *Lincoln President-Elect: Abraham Lincoln and the Great Secession Winter 1860–1861* (New York: Simon and Schuster, 2008), 186.

110 Murdoch, however, published an account in 1864 of that part of his conversation with Lincoln relating to the secession crisis. See James Edward Murdoch, Thomas Buchanan Read, and George H. Boker, *Patriotism in Poetry and Prose: Being Selected Passages from Lectures and Patriotic Readings* (Philadelphia: J. B. Lippincott, 1864), 23–29.

111 James Murdoch, quoted in Osborn H. Oldroyd, *The Lincoln Memorial: Album-immortelles* (New York: G. W. Carleton, 1882), 347–348.

112 *New York Herald*, September 17, 1863.

113 Charles Lamb, cited in *Hamlet: A New Variorum Edition of Shakespeare*, ed. Horace Howard Furness, 2 vols. (New York: Dover Publications, 1963), 1: 205.

114 David Bromwich, *Moral Imagination* (Princeton and Oxford: Princeton University Press, 2014), 162.

115 Allen C. Guelzo, review of *Reading with Lincoln*, by Robert Bray, *JALA* 33, no. 1 (2012): 212.

116 John W. Forney, *Anecdotes of Public Men* (New York, 1873), 180. Lincoln saw Edwin Forrest as Lear on April 8, 1864.

117 Basler, *Touchstone for Greatness*, 223.

118 Burlingame, *Abraham Lincoln*, print edition, 2: 737.

119 Charles Adolphe de Pineton, Marquis de Chambrun, "Personal Recollections of Mr. Lincoln," *Scribner's Magazine*, January 1893, 26–39, 34.

120 Edward Lillie Pierce and Charles Sumner, *Memoir and Letters of Charles Sumner* (Boston: Roberts Brothers, 1877), 235.

121 Ward Hill Lamon and Dorothy (Lamon) Teillard, *Recollections of Abraham Lincoln, 1847–1865* (Chicago: A. C. McClurg, 1895), 114.

122 Ibid., 116.

123 Ibid., 117.

124 Fehrenbachers, in Lincoln, *Recollected Words*, 281 and liii.

125 Lamon, *Recollections of Abraham Lincoln*, 117.

126 Jonathan White, "Did Lincoln Dream He Died?," *For the People: A Newsletter of the Abraham Lincoln Organization* 16, no. 3 (Fall 2014): 1–5, 5.

127 Dwight G. Anderson, "Quest for Immortality: A Theory of Abraham Lincoln's Political Psychology," in *The Historian's Lincoln: Pseudohistory, Psychohistory, and History*, ed. G. S. Boritt and Norman O. Forness (Urbana: University of Illinois Press, 1988), 253–274, 270. See also Dwight G. Anderson, *Abraham Lincoln, the Quest for Immortality* (New York: Alfred A. Knopf, 1982), 196–198.

128 Anderson gets around this problem by making the assassinated president George Washington, "killed," at least symbolically, by his "son," Lincoln; see Anderson, "Quest for Immortality," 253–254.

129 Michael Beran, "Lincoln, *Macbeth*, and the Moral Imagination," *Humanitas* 11, no. 2 (1998), http://www.nhinet.org/beran.htm.

130 Don E. Fehrenbacher, *Lincoln in Text and Context: Collected Essays* (Stanford, Calif.: Stanford University Press, 1987), 161.

131 Briggs, *Lincoln's Speeches Reconsidered*, 57.

132 Chambrun, "Personal Recollections," 35.

133 Some have seen Lincoln's famous "spot" speech delivered to Congress in 1847 as referring to *Macbeth* ("Out, damned spot!" [act 5, scene 1, line 30]), but the connection is slight at best. See Briggs, *Lincoln's Speeches Reconsidered*, 104. For a nuanced view of how Lincoln understood *Macbeth*, see David Bromwich, "Shakespeare, Lincoln, and Ambition," *New York Review of Books* (blog), April 11, 2014, http://www.nybooks.com/blogs/nyrblog/2014/apr/11/shakespeare-lincoln-ambition/?insrc=rel. Bromwich concludes, "Conscience, often if not always, stopped him short of the grand assertions of arbitrary power that the ambitious have no second thoughts about."

134 Adam Gopnik, *Angels and Ages: A Short Book about Darwin, Lincoln, and Modern Life* (New York: Alfred A. Knopf, 2009), 139.

135 George B. Forgie, *Patricide in the House Divided: A Psychological Interpretation of Lincoln and His Age* (New York: W. W. Norton, 1979), 247.

136 Carpenter's actual words are "unconsciously assuming the character, Mr. Lincoln repeated, also from memory, Richard's soliloquy, rendering it with a degree of force and power that made it seem like a new creation to me" (Carpenter, *Six Months at the White House*, 52).

137 Forgie, *Patricide*, 247.

138 Ibid.

139 Forgie, *Patricide*, 246, citing Charles Adolphe de Pineton, Marquis de Chambrun, *Impressions of Lincoln and the Civil War: A Foreigner's Account*, trans. Aldebert de Chambrun (New York: Random House, [1952]), 83.

140 Forgie, *Patricide*, 246.

141 Anderson, *Abraham Lincoln*, 195.

142 For a critique of Anderson and Forgie, see Richard N. Current, "Lincoln after 175 Years: The Myth of the Jealous Son," *Journal of the Abraham Lincoln Association* 6, no. 1 (1984): 15–24; and Michael Burlingame, *The Inner World of Abraham Lincoln* (Urbana: University of Illinois Press, 1994), 253–255.

143 Hay, *At Lincoln's Side*, 139.

144 Johnson Brigham, *James Harlan* (Iowa City: State Historical Society of Iowa, 1913), 338.

145 Hay, *At Lincoln's Side*, 137

146 Carpenter gives a slightly different account of what is clearly the same episode, quoting these lines: "And, father cardinal, I have heard you say / That we shall see and know our friends in heaven: / If that be true, I shall see my boy again" (Carpenter, *Six Months at the White House*, 116). The words I have quoted in the text better fit Le Grand Cannon's own account, however.

147 Le Grand B. Cannon, *Personal Reminiscences of the Rebellion, 1861–1866* (New York: [Burr Printing House], 1895), 167–168. In an 1889 letter to Herndon, Cannon writes "direct communion" rather than "sweet communion" (Wilson et al., *Herndon's Informants*, 679). Carpenter writes "sweet communion" (*Six Months at the White House*, 116).

148 Shenk, *Lincoln's Melancholy*, 107.

149 Fred Kaplan, *Lincoln: The Biography of a Writer* (New York: HarperCollins, 2008), 41.

150 Chambrun, "Personal Recollections," 34.

151 So familiar was the play that a November 19, 1842, announcement of Lincoln's marriage that appeared in the *Winchester (Ill.) Battle Axe, and Political Reformer* cites Richard's opening soliloquy: "Linco[l]n [who was recently involved in a near duel] . . . is married! 'Grim visaged war hath smoothed his wrinkled front,' and now 'he capers nimbly in a ladys'—don't recollect the rest of the quotation." Thomas F. Schwartz, "'—In Short, He Is *Married!*': A Contemporary Newspaper Account," *For the People: A Newsletter of the Abraham Lincoln Association* 1, no. 4 (Winter 1999): 4.

152 For a brief discussion of Lincoln's awareness of the difference between the standard texts of Shakespeare's plays and the acting versions, see Douglas L. Wilson, "His Hour upon the Stage," *American Scholar* 81, no. 1 (Winter 2012): 60–69.

CHAPTER 3. LINCOLN AT THE THEATER

1 Roy Basler, *A Touchstone for Greatness: Essays, Addresses, and Occasional Pieces about Abraham Lincoln* (Westport, Conn.: Greenwood Press, 1973), 207.

2 Mark E. Neely, *The Abraham Lincoln Encyclopedia* (New York: McGraw-Hill, 1982), 275.

3 Gertrude Garrison, in William Henry Herndon and Jesse William Weik, *Herndon's Lincoln*, ed. Douglas L. Wilson and Rodney O. Davis ([Galesburg, Ill.?]: Knox College Lincoln Studies Center, 2006), 339.

4 Henry Clay Whitney, *Life on the Circuit with Lincoln. With Sketches of Generals Grant, Sherman and McClellan, Judge Davis, Leonard Swett, and Other Contemporaries* (Boston: Estes and Lauriat, 1892), 198–199. "[Whitney's memoir] remains important for its eyewitness observations of Lincoln in the latter 1850s, but Whitney has proved unreliable on important aspects of Lincoln's life and political career—most notoriously, he claimed in 1895 to have found his long-forgotten notes from Lincoln's 'Lost Speech' in Bloomington, Illinois (1856), and published what he said was a near-verbatim account of its text." Robert C. Bray, "What Abraham Lincoln Read—An Evaluative and Annotated List," *Journal of the Abraham Lincoln Association*, Summer 2007, http://www.historycooperative .org/journals/jala/28.2/bray.html.

5 Katherine Helm, *The True Story of Mary, Wife of Lincoln: Containing the Recollections of Mary Lincoln's Sister Emilie (Mrs. Ben Hardin Helm), Extracts from Her War-Time Diary, Numerous Letters and Other Documents Now First Published* (New York: Harper, 1928), 119.

6 Rosemarie K. Bank, *Theatre Culture in America, 1825–1860* (Cambridge: Cambridge University Press, 1997), 113.

7 Philip C. Kolin, ed., *Shakespeare in the South: Essays on Performance* (Jackson: University Press of Mississippi, 1983), 12.

8 Herndon and Weik, *Herndon's Lincoln*, 264.

9 Richard Campanella, *Lincoln in New Orleans: The 1828–1831 Flatboat Voyages and Their Place in History* (Lafayette: University of Louisiana at Lafayette Press, 2010), 85.

10 Ibid., 125.

11 Nelle Kroger Smither, *A History of the English Theatre in New Orleans* (New York: Benjamin Blom, 1967), 222.

12 See Sol Smith, *Theatrical Management in the West and South for Thirty Years: Interspersed with Anecdotical Sketches* (New York: Harper and Brothers, 1868), 49. Stephen M. Archer records Booth's performances in New Orleans during both the 1827–1828 and the 1828–1829 seasons. Archer, *Junius Brutus Booth: Theatrical Prometheus* (Carbondale: Southern Illinois University Press, 1992). See also Smither, *A History of the English Theatre in New Orleans*, 65.

13 Accessible at Jefferson Parish Library, "Genealogy: New Orleans Bee," http:// nobee.jefferson.lib.la.us.

14 "In Flatboat and Keelboat Times," *Daily Picayune*, March 19, 1896, cited from Campanella, *Lincoln in New Orleans*, 68.

15 John Hay, *Inside Lincoln's White House: The Complete Civil War Diary of John Hay*, ed. Michael Burlingame and John R. T. Ettlinger (Carbondale: Southern Illinois University Press, 1999), xii.

16 "Springfield, Illinois, and probably, Chicago were among other towns where

such [amateur] performances were known before 1841." Ralph L. Rusk, *The Literature of the Middle Western Frontier*, 2 vols. (New York: Columbia University Press, 1925), 1: 364.

17 Paul M. Angle, *"Here I Have Lived": A History of Lincoln's Springfield, 1821–1865* (Springfield, Ill.: Abraham Lincoln Association, 1935), 52. See also *Illinois Weekly State Journal*, December 3, 1836.

18 *Illinois Weekly State Journal*, January 28 and February 4, 1837.

19 *Illinois Weekly State Journal*, March 3, 1838, cited in Angle, *"Here I Have Lived,"* 80.

20 *Illinois Weekly State Journal*, March 10, 1838.

21 *Sangamo Journal*, June 21, 1839.

22 *Sangamo Journal*, November 29, 1839.

23 Joseph Jefferson, *The Autobiography of Joseph Jefferson*, ed. Alan Seymour Downer (Cambridge, Mass.: Belknap Press, 1964), 26.

24 Ibid., 27–28.

25 Benjamin McArthur, *The Man Who Was Rip Van Winkle: Joseph Jefferson and Nineteenth-Century American Theatre* (New Haven: Yale University Press, 2007), 41.

26 Martha L. Benner and Cullom Davis, *The Law Practice of Abraham Lincoln: Complete Documentary Edition* (Champaign: University of Illinois Press, 2000).

27 Benjamin McArthur, "Joseph Jefferson's Lincoln: Vindication of an Autobiographical Legend," *Journal of the Illinois State Historical Society* 93, no. 2 (Summer 2000): 155–166.

28 Sarah Rickard Barret to William Henry Herndon, August 12, 1888, in *Herndon's Informants: Letters, Interviews, and Statements about Abraham Lincoln*, by Douglas L. Wilson et al. (Urbana: University of Illinois Press, 1998), 665, cited in *The Inner World of Abraham Lincoln*, by Michael Burlingame (Urbana: University of Illinois Press, 1994), 135.

29 Michael Burlingame, *Abraham Lincoln: A Life*, print edition, 2 vols. (Baltimore: Johns Hopkins University Press, 2008), 1: 187.

30 McArthur, *Rip Van Winkle*, 38.

31 Robert Lowery Sherman, *Chicago Stage, Its Records and Achievements*, vol. 1, *Gives a Complete Record of All Entertainment and, Substantially, the Cast of Every Play Presented in Chicago, on Its First Production in the City, from the Beginning of Theatricals in 1834 Down to the Last before the Fire of 1871* (Chicago: Robert L. Sherman, 1947), 49–53.

32 Don B. Wilmeth, "The MacKenzie-Jefferson Theatrical Company in Galena, 1838–1839," *Journal of the Illinois State Historical Society* 60, no. 1 (Spring, 1967): 23–36, 35.

33 Catherine Clinton, *Mrs. Lincoln: A Life* (New York: Harper, 2009), 31–33. Mary "may or may not" have met Lincoln in the summer of 1837 (ibid., 31).

34 Helm, *True Story of Mary*, 119.

35 Emmett, under what appears to have been his real name, Fairclough, played Othello in Washington, D.C., in 1856.

36 *Daily Illinois State Journal*, February 24 and March 5, 1855; *Daily Illinois State Register*, March 13, 1855. In his novel *Love Is Eternal*, Irving Stone writes, "Mary

and Abraham went downtown to the Masonic Hall to hear Boothroyd Emmett read *Richard III,*" but, unsurprisingly, he gives no source. *Love Is Eternal: A Novel about Mary Todd Lincoln and Abraham Lincoln* (Garden City, N.Y.: Doubleday, 1954), 254.

37 See *The Lincoln Log: A Daily Chronology of the Life of Abraham Lincoln*, http://www.thelincolnlog.org/Home.aspx (hereafter *Lincoln Log*), June 10, 1856.

38 So obscure has Couldock become that he is not even listed in the index to Charles Harlen Shattuck's *Shakespeare on the American Stage: From the Hallams to Edwin Booth* (Washington, D.C.: Folger Shakespeare Library, 1976). He became known in later life (he died in 1898) for playing older character parts in various melodramas. In 1858 he became a member of Laura Keene's company, where he created the role of Abel Murcott in the first American production of Tom Taylor's *Our American Cousin.* John A. Garraty and Mark C. Carnes, *American National Biography* (New York: Oxford University Press, 1999), 581.

39 Garraty and Carnes, *American National Biography*, 581.

40 Charles W. Couldock as Cardinal Wolsey, Folger Shakespeare Library, art file C855 no. 3, copy 1.

41 *Daily Illinois State Journal*, February 9, 1857.

42 *Daily Illinois State Journal*, February 10, 1857.

43 *Daily Illinois State Register*, February 12, 1857.

44 *Daily Illinois State Register*, February 14 and 18, 1857.

45 "Early in 1857, during the 'gay season,' the great actor Charles Walter Couldock played for several weeks" (Angle, *"Here I Have Lived,"* 189).

46 Justin G. Turner, Linda Levitt Turner, and Mary Todd Lincoln, *Mary Todd Lincoln: Her Life and Letters* (New York: Alfred A. Knopf, 1972), 48.

47 In a letter dated February 12, Lincoln wrote, "I am going to Chicago, if nothing prevents, on the 21st. Inst." Abraham Lincoln to James Steele and Charles Summers, in *The Collected Works of Abraham Lincoln*, ed. Roy Prentice Basler, 11 vols. (New Brunswick, N.J.: Rutgers University Press, 1953), 2: 389. Hereafter cited as *CW*. See *Lincoln Log*, February 23 and 28 and March 4, 1857.

48 *Daily Illinois State Register*, February 12, 1857.

49 *Cleveland (Ohio) Plain Dealer*, October 10, 1856.

50 *Cleveland (Ohio) Plain Dealer*, March 14, 1857.

51 *Chicago Daily Tribune*, November 12, 1853.

52 *Daily Ohio Statesman*, January 16, 1858.

53 Cited in Mary Duggar Toulmin, "Shakespeare in Mobile, 1822–1861," in Kolin, *Shakespeare in the South*, 128–156, 149–150.

54 *Frank Leslie's Illustrated Newspaper*, November 17, 1860.

55 Angle, *"Here I Have Lived,"* 188. "After [Ralph Waldo] Emerson and [Bayard] Taylor, the leading lecturers of the country followed in quick succession— Horace Greeley ('Reform and Reformers') and Henry Ward Beecher ('Conservatism and Progression') in 1855, Theodore Parker ('The Progressive Development of Mankind') in 1856, and Parke Benjamin ('Hard Times') in 1857" (ibid., 188). For Emerson's lectures and how they were received in Illinois, see Donald

F. Tingley, "Ralph Waldo Emerson on the Illinois Lecture Circuit," *Journal of the Illinois State Historical Society* 64, no. 2 (Summer 1971): 192–205.

56 *Daily Illinois State Register*, December 15, 1858.

57 *Daily Illinois State Journal*, January 29, 1855.

58 *Daily Illinois State Register*, March 17, 1858; and *Daily Illinois State Register*, July 2, 1858.

59 *Daily Illinois State Journal*, February 18, 1854.

60 *Daily Illinois State Register*, February 24, 1857.

61 *Daily Illinois State Register*, November 14, 1849.

62 *Daily Illinois State Journal*, January 11, 1861.

63 Murdoch described the lectures he generally gave in a December 19, 1860, letter to an unknown recipient: "I have *Hamlet Othello*, & *Macbeth* arranged for Reading Recitation & Remarks: each 'evening' reserved to the Reading and Recitation of the Principal scenes and soliloquies." Ms.Yc. 1963 (2), Folger Library. The promptbook for his *Hamlet* reading at the Folger (PROMPT Ham.83) indicates that he skipped the Claudius prayer scene, along with much else.

64 *Daily Illinois State Journal*, January 9, 1861.

65 Harold Holzer, *Lincoln President-Elect: Abraham Lincoln and the Great Secession Winter 1860–1861* (New York: Simon and Schuster, 2008), 186. A notice in the *Daily Illinois State Journal* for January 10, 1861, reports that a request "for a repetition of the entertainment given by Mr. Murdoch on Tuesday evening" was made by many prominent citizens; "A. Lincoln" heads the list of sponsors.

66 Quoted in Osborn H. Oldroyd, *The Lincoln Memorial: Album-immortelles* (New York: G. W. Carleton, 1882), 347.

67 "While this is attractive—for who would not like for the works of Dickens and Lincoln to have found each other?—and even somewhat plausible, since Murdoch was an 'actor and elocutionist'; yet, given Lincoln's own purported statement [of not having read novels] and the lack of corroboration from other sources, we must discount Murdoch's claim, as do the Fehrenbachers. (Bray, "What Abraham Lincoln Read," citing Don E. Fehrenbacher and Virginia Fehrenbacher in *Recollected Words of Abraham Lincoln*, comp. and ed. Don E. Fehrenbacher and Virginia Fehrenbacher [Stanford: Stanford University Press, 1996], 337).

68 Sherman, *Chicago Stage*, 2–3. "This entertaining mélange consisted of magic, ventriloquism and other stunts that could be provided by a single individual" (ibid., 3).

69 *The Diary of Orville Hickman Browning*, ed. Theodore Calvin Pease and James G. Randall, 2 vols., Illinois State Historical Library Collections, vols. 20, 22 (Springfield: Illinois State Historical Library, 1925–1933), 1: 505–506. "Burton took an apparently conventional stage sot and managed to imbue him with a bumbling pathos" (McArthur, *Rip Van Winkle*, 89). Burton was more than a comic performer: as an actor-manager, he championed the restoration of Shakespeare's texts to the stage. See also David L. Rinear, *Stage, Page, Scandals, and Vandals: William E. Burton and Nineteenth-Century American Theatre*, Theater in the Americas (Carbondale: Southern Illinois University Press, 2004).

70 Whitney, *Life on the Circuit*, 156–157.

71 Sherman, *Chicago Stage*, 87.

72 Ibid., 102–104.

73 Ibid., 312.

74 Mary Lincoln to Hannah Shearer, January 1, 1860; in Turner and Turner, *Mary Todd Lincoln*, 61.

75 *Daily National Intelligencer*, March 28, 1849.

76 "Congressman Lincoln was very fond of bowling, and would frequently join others of the mess, or meet other members in a match game, at the alley of James Casparis, which was near the boarding-house." Samuel C. Busey, *Personal Reminiscences and Recollections of Forty-Six Years' Membership in the Medical Society of the District of Columbia and Residence in This City, with Biographical Sketches of Many of the Deceased Members* (Washington, D.C. [Philadelphia: Dornan, printer], 1895), 27.

77 See Abraham Lincoln to Mary Todd Lincoln, 2 July, 1848; in *CW* 1: 495. In this letter, Lincoln refers to the visit to Carusi's: "The music in the Capitol grounds on saturdays, [*sic*] or, rather, the interest in it, is dwindling down to nothing. Yesterday evening the attendance was rather thin. Our two girls, whom you remember seeing first at Carusis, at the exhibition of the Ethiopian Serenaders, and whose peculiarities were the wearing of black fur bonnets, and never being seen in close company with other ladies, were at the music yesterday. One of them was attended by their brother, and the other had a member of Congress in tow. He went home with her; and if I were to guess, I would say, he went away a somewhat altered man—most likely in his pockets, and in some other particular. The fellow looked conscious of guilt, although I believe he was unconscious that every body around knew who it was that had caught him" (ibid., 495–496).

78 David Herbert Donald, *Lincoln* (New York: Simon and Schuster, 1995), 131. As Michael Burlingame notes (*Abraham Lincoln*, 1: 280), "Lincoln stumped vigorously for [presidential candidate Zachary] Taylor" on this trip: to give one example, he spoke at Dorchester on September 18, at Chelsea on the nineteenth, and attended a meeting at Dedham and spoke at Cambridge, both on the twentieth. See *Lincoln Log* for those dates.

79 George Clinton Densmore Odell, *Annals of the New York Stage*, 15 vols. (New York: Columbia University Press, 1927–1949), 7: 311.

80 LeRoy Ashby, *With Amusement for All: A History of American Popular Culture since 1830* (Lexington: University Press of Kentucky, 2006), 109.

81 Leonard Grover, proprietor of Grover's National Theatre, claimed that Tad Lincoln saw his production of *The Seven Sisters* in Washington. Grover, "Lincoln's Interest in the Theater," *Century Magazine*, April 1909, 943–950, 945.

82 Turner and Turner, *Mary Todd Lincoln*, 87.

83 Thomas A. Bogar, *American Presidents Attend the Theatre: The Playgoing Experiences of Each Chief Executive* (Jefferson, N.C.: McFarland, 2006), 92.

84 The playbill for this production is reproduced in Shattuck, *Shakespeare on the American Stage*, 24. For a brief history of Washington theaters, see two essays by

Alysius I. Mudd: "Early Theater in Washington D.C.," *Records of the Columbia Historical Society* 5 (1902): 64–86; and "The Theatres of Washington from 1835 to 1850," *Records of the Columbia Historical Society* 6 (1903): 222–266. Thomas Bogar, updating Mudd, finds theatrical activity taking place in both Alexandria and Georgetown as early as the 1760s. See Bogar, "The Origins of Theater in the District of Columbia, 1789–1800," *Washington History* 22 (2010): 4–16; and Roger Meersman and Robert Boyer, "The National Theatre in Washington: Buildings and Audiences, 1835–1972," *Records of the Columbia Historical Society, Washington, D.C.* 71–72 (1971–1972): 190–242.

85 Theater buildings in the 1800s were so vulnerable to fire, due to flame-operated lighting and the flammable materials used in sets and costumes, that they seldom lasted more than twenty years. See Amy Hughes, *Spectacles of Reform: Theater and Activism in Nineteenth-Century America* (Ann Arbor: University of Michigan Press, 2012), 30.

86 Grover, "Lincoln's Interest in the Theater," 943.

87 The Fehrenbachers reasonably comment, "[Grover's] assertion that Lincoln attended his theatre 'probably more than a hundred times' and Ford's Theatre not once until the night of the assassination, contributes to doubt about his recollective accuracy in general" (in Lincoln, *Recollected Words*, 188). Grover and Ford appear to have been, at least at times, bitter rivals. Theater historian Thomas A. Bogar estimates that "Lincoln attended Grover's twenty-one times and Ford's ten," which is reasonable (Bogar, *American Presidents Attend the Theatre*, 374n1).

88 Grover, "Lincoln's Interest in the Theater," 944.

89 William E. Sinn, "A Theatrical Manager's Reminiscences," in *Abraham Lincoln: Tributes from His Associates, Reminiscences of Soldiers, Statesmen and Citizens*, ed. William Hayes Ward (New York: T. Y. Crowell, 1895), 169–174, 169. It does not appear that anyone, apart from Sinn, ever referred to the theater as "Grover and Sinn's."

90 Sinn, "A Theatrical Manager's Reminiscences," 170.

91 As Douglas Wilson notes, "Lincoln's pursuit of Shakespeare in Washington theaters has long been overstated," adding that "circumstances kept Lincoln away from the theater during his first two years in office—the rebuilding of one of the major theaters, the burning of another, the death of his son, and his almost total immersion in a grave national crisis that was going badly." Wilson, "His Hour upon the Stage," *American Scholar* 81, no. 1 (Winter 2012): 60–69, 61–62. Grover's theater had burned down in 1857 and did not reopen until 1862. It is possible that Lincoln sometimes snuck into theaters unobserved, as Wilson and others have suggested, but it is unlikely: the president's height and distinctive appearance would count against it.

92 Noah Brooks, "Glimpses of Lincoln in War Time," *Century*, January 1895, 457–467, 464. Brooks, however, may not be entirely reliable; see Fehrenbacher's comment: "Brooks's claim to have frequently attended the theater with Lincoln is uncorroborated" (in Lincoln, *Recollected Words*, 518n45). On the other hand, Michael Burlingame claims that Brooks's letters and dispatches "are trustworthy sources"; see Noah Brooks, *Lincoln Observed: Civil War Dispatches of Noah*

Brooks, ed. Michael Burlingame (Baltimore: Johns Hopkins University Press, 1998), 12.

93 William Osborn Stoddard, *Lincoln's White House Secretary: The Adventurous Life of William O. Stoddard*, ed. Harold Holzer (Carbondale: Southern Illinois University Press, 2007), 304. I have slightly altered the paragraphing.

94 The *Lincoln Log* entry for June 8, 1864, reads, "Attends Grover's Theatre in evening alone. Leonard Grover, 'Lincoln's Interest in the Theater,' *Century Magazine* 77 (April 1909): 947." The at-times unreliable *National Theater* Web site "timeline" (http://thenationaldc.org/timeline/) indicates that Lincoln went to see *Mazeppa, the Wild Horse of Tartary* on the evening of June 8; according to another source, that play was also playing on April 15, 1865, when Tad was there. See Douglas Bennett Lee, Roger L. Meersman, and Donn B. Murphy, *Stage for a Nation: The National Theatre, 150 Years* (Lanham, Md.: University Press of America, 1985). This last claim is clearly wrong. *Aladdin and His Wonderful Lamp* was playing that night; the playbill is reproduced in M. Helen Palmes Moss, "Lincoln and Wilkes Booth as Seen on the Day of the Assassination," *Century Magazine*, April 1909, 950–953, 952.

95 *New York Times*, March 23, 1918.

96 *Washington National Republican*, January 22, 1864.

97 See Bruce A. McConachie, *Melodramatic Formations: American Theatre and Society, 1820–1870* (Iowa City: University of Iowa Press, 1992), 241–242.

98 Ibid., 241.

99 Lorraine Commeret, "Edwin Booth's Bertuccio: Tom Taylor's Fool Revised," in *When They Weren't Doing Shakespeare: Essays on Nineteenth-Century British and American Theatre*, ed. Judith Law Fisher and Stephen Watt (Athens: University of Georgia Press, 1989), 64–87, 64.

100 David Grimsted, *Melodrama Unveiled: American Theater and Culture, 1800–1850* (Chicago: University of Chicago Press, 1968), 155.

101 David Francis Taylor, "Shakespeare and Drama," in *Shakespeare in the Nineteenth Century*, ed. Gail Marshall (Cambridge: Cambridge University Press, 2012), 129–147, 133.

102 Shattuck, *Shakespeare on the American Stage*, 117.

103 McArthur, *Rip Van Winkle*, 103.

104 "[The] third tier at the National had [in the 1840s] long been a resort for the city's prostitutes, and the saloons did tremendous business in liquor sales" (Rinear, *Stage, Page, Scandals, and Vandals*, 89).

105 Theodore J. Shank, "Shakespeare and Nineteenth-Century Realism," *Theater Survey* 4 (1963): 59–75, 60.

106 Grimsted, *Melodrama Unveiled*, 83.

107 Ibid.

108 Of a production of James Wallack and E. L. Davenport in *Macbeth*, we read that "Mr. Grover spares no pains or expense in the properties and costumes and scenery, and the mounting of the piece was equal to anything of the kind in this country—with the exception, perhaps, of the New York theatres." *Daily National Republican*, March 25, 1863. As an amusing side note, the reviewer adds, "The

witch cauldron lacked only one ingredient, not known however in Shakespeare's time, a Copperhead's gizzard. That, in addition to the 'baboon's blood,' etc., would have made the charm complete."

109 James Edward Murdoch and J. Bunting, *The Stage; or, Recollections of Actors and Acting from an Experience of Fifty Years* (Philadelphia: J. M. Stoddart, 1880), 49.

110 Herndon and Weik, *Herndon's Lincoln*, 248.

111 Murdoch and Bunting, *The Stage; or, Recollections of Actors and Acting from an Experience of Fifty Years*, 29.

112 Shattuck, *Shakespeare on the American Stage*, xiv.

113 *Daily National Intelligencer*, August 13, 1822, cited in Archer, *Junius Brutus Booth*, 77.

114 *Baltimore American and Commercial Daily Advertiser*, October 23, 1822, cited in Archer, *Junius Brutus Booth*, 81.

115 *London Times*, October 10, 1825, cited in Archer, *Junius Brutus Booth*, 99.

116 *Theatrical Journal and Stranger's Guide* (London), xxxiii (1872), 212, cited in Alan S. Downer, "Players and Painted Stage: Nineteenth Century Acting," *PMLA* 61, no. 2 (June, 1946): 522–576, 527.

117 Lewes, *On Actors and the Art of Acting* (London, 1875), 147–148, cited in Downer, "Players and Painted Stage," 552.

118 Garff B. Wilson, *A History of American Acting* (Bloomington: Indiana University Press, 1966), 108.

119 McArthur, *Rip Van Winkle*, 20.

120 *New York Herald*, October 30, 1860. One critic, reviewing Forrest in *The Gladiator*, complimented the manager for "'having taken great care' to cast the most incompetent actors as characters who are killed so that their 'timeless deaths do not draw to an unnecessary extent upon the sympathies of the audience'" (cited in McConachie, *Melodramatic Formations*, 78).

121 *Daily National Intelligencer*, April 20, 1864.

122 *Daily National Republican*, October 13, 1863, 2nd ed.

123 "Ford's Theatre—Benefit to the Sanitary Commission," *Daily National Republican*, October 13, 1863. According to Fanny Seward's diary entry for October 12, Cushman had talked to Leonard Grover, who visited the Seward home, where the actress was staying, to offer her both his facilities and the services of the two stars who were then appearing at his theater, James Wallack and E. L. Davenport. Cited in Alexander Nemerov, *Acting in the Night: Macbeth and the Places of the Civil War* (Berkeley: University of California Press, 2010), 18, 230n3.

124 *Spirit of the Times*, May 21, 1864, cited in Charles Harlen Shattuck, *The Hamlet of Edwin Booth* (Urbana: University of Illinois Press, 1969), 53. As late as 1883, one observer commented (here, of Booth's *Lear*), "The support is so miserably poor and inadequate . . . that the play as a whole on the stage seems far inferior to the same when read." Mary Isabella Stone, *Edwin Booth's Performances: The Mary Isabella Stone Commentaries*, ed. Daniel J. Watermeier (Ann Arbor, Mich.: UMI Research Press, 1990), 215.

125 *New World*, November 26, 1842, cited in Grimsted, *Melodrama Unveiled*, 106.

126 Richard Moody, *Edwin Forrest, First Star of the American Stage* (New York: Alfred A. Knopf, 1960), 232.

127 See the program reproduced in Gordon Samples's *Lust for Fame: The Stage Career of John Wilkes Booth* (Jefferson, N.C.: McFarland, 1982), 101.

128 *Daily National Republican,* October 9, 1862.

129 Archer, *Junius Brutus Booth,* 111.

130 McArthur, *Rip Van Winkle,* 21.

131 *Richard III,* ed. Julie Hankey (London: Junction Books, 1981), 158.

132 Charles Lamb, *The Portable Charles Lamb,* ed. John Mason Brown (New York: Viking Press, 1949), 562. *King Lear,* in particular, "cannot be acted" (ibid., 574).

133 F. B. Carpenter, *Six Months at the White House with Abraham Lincoln: The Story of a Picture* (New York: Hurd and Houghton, 1866), 49.

134 Ibid., 51.

135 As Mark Neely notes, Carpenter "sometimes betrayed a tin ear in retelling Lincoln anecdotes." Neely, introduction to *The Inner Life of Abraham Lincoln: Six Months at the White House,* by Francis Bicknell Carpenter (Lincoln: University of Nebraska Press, 1995), xi.

136 *Richard III,* ed. Hankey, 27, 28.

137 Lincoln, *Recollected Words,* 277.

138 Walt Whitman, quoted in Shattuck, *Shakespeare on the American Stage,* 48.

139 John Finlay, *Miscellanies. The Foreign Relations of the British Empire: The Internal Resources of Ireland: Sketches of Character: Dramatic Criticism* (Dublin, 1835), 211–212.

140 Cited in Gāmini Salgādo, *Eyewitnesses of Shakespeare: First Hand Accounts of Performances, 1590–1890* (New York: Barnes and Noble Books, 1975), 102.

141 Shattuck, *Shakespeare on the American Stage,* 46.

142 William Dunlap, *Memoirs of the Life of George Frederick Cooke, Esquire: Late of the Theatre Royal, Covent Garden,* 2 vols. (New York: D. Longworth, 1813), 2: 181–182.

143 *Remarks on the Character of Richard the Third; As Played by Cooke and Kemble.* (London, 1801), 18.

144 Dunlap, *Memoirs of the Life of George Frederick Cooke,* 353.

145 *Daily National Intelligencer,* April 9, 1862, and March 26, 1864. The claim that Lincoln saw Forrest in *Richard III* appears to rest on David C. Mearns's *Largely Lincoln* (New York: St. Martin's Press, 1961), 147; Mearns may have relied on an undocumented statement in the reminiscences of the actress Helen Truman, who, as a nineteen-year-old, played a juvenile role in *Our American Cousin* on the fateful night of April 14, 1865. Nearly sixty years later she gave interviews in which she related that she had often seen Lincoln at Ford's Theatre; her recollections are sometimes supported by other evidence, but in other cases they are clearly wrong (she says, for example, that Lincoln was never accompanied by his wife at the theater apart from the night of the assassination) or cannot be verified. See "Eyewitnesses to Lincoln's Assassination Live Here," *Los Angeles Times,* February 11, 1923, and "Ford Theater Actress Tells of Emancipator," *Los Angeles Times,* February 10, 1924. She also claimed that Lincoln saw Junius

Brutus Booth, Jr., in *The Merchant of Venice* as well as Forrest in *Jack Cade* and *Metamora*.

146 William Rounseville Alger, *Life of Edwin Forrest, the American Tragedian*, 2 vols. (Philadelphia: J. B. Lippincott, 1877), 2: 747. The critic and future Dickens biographer John Forster, who was a friend of Forrest's enemy Macready, wrote that in *Richard III* Forrest "looked like a savage newly caught from out of the American backwoods" (cited in Moody, *Edwin Forrest*, 157).

147 Shattuck, *Shakespeare on the American Stage*, 66.

148 Katherine Molony Goodale, *Behind the Scenes with Edwin Booth* (Boston: Houghton Mifflin, 1931), 57–58.

149 "Chronology—the National Theater—1835–Present," October 19, 2010, http://thenationaldc.org/files/2013/10/timeline.pdf. The same information appears in Lee, Meersman, and Murphy, *Stage for a Nation*, 50.

150 *Washington Evening Star*, April 13, 1863, cited in *Lincoln Log*, April 11, 1863.

151 Carpenter, *Six Months at the White House*, 52.

152 James G. Randall, *Last Full Measure* (New York: Dodd, Mead, 1955), 378.

153 Ronald C. White, *A. Lincoln: A Biography* (New York: Random House, 2009), 5.

154 Horace White, "Abraham Lincoln in 1854," *Transactions* 1908, no. 13 (1909): 32, cited in Waldo Warder Braden, *Abraham Lincoln: Public Speaker* (Baton Rouge: Louisiana State University Press, 1988), 99.

155 Carl Schurz, Agathe Schurz, Marianne Schurz, and Carl Lincoln Schurz, *The Reminiscences of Carl Schurz*, 3 vols. (New York: McClure, 1907), 2: 93

156 Herndon and Weik, *Herndon's Lincoln*, 249.

157 *Daily National Intelligencer*, March 5, 1861, cited, in part, in Ronald C. White, *The Eloquent President: A Portrait of Lincoln through His Words* (New York: Random House, 2005), 80.

158 Herndon and Weik, *Herndon's Lincoln*, 248.

159 *Cincinnati Daily Commercial*, September 19, 1859, cited in Braden, *Abraham Lincoln*, 97.

160 *New York Tribune*, February 28, 1860.

161 Herndon and Weik, *Herndon's Lincoln*, 194.

162 Ibid., 394.

163 Ibid., 389.

164 Ibid., 236, 221.

165 Wilson et al., *Herndon's Informants*, 485–486.

166. Isaac N. Arnold, *The Life of Abraham Lincoln* (Chicago: Jansen, McClurg, 1885), 444.

167 "Recollections of one who studied law with Lincoln," in Ward, *Abraham Lincoln*, 200–206, 203.

168 Josiah Bushnell Grinnell, *Men and Events of Forty Years. Autobiographical Reminiscences of an Active Career from 1850 to 1891*, ed. Henry W. Parker (Boston: D. Lothrop, 1891), 173.

169 "He was a good Mimic in Words & Jestures," Abner Y. Ellis told Herndon (Wilson et al., *Herndon's Informants*, 102, 161). See also Burlingame, *Abraham Lincoln*, 1: 41.

170 Carpenter, *Six Months at the White House*, 52.

171 *Remarks on Mr. John Kemble's Performance of Hamlet and Richard the Third* (London: 1802), cited in John Scott Colley, *Richard's Himself Again: A Stage History of Richard III* (New York: Greenwood Press, 1992), 46.

172 Lincoln to Hackett, in *CW* 6: 392.

CHAPTER 4. LINCOLN'S FALSTAFF: JAMES H. HACKETT

1 William Osborn Stoddard, *Inside the White House in War Times: Memoirs and Reports of Lincoln's Secretary*, ed. Michael Burlingame (Lincoln: University of Nebraska Press, 2000), 105–106.

2 James H. Hackett to Abraham Lincoln, Friday, March 20, 1863, Abraham Lincoln Papers, series 1, General Correspondence, 1833–1916, Library of Congress. These letters are digitized and provided with transcripts online; see http://www.loc.gov/manuscripts/?q=James+Hackett&sp=1 (hereafter Lincoln Papers, Library of Congress).

3 Abraham Lincoln, *The Collected Works of Abraham Lincoln*, ed. Roy Prentice Basler, 11 vols. (New Brunswick, N.J.: Rutgers University Press, 1953–1990), 6: 392. Hereafter cited as *CW*.

4 "I went with [the president] to the Soldiers' Home & he read Shakespeare to me, the end of Henry VI and the beginning of Richard III till my heavy eye-lids caught his considerate notice & he sent me to bed." John Hay, *Inside Lincoln's White House: The Complete Civil War Diary of John Hay*, ed. Michael Burlingame and John R. T. Ettlinger (Carbondale: Southern Illinois University Press, 1999), 75–76.

5 James H. Hackett to Abraham Lincoln, September 4, 1863, Lincoln Papers, Library of Congress.

6 James H. Hackett to Abraham Lincoln, October 3, 1863, Lincoln Papers, Library of Congress.

7 "Who can remember the names of *any* American actors of the nineteenth century, except perhaps Edwin Booth and his notorious brother, John Wilkes?" Robert Gottlieb, review of three books on Joseph Jefferson, *New York Review of Books*, October 22, 2009, 57.

8 For a thorough discussion of Hackett's career, see John Jerome Sommers, "James H. Hackett: The Profile of a Player" (Ph.D. diss., University of Iowa, 1966). Francis Hodge's *Yankee Theatre: The Image of America on the Stage, 1825–1850* (Austin: University of Texas Press, 1964) is concerned primarily with Hackett's portrayal of American "types."

9 Joseph Norton Ireland, *Records of the New York Stage: From 1750 to 1860* (New York: T. H. Morrell, 1866), 473.

10 Don B. Wilmeth and C. W. E. Bigsby, eds., *The Cambridge History of American Theatre*, 3 vols. (Cambridge: Cambridge University Press, 2006), 1: 344.

11 Ibid.

12 Hodge, *Yankee Theatre*, 123.

13 See Esther Cloudman Dunn, *Shakespeare in America* (New York: Macmillan, 1939), 160.

14 "[John Barnes] saw himself aped by his associate to a startling degree; every motion, every intonation of the voice, every little vagary in costume, was so well studied as to defy detection." Montrose Jonas Moses, *Famous Actor-Families in America* (New York: T. Y. Crowell, 1906), 147.

15 See Shakespeare, *Oxberry's 1822 Edition of King Richard III, with Descriptive Notes Recording Edmund Kean's Performance Made by James Hackett*, ed. W. Oxberry; reprinted in facsimile and edited with an introduction and notes by Alan Seymour Downer (London: Society for Theatre Research, 1959). Downer cites a review from the *New York Evening Post* that reported that Hackett achieved "a success which exceeded even the anticipation of his friends" (ibid., xiii).

16 Charles H. Shattuck, *Shakespeare on the American Stage: From the Hallams to Edwin Booth* (Washington, D.C.: Folger Shakespeare Library, 1976), 59.

17 Ibid., 59.

18 *North American and United States Gazette* (Philadelphia), January 28, 1863.

19 *New York Morning Herald*, March 30, 1840.

20 His Richard, presented in New Orleans in 1843, was described by a critic as "a horrid abortion." *New York Herald*, March 7, 1843.

21 James Henry Hackett, *Notes and Comments upon Certain Plays and Actors of Shakespeare with Criticisms and Correspondence* (New York: Carleton, 1863), 87.

22 "Hackett's whole career," as one writer has noted, "in its international aspects, its combination of acting and critical writing, marks a new stage in Shakespearean prestige" (Dunn, *Shakespeare in America*, 150).

23 See the *New York Spectator*, February 1, 1828; and *New York Herald*, December 6, 1860. Edwin Booth, together with his brothers Junius Brutus Jr. and John Wilkes, acted in a special performance of *Julius Caesar* to raise funds for the statue. For an account of the placing of the cornerstone for the monument, see "The Shakespeare Tercentenary; Interesting Commemorative Exercises," *New York Times*, April 24, 1864.

24 James Henry Hackett, "Merchant Princes and Parvenus," *Crayon* 6, no. 2 (February 1859): 40.

25 It must have been particularly galling to Hackett to read that "Mr. Hill's performance of Solomon Swap, . . . if not equal to Hackett's, was highly amusing, and entitled him to strong approbation. . . . His *militia training* [another of Hackett's pieces] is, we are informed, equal to Hackett's." *Washington, D.C., Daily National Intelligencer*, December 31, 1832.

26 *Morning Herald*, September 7, 1837. Hackett got his injunction; Hill simply changed the character's name to Solomon Gundy, evidently the original of Solomon Swap. *Morning Herald*, September 9, 1837.

27 "Court Calendar," *Boston Daily Atlas*, May 3, 1847.

28 "A bill was presented by James H. Hackett, as one of the lessees of the Astor Place Opera House, for damages sustained in the riot of the 10th of May, 1849; also 23 days' rent, payable by the lessee to the owners of the Opera House, one week of which time the premises were taken exclusive possession of by the police authorities. . . . For breach of contract with Mr. Macready, in consequence of the house being rendered unfit for his performances, for 17 nights, averaging perspectively

at least $900 per night." After various deductions, Hackett asked the council for $5,005.29. *New York Herald*, June 5, 1849. In his brief "autobiography," written to be published on his death by the *New York Post*, Hackett quotes a figure of $4,400, "which sum, owing to the fact that then (1849) no law existed in New York to indemnify sufferers by riots, was a total and irrecoverable loss." *New York Evening Post*, December 28, 1871.

29 *New York Times*, December 29, 1871.

30 "Mr. Hackett to His Theatrical Friends," *Boston Courier*, February 1, 1841.

31 Shattuck, *Shakespeare on the American Stage*, 62.

32 There may be an echo of "Baron" Hackett in Mark Twain's two supposed Shakespearean actors, the King and the Duke, in *Adventures of Huckleberry Finn*, published in 1884.

33 Hackett, *Notes and Comments*, 67.

34 Ibid., 89.

35 *CW* 6: 393n.

36 Hackett, *Notes and Comments*, 67–68. Adams, it should be noted, was pleased by Hackett's attentions, writing in his diary, "Mr. Hackett, in his letter mentions . . . that he has very recently heard of an analysis by me of the tragedy of 'Othello,' and enquires where he can procure it. This extension of my fame is more tickling to my vanity than it was to be elected president of the United States." Cited in Gary V. Wood, *Heir to the Fathers: John Quincy Adams and the Spirit of Constitutional Government* (Lanham, Md.: Lexington Books, 2004), 83.

37 Roy Basler, *A Touchstone for Greatness: Essays, Addresses, and Occasional Pieces about Abraham Lincoln* (Westport, Conn.: Greenwood Press, 1973), 209.

38 *New York Herald*, September 17, 1861, cited in ibid., 210.

39 Basler reproduces the column; the original clipping that Hackett sent to Lincoln is in the Sloan Collection, Library of Congress, Lincoln Papers, Library of Congress. A brief analysis of the episode can be found online: "Abraham Lincoln To James H. Hackett, November 2, 1863," YouTube video by Andrew Willwok, posted September 24, 2013, https://www.youtube.com/watch?v=cMK4FfkdA9c.

40 James H. Hackett to Abraham Lincoln, October 22, 1863, Lincoln Papers, Library of Congress.

41 *CW* 6: 559. In what may be his earliest published remarks, Lincoln wrote, "I have been too familiar with disappointments to be very much chagrined" ("Communication to the People of Sangamo County," *CW* 1: 9).

42 *New York Times*, October 2, 1865.

43 See, for example, this note: "Seized upon by political enemies, the letter thus distributed was soon carried in the newspapers with sarcastic comments on the president's lack of critical sense" (*CW* 6: 393).

44 Albert Furtwangler, *Assassin on Stage: Brutus, Hamlet, and the Death of Lincoln* (Urbana: University of Illinois Press, 1991), 70.

45 See Robert S. Harper, *Lincoln and the Press* (New York: McGraw-Hill, 1951), 320; and Harold Holzer, *Lincoln and the Power of the Press: The War for Public Opinion* (New York: Simon and Schuster, 2014), passim.

46 *Living Age*, November 21, 1863.

47 *San Francisco Daily Evening Bulletin*, October 14, 1863.

48 *Chicago Tribune*, September 22, 1863. There is no evidence that King James ever wrote to Shakespeare.

49 *New Haven Daily Palladium*, September 23, 1863.

50 One newspaper published a racist parody of Lincoln's letter with the heading "The King of Dahomy to Mr. Christy." *(Madison) Wisconsin Daily Patriot*, October 15, 1863. George Christy was a famous blackface minstrel.

51 *Savannah (Ga.) Daily Morning News*, October 28, 1863.

52 *Richmond (Va.) Sentinel*, November 4, 1863.

53 Ibid.

54 *Mobile (Ala.) Daily Tribune*, March 26, 1864. For similar comments by an Illinois Democrat, see the *Illinois State Register*, October 2, 1863.

55 James H. Hackett to Abraham Lincoln, November 14, 1863, Lincoln Papers, Library of Congress.

56 James H. Hackett to Abraham Lincoln, December 11, 1863, Lincoln Papers, Library of Congress.

57 John Hay records in his diary that he accompanied Lincoln to a performance on December 15, but unless Lincoln went twice, it is very likely that Hay got the date wrong. See the *Daily National Republican*, December 15, 1863: "Falstaff will be played by Hackett to-night. . . . The President with numerous other distinguished gentlemen occupied seats and boxes last evening." A handbill advertising Hackett's December 14 appearance announces, "This evening the performance will be honored by the presence of President Lincoln." Brown University Library, http://library.brown.edu/jpegs/1188248112609375.jpg.

58 See Arthur Colby Sprague, "Falstaff Hackett," *Theater Notebook* 9 (April–June, 1955): 61–67, 61. A promptbook of *Merry Wives* preserved at the Folger Shakespeare Library (MW 25) includes a newspaper clipping informing the reader that "Mr. Hackett has carefully expunged from his acting copy . . . every word and phrase deemed coarse, and hence the most refined can take no exception to the text as spoken by Mr. Hackett."

59 Sprague, "Falstaff Hackett," 63.

60 Sommers, "James H. Hackett," 345–346.

61 Josiah Bushnell Grinnell, *Men and Events of Forty Years: Autobiographical Reminiscences of an Active Career from 1850 to 1890*, ed. Henry W. Parker (Boston: D. Lothrop, 1891), 173–174. This sounds a bit too circumstantial as reported conversation, but the essence may be accurate.

62 Shattuck, *Shakespeare on the American Stage*, 62. The songs, evidently, were not always left out: Odell takes note of an 1845 performance in which Hackett is supported by a "Miss Moss as Anne (of course to sing the music now encrusted on the part)." See George Clinton Densmore Odell, *Annals of the New York Stage*, 15 vols. (New York: Columbia University Press, 1927–1949), 5: 165.

63 Hay, *Inside Lincoln's White House*, 127–128.

64 Letter from Robert Todd Lincoln to James H. Hackett, March 17, 1871, the Alfred Withal Stern Collection of Lincolniana, Library of Congress, Rare Book and Special Collections Division.

65 Arthur Colby Sprague, *Shakespeare and the Actors: The Stage Business in His Plays (1660–1905)* (New York: Russell, 1963), 87.

66 John Russell Brown, in *Shakespeare in Performance: An Introduction through Six Major Plays*, ed. John Russell Brown (New York: Harcourt Brace Jovanovich, 1976), 154.

67 For evidence that Hackett had, at one point, intended to restore this scene in performance, see Sprague, "Falstaff Hackett," 61; and Sommers, "James H. Hackett," 348–349.

68 A similar account can be found in David Homer Bates, *Lincoln in the Telegraph Office: Recollections of the United States Military Telegraph Corps during the Civil War* (New York: Century, 1907), 223–224.

69 *Boston Daily Atlas*, September 20, 1852.

70 Hackett, *Notes and Comments*, 324–325. On a blank page in an 1840 promptbook (but perhaps written much later) at the Folger Library ("I Henry IV, 5"), Hackett notes, "It is only as the performer's effects upon the stage are reflected upon his own mind by his audience, that he, who undertakes to personate this part, can confirm the value of his own perceptions, learn to correct his errors in taste, judgment or execution, acquire the necessary ease, give unrestrained vent to his humour & thus gradually approach the perfection of his own capability. J.H.H."

71 Samuel Johnson, *Samuel Johnson on Shakespeare*, ed. William K. Wimsatt (New York: Hill and Wang, 1960), 89.

72 Ibid. Hackett's Falstaff in *Merry Wives*, according to Charles Shattuck, "for all of its lustiness and strong jollification . . . was an example of wickedness set out to be condemned." Shakespeare, *The Merry Wives of Windsor*, edited by Charles Jasper Sisson and Charles Harlen Shattuck (New York: Dell, 1966), 28.

73 Cited in James C. Bulman, "Performing the Conflated Text of *Henry IV*: The Fortunes of *Part Two*," in *Shakespeare Survey* 63 (2010): 89–101, 90.

74 Maurice Morgann, *Essay on the Dramatic Character of Sir John Falstaff* (London, 1777), cited in Scott McMillin, *Henry IV, Part One* (Manchester, U.K.: Manchester University Press, 1991), 6.

75 Hackett, *Notes and Comments*, 175.

76 George William Curtis, Editor's Easy Chair, *Harper's New Monthly Magazine*, August, 1867, 393–397, 395. "Unctuous" is a favorite word of critics attempting to characterize Falstaff performances. One critic found that the English actor Samuel Phelps was superior to Hackett despite having "far less unctuousness." Cited in Shakespeare, *Henry the Fourth, Part I*, ed. Samuel Burdett Hemingway (Philadelphia: J. B. Lippincott, 1936), 491. But then, Phelps, like Hackett, was "both noted for 'unctuousity' and pronounced lacking in 'unction.'" See Shakespeare, *The First Part of King Henry IV*, ed. Herbert Weil and Judith Weil, updated ed. (Cambridge: Cambridge University Press, 2007), 46.

77 Shattuck, *Shakespeare on the American Stage*, 59.

78 *New York Morning Herald*, May 16, 1838.

79 *Washington, D.C., Daily National Intelligencer*, January 28, 1839.

80 *New York Herald*, September 27, 1841.

81 All reprinted in the *Boston Daily Atlas*, March 25, 1845.

82 Hackett reproduces this review himself, from the *London Times*, June 27, 1851 in *Notes and Comments* (328).

83 Hackett, *Notes and Comments*, 325.

84 Hackett reprints a highly laudatory "Sketch of James H. Hackett" by Charles J. Foster (originally published in *Wilkes's Spirit of the Times*, February, 1862), from which these phrases are taken (Hackett, *Notes and Comments*, 329–348, 333).

85 *Daily National Intelligencer*, December 17, 1863.

86 Curtis, Editor's Easy Chair, 395.

87 There were few Falstaffs of note in either England or America in the nineteenth century; as a consequence, the "literary Falstaff . . . the Falstaff of humane wit and courage, flourished in the vacuum created by lack-lustre and unsubtle stage performances." David Bevington, introduction to *Henry IV, Part I*, ed. David M. Bevington (Oxford: Oxford University Press, 1987), 75.

88 Stoddard, *Inside the White House in War Times*, 107.

89 Ibid., 190.

90 Bates, *Lincoln in the Telegraph Office*, 223.

91 Hay, *Inside Lincoln's White House*, 128. "Orson Welles, playing Falstaff in *Chimes at Midnight*, reads the disputed line Lincoln's way, not Hay's," Garry Wills writes. "There was very little Hay, or any other man, could teach Lincoln about how to milk a comic remark for maximum effect." Wills, *Lincoln at Gettysburg: The Words That Remade America* (New York: Simon and Schuster, 1992), 152. Hay is technically right, but Lincoln's reading has more flair.

92 John Edwin McDonough. In *Team of Rivals*, McDonough is identified as the actor Lincoln saw in *King Lear*, but that was John M. McCullough (see chapter 5 below).

93 The conversation was recalled by Congressman William Kelly; see *Recollected Words of Abraham Lincoln*, comp. and ed. Don E. Fehrenbacher and Virginia Fehrenbacher (Stanford: Stanford University Press, 1996), 277.

94 James H. Hackett to Abraham Lincoln, February 4, 1864, Lincoln Papers, Library of Congress.

95 A popular lecturer, Bayard Taylor—poet, essayist, journalist, and diplomat—was especially well known for his travel writings; the Lincolns went to hear him talk about Russia. Taylor, who had lectured in Springfield in the 1850s, had interviewed Lincoln for the *New York Tribune* early in the president's first term. See *The Lincoln Log: A Daily Chronology of the Life of Abraham Lincoln*, http://www.thelincolnlog.org/Home.aspx, April 18, 1861.

96 James H. Hackett to Abraham Lincoln, March 9, 1864, Lincoln Papers, Library of Congress.

97 Ibid.

98 James H. Hackett to Abraham Lincoln, July 1, 1864, Lincoln Papers, Library of Congress.

99 James H. Hackett to Abraham Lincoln, July 19, 1864, Lincoln Papers, Library of Congress.

100 James H. Hackett to Abraham Lincoln, August 1, 1864, Lincoln Papers, Library of Congress.

101 On hearing that his father might want to marry again, Hackett's oldest son, John, wrote to a younger brother, "I would pity in advance any woman who would become his wife, for his disposition, naturally unequal, has of late become peevish, if not malicious and tyrannical" (cited in Sommers, "James H. Hackett," 402).

102 James H. Hackett to Abraham Lincoln, August 2, 1864, Lincoln Papers, Library of Congress.

103 James H. Hackett to Abraham Lincoln, January 1, 1865, Lincoln Papers, Library of Congress.

104 *Boston Daily Advertiser*, January 18, 1865.

105 Hackett's letter to Hay is in the John Hay Manuscript Collection at Brown University (series 2, Correspondence, reel F5701: 5), and is cited in Ulysses S. Grant, *The Papers of Ulysses S. Grant*, ed. John Y. Simon, 32 vols. (Carbondale: Southern Illinois University Press, 1967), 21: 480.

106 Cited in Sommers, "James H. Hackett," 405.

107 There is extant a calling card of John Hay's on which Hay has written the following: "Mr. Hay called at the request of the President to say that the President will be pleased to see Mr. Hackett either this evening or tomorrow morning, or at any time when Mr. Hackett may find it convenient to wait upon him." The Alfred Withal Stern Collection of Lincolniana, Library of Congress, Rare Book and Special Collections Division. Unfortunately, there is no date on the card.

108 Noah Brooks, "Personal Reminiscences of Lincoln," *Scribner's Monthly*, March 1878, 673–681, 675; see also Noah Brooks, *Lincoln Observed: Civil War Dispatches of Noah Brooks*, ed. Michael Burlingame (Baltimore: Johns Hopkins University Press, 1998), 157.

109 "A hundred times this experience was repeated." Hay adds, "A man would be introduced to the President whose disposition and talk were agreeable; he took pleasure in his conversation for two or three interviews and then this congenial person would ask for some favor impossible to grant, and go away in bitterness of spirit. It is a cross that every President must bear." Hay, *At Lincoln's Side: John Hay's Civil War Correspondence and Selected Writings*, ed. Michael Burlingame (Carbondale: Southern Illinois University Press, 2000), 136.

110 Hay, *Inside Lincoln's White House*, 128.

111 Chas. H. Haswell, *Reminiscences of New York by an Octogenarian* (New York: Harper and Brothers, 1896), 185.

112 *Frank Leslie's Illustrated Newspaper*, January 20, 1872, 293.

113 Letter from Robert Todd Lincoln to James H. Hackett, March 17, 1871, Alfred Withal Stern Collection of Lincolniana, Library of Congress, Rare Book and Special Collections Division.

CHAPTER 5. PRESIDENT LINCOLN AND THE GREAT SHAKESPEAREANS

1 "Sometimes he would run away to a lecture or concert or theatre for the sake of a little rest." John Hay to Herndon, September 5, 1866, in *Herndon's Informants: Letters, Interviews, and Statements about Abraham Lincoln*, by Douglas L. Wilson et al. (Urbana: University of Illinois Press, 1998), 331. Hay reports an amusing

instance of combining duty with pleasure: "I went last night to a Sacred Concert of profane music at Ford's. . . . The Tycoon [Lincoln] & I occupied private box & (both of us) carried on a hefty flirtation with the Monk girls in the flies." John Hay to John Nicolay, June 20, 1864, John Hay Papers, box 14, reel 10, General Correspondence, 1856–1905, Manuscript Division, Library of Congress. Ada, Minnie, and Jennie Monk were artistes (evidently sisters) who appeared at both Ford's and Grover's, mainly in popular entertainments.

2 *Daily National Republican*, October 7, 1863.

3 Ibid.

4 *New York Herald*, October 9, 1863. See also the *Washington Evening Star*, October 6, 1863, and October 7, 1863, and *The Lincoln Log: A Daily Chronology of the Life of Abraham Lincoln*, http://www.thelincolnlog.org/Home.aspx (hereafter *Lincoln Log*), October 6, 1863.

5 *Daily National Republican*, November 14, 1863.

6 *Daily National Republican*, October 19, 1863.

7 See David R. Barbee, "The Musical Mr. Lincoln," *Abraham Lincoln Quarterly* 5, no. 8 (December 1949): 435–451.

8 Three days later, Williams, in a letter now lost, asked a favor from the president. Lincoln's response to Williams is dated February 27, 1863: "My Dear Sir, Your note of today is received. I do not think I can put your nephew among the first ten appointments [to the Naval Academy] now soon to be made. I really wish to oblige you; but the best I can do is to keep the papers, and try to find a place before long. Yours truly, A. LINCOLN." Lincoln, *The Collected Works of Abraham Lincoln*, ed. Roy Prentice Basler, 11 vols. (New Brunswick, N.J.: Rutgers University Press, 1953), 6: 120. Hereafter cited as *CW*.

9 Douglas McDermott, "Structure and Management in the American Theatre from the Beginning to 1870," in *The Cambridge History of American Theatre*, ed. Don B. Wilmeth and C. W. E. Bigsby, 3 vols. (Cambridge: Cambridge University Press, 2006), 1: 192. On at least one occasion in 1863, Lincoln attended a Shakespeare recitation at a private home. Samuel Peter Heintzelman Papers, Journals, box 5, reel 7, Manuscript Division, Library of Congress.

10 Leonard Grover to Abraham Lincoln, March 24, 1863, Abraham Lincoln Papers, Library of Congress, http://www.memory.loc.gov/cgi-bin/query/P?mal:3:./temp/~ammem_mjL2::.

11 William Winter, *Life and Art of Edwin Booth* (New York: Greenwood Press, 1968), 147–148.

12 Cited in Edwin Francis Edgett, *Edward Loomis Davenport: A Biography* (New York: Dunlap Society, 1901), 62.

13 *New York Daily Tribune*, May 17, 1855.

14 *North American and United States Gazette*, November 10, 1862.

15 "Death of E. L. Davenport: The History of One of the Brightest Ornaments of the American Stage," *New York Times*, September 2, 1877.

16 *Daily National Republican*, October 13, 1863.

17 Clara Morris, *Life on the Stage: My Personal Experiences and Recollections* (New York: McClure, Phillips, 1901), 185, cited in Charles Shattuck, *Shakespeare on*

the American Stage: From the Hallams to Edwin Booth (Washington, D.C.: Folger Shakespeare Library, 1976), 122.

18 *Daily National Republican*, March 25, 1863, 2nd ed.

19 *New York Daily Tribune*, May 17, 1855. The reviewer writes primarily of Davenport's performance, which he does not much like.

20 *San Francisco Daily Evening Bulletin*, June 9, 1868.

21 *Daily National Republican*, October 10, 1863.

22 *Daily National Republican*, October 7, 1863.

23 Ibid. The reviewer only regretted "the heathenish conduct of boys in the gallery, who must be taught to keep still. However, on an opening night perfect order can hardly be expected in Washington, where a handsome theatre is such a novelty that it makes the juveniles wild."

24 William Osborn Stoddard, *Inside the White House in War Times: Memoirs and Reports of Lincoln's Secretary*, ed. Michael Burlingame (Lincoln: University of Nebraska Press, 2000), 189.

25 *New York Daily Tribune*, May 22, 1855. A column immediately adjoining this review reports on the veto (overturned) of a personal liberty bill passed by the Massachusetts Legislature in opposition to provisions of the Fugitive Slave Acts.

26 *New York Herald*, December 26, 1861.

27 *Atheneum*, May 21, 1881, cited in Shattuck, *Shakespeare on the American Stage*, 131.

28 See Joyce Green MacDonald, "Acting Black: 'Othello,' 'Othello' Burlesques, and the Performance of Blackness," *Theatre Journal* 46 (May 1994): 231–249.

29 Sylvan Barnet, "*Othello* on Stage and Screen," in Shakespeare, *The Tragedy of Othello: The Moor of Venice*, ed. Alvin B. Kernan (New York: Signet Classic, 1998), 220–221.

30 Charles B. Lower, "Othello as Black on Southern Stages, Then and Now," in *Shakespeare in the South: Essays on Performance*, ed. Philip C. Kolin (Jackson: University Press of Mississippi, 1983), 199–228, 202, 206.

31 Ibid., 211.

32 Mary Preston, *Studies in Shakspeare: A Book of Essays* (Philadelphia: Claxton, Remson and Haffelfinger, 1869), 71.

33 *New York Daily Tribune*, May 22, 1855.

34 Charles Lamb, *The Portable Charles Lamb*, ed. John Mason Brown (New York: Viking Press, 1949), 299. Kitty Molony, who was a member of Edwin Booth's acting company in the 1880s, remembered once saying to the actor, "You are the first Othello I have seen, Mr. Booth, whose skin does not make me shudder at the very thought of Desdemona's marriage." Katherine Molony Goodale, *Behind the Scenes with Edwin Booth* (Boston: Houghton Mifflin, 1931), 208.

35 John Quincy Adams, quoted in James Henry Hackett, *Notes and Comments upon Certain Plays and Actors of Shakespeare with Criticisms and Correspondence* (New York: Carleton, 1863), 225, 224.

36 James R. Andreas, "Othello's African American Progeny," *South Atlantic Review* 57, no. 4 (November 1992): 39–57, 41.

37 Woodrow L. Holbein, "Shakespeare in Charleston, 1800–1860," in Kolin, *Shakespeare in the South*, 88–111, 98.

38 Lower, "Othello as Black on Southern Stages," 201. "By the end of the ante bellum period," however, "Othello had to be played as near white, or not at all." James H. Dormon, *Theater in the Ante Bellum South, 1815–1861* (Chapel Hill: University of North Carolina Press, 1967), 277.

39 A story is told of an 1822 performance of *Othello* in Baltimore "during which a soldier on guard duty, 'seeing Othello . . . about to kill Desdemona, shouted "It will never be said that in my presence a confounded negro has killed a white woman!"' whereupon 'he fired his gun and broke the arm of the actor who was playing Othello.'" The actor playing Othello, of course, was white. Edward Pechter, *"Othello" and Interpretive Traditions* (Iowa City: University of Iowa Press, 2012), 12.

40 Joseph Leach, *Bright Particular Star: The Life and Times of Charlotte Cushman* (New Haven: Yale University Press, 1970), 44.

41 William Winter, *The Wallet of Time; Containing Personal, Biographical, and Critical Reminiscence of the American Theatre*, 2 vols. (New York: Moffat, Yard, 1913), 1: 160.

42 Walter Stahr, *Seward: Lincoln's Indispensable Man* (New York: Simon and Schuster, 2012), 381. See also David C. Mearns, "Charlotte Cushman's 'True and Faithful' Lincoln: Some Documents with Some Observations," *Lincoln Herald* 59, no. 2 (Summer 1957), 3–10.

43 Charlotte Cushman to [William H. Seward], July 9, 1861, Abraham Lincoln Papers, series 2, General Correspondence, 1858–1864, Library of Congress.

44 "Miss Cushman does not come until 4 o'clock, so it will be evening before I shall be able to bring her over to call upon you." William H. Seward to Abraham Lincoln, October 11, 1863, Abraham Lincoln Papers, Library of Congress, http://www.memory.loc.gov/cgi-bin/query/P?mal:1:./temp/~ammem_piBB::.

45 Heather S. Nathans, "Blood Will Have Blood: Violence, Slavery, and *Macbeth* in the Antebellum American Imagination," in *Weyward Macbeth: Intersections of Race and Performance*, ed. Scott L. Newstok and Ayanna Thompson (Basingstoke, U.K.: Palgrave Macmillan, 2010), 23–33, 33.

46 Charlotte Cushman Papers, box 18, Manuscript Division, Library of Congress.

47 *Daily National Republican*, October 19, 1863.

48 "Miss Charlotte Cushman, the first of American tragediennes, and whose talent has ridden safely on the tide of public favor, will visit [Ford's] theatre during tonight's performance [of Maggie Mitchell in *Fanchon the Cricket*]." *Daily National Republican*, October 12, 1863. Lincoln, according to the same article, was expected to attend but apparently did not; he saw Maggie Mitchell on October 30 (see *Lincoln Log*: "President and Mrs. Lincoln visit Ford's Theatre on occasion of Maggie Mitchell's benefit in performance of 'Fanchon, the Cricket.'" *Washington National Republican*, October 31, 1863; *Washington Star*, October 31, 1863).

49 *Daily National Republican*, October 12, 1863.

50 *North American and United States Gazette*, June 16, 1851.

51 *Daily Cleveland Herald*, December 4, 1857.

52 James Edward Murdoch and J. Bunting, *The Stage; or, Recollections of Actors and Acting from an Experience of Fifty Years* (Philadelphia: J. M. Stoddart, 1880), 240. A touch of professional jealousy emerges at several points in Murdoch's account of Cushman, as when he writes, "To a determined disposition to make the most of social advantages she added a fine tact in the management of people whom she considered necessary to her personal interests or professional advancement" (239).

53 George Vandenhoff and Henry Seymour Carleton, *Dramatic Reminiscences; or, Actors and Actresses in England and America* (London, 1860), 184.

54 Florence Marion Hall, "The Friendship of Edwin Booth and Julia Ward Howe," *New England Magazine*, November 1893, 315–321, 317.

55 *New York Times*, February 19, 1876.

56 Benjamin Brown French Papers, box 1, reel 3, 153, Manuscript Division, Library of Congress, http://lccn.loc.gov/mm80021550, cited in Alexander Nemerov, *Acting in the Night: Macbeth and the Places of the Civil War* (Berkeley: University of California Press, 2010), 12.

57 M. A. De Wolfe Howe and Annie Fields, *Memories of a Hostess: A Chronicle of Eminent Friendships, Drawn Chiefly from the Diaries of Mrs. James T. Fields* (Boston: Atlantic Monthly Press, 1922), 220.

58 Benjamin Brown French Papers, box 1, reel 3, 152–153, Manuscript Division, Library of Congress, cited in Nemerov, *Acting in the Night*, 95–96.

59 Benjamin B. French, *Witness to the Young Republic: A Yankee's Journal, 1828–1870*, ed. Donald B. Cole and John J. McDonough (Hanover, N.H.: University Press of New England, 1989), 58, entry for November 6, 1835.

60 Howe and Fields, *Memories of a Hostess*, 220.

61 *Daily National Republican*, March 25, 1863, 2nd ed.

62 *Boston Daily Atlas*, February 8, 1853.

63 *Advertiser*, January 20, 1858, cited in Mary Duggar Toulmin, "Shakespeare in Mobile, 1822–1861," in Kolin, *Shakespeare in the South*, 128–156, 152.

64 Dennis Bartholomeusz, *Macbeth and the Players* (Cambridge: Cambridge University Press, 1969), 193.

65 According to Noah Ludlow, a theater manager, "The public did not seem to appreciate the acting of Mr. Wallack, Sr., in his Shakesperian representations; but whenever he performed *Rolla, Don Cæsar de Bazan, Massaroni*, or any of his fine comedy characters, they came to see him act." N. M. Ludlow, *Dramatic Life As I Found It; A Record of Personal Experience, Etc.* (St. Louis, Mo.: G. I. Jones, 1880), 651.

66 "President Lincoln and Gen. Sickles at the Theatre," *Chicago Tribune*, October 21, 1863. This account was reprinted in Frazar Kirkland [Richard Miller Devens], *The Pictorial Book of Anecdotes and Incidents of the War of the Rebellion* (Hartford, Conn., 1866), 134, which is usually cited as the source.

67 *CW* 6: 524, cited in Nemerov, *Acting in the Night*, 60.

68 Civil War Trust, "Bristoe Station," http://www.civilwar.org/battlefields/bristoe-station.html.

69 Nemerov, *Acting in the Night*, 185. Nemerov's fascinating attempt to connect this performance of *Macbeth* with the Civil War people and events that coincide with it includes a good deal of highly speculative assumptions.

70 Jean H. Baker, *Mary Todd Lincoln* (New York: W. W. Norton, 1987), 147–148; Gay Smith, *Lady Macbeth in America: From the Stage to the White House* (New York: Palgrave Macmillan, 2010), 116.

71 Gay Smith, in her *Lady Macbeth in America*, places Mary Lincoln in the context of first ladies who have been seen as exerting undue influence on their husbands, though she does not directly compare her to Lady Macbeth.

72 Baker, *Mary Todd Lincoln*, 144.

73 William Henry Herndon and Jesse William Weik, *Herndon's Lincoln*, ed. Douglas L. Wilson and Rodney O. Davis, Knox College Lincoln Studies Center series ([Galesburg, Ill.]: Knox College Lincoln Studies Center, 2006), 135, cited in Michael Burlingame, *The Inner World of Abraham Lincoln* (Urbana: University of Illinois Press, 1994), 308.

74 William Hayes Ward, ed., *Abraham Lincoln: Tributes from His Associates, Reminiscences of Soldiers, Statesmen and Citizens* (New York: T. Y. Crowell, 1895), 32.

75 Burlingame, *Inner World of Abraham Lincoln*, 311.

76 Adam Badeau, *Grant in Peace: From Appomattox to Mount McGregor, a Personal Memoir* (Hartford, Conn.: S. S. Scranton, 1887), 355; see *Macbeth*, act 1, scene 3.

77 Catherine Clinton, *Mrs. Lincoln: A Life* (New York: Harper, 2009), 191.

78 Leach, *Bright Particular Star*, 324.

79 *New York Herald*, September 29, 1857.

80 See John F. Andrews, "Shakespeare Aspects of Lincoln Assassination," interview by Liane Hansen, *Weekend Edition Sunday*, National Public Radio, March 15, 1992.

81 For the sake of a weak verbal joke, a Southern newspaper notice joined Lincoln and Edwin Booth long before there would have been any reason to make a connection: "Edwin Booth has arrived in London, and has appeared at the Haymarket in the character of Iago. Lincoln will probably appear shortly in the character of I am gone—from Washington." *Atlanta Daily Constitutionalist*, September 29, 1861.

82 "Just here the phonograph expert came with his machine. . . . I recited *Othello's* and *Hamlet's* speeches for you; . . . but, of course, it is impossible (for me, at least) to recite with full feeling and warmth of expression in cold blood, as it were; still, the effect is nearly perfect." Edwin Booth to Edwina Booth Grossmann, March 19, 1890, in Edwin Booth and Edwina Booth Grossmann, *Edwin Booth: Recollections by His Daughter, Edwina Booth Grossmann, and Letters to Her and to His Friends* (New York: Century, 1894), 107. Only the *Othello* recording appears to have survived.

83 *Daily National Republican*, February 13, 1864, 2nd ed.

84 Tice L. Miller, *Entertaining the Nation: American Drama in the Eighteenth and Nineteenth Centuries* (Carbondale: Southern Illinois University Press, 2007), 51.

85 H. J. Oliver, in Shakespeare, *The Taming of the Shrew*, ed. H. J. Oliver (Oxford: Clarendon Press, 1982), 2.

86 See Leonard Grover to Abraham Lincoln, Abraham Lincoln Papers, Library of Congress, February 20 and February 25, 1864.

87 *Daily National Republican*, February 26, 1864.

88 *Daily National Republican*, March 1, 1864; see also the *Evening Star*, March 2, 1864: "Mr. Grover announces that this play is produced at the request of President and Mrs. Lincoln, who desires [*sic*] to see Booth in the character of the melancholy prince. It may, therefore, be expected that a brilliant audience will be in attendance."

89 H. L. Mencken, quoted in Walter J. Meserve, "Winter, William," in *American National Biography*, ed. John A. Garraty and Mark C. Carnes, 24 vols. (New York: Oxford University Press, 1999), 23: 658.

90 Winter, *Life and Art of Edwin Booth*, 253.

91 William Winter, *Shakespeare on the Stage*, first series (New York: Moffat, Yard, 1911), 340.

92 Ibid.

93 Lucia Gilbert Calhoun, "Edwin Booth," *Galaxy*, January 1869, 77–87, 78.

94 Winter, *Shakespeare on the Stage*, 344.

95 Charles Harlen Shattuck, *The Hamlet of Edwin Booth* (Urbana: University of Illinois Press, 1969), xvi.

96 Mary Isabella Stone, *Edwin Booth's Performances: The Mary Isabella Stone Commentaries*, ed. Daniel J. Watermeier (Ann Arbor, Mich.: UMI Research Press, 1990), 109.

97 Thomas Hamner, quoted in *Hamlet: A New Variorum Edition of Shakespeare*, ed. Horace Howard Furness, 2 vols. (New York: Dover Publications, 1963), 1: 281.

98 "Amusements," *New York Times*, November 27, 1860.

99 Shattuck, *Hamlet of Edwin Booth*, 37.

100 Ibid., 218.

101 See William Winter, ed., *William Shakespeare's Tragedy of Hamlet* (New York: Printed for William Winter, by Francis Hart, 1879), 80–82, online at the Furness collection, University of Pennsylvania, http://sceti.library.upenn.edu/sceti /printedbooksNew/index.cfm?textID=hamlet_booth&PagePosition=1.

102 "The Playhouses," *Illustrated London News*, November 13, 1880, 471.

103 Otis Skinner, Edwin Booth, and Mary Devlin Booth, *The Last Tragedian: Booth Tells His Own Story* (New York: Dodd, Mead, 1939), 197.

104 Stone, *Edwin Booth's Performances*, 2.

105 Adam Badeau, "Edwin Booth On and Off the Stage," *McClure's Magazine*, August 1893, 255–267, 258.

106 William Winter, *Shakespeare on the Stage*, 347.

107 Johann Wolfgang von Goethe, *The Collected Works*, vol. 9, *Wilhelm Meister's Apprenticeship*, ed. and trans. Eric A. Blackall in cooperation with Victor Lange (Princeton: Princeton University Press, 1995), 146.

108 From a review of the 100-nights *Hamlet*, cited in George Clinton Densmore Odell, *Annals of the New York Stage*, 15 vols. (New York: Columbia University Press, 1927–1949), 7: 640.

109 *New York Times*, September 22, 1863.

110 *New York Times*, January 7, 1870.

111 *Daily National Intelligencer*, February 17, 1864.

112 *Daily National Intelligencer*, February 22, 1864.

113 Tori Haring-Smith, *From Farce to Metadrama: A Stage History of "The Taming of the Shrew," 1594–1983* (Westport, Conn.: Greenwood Press, 1985), 37.

114 Charlotte Endymion Porter, *Shakespeariana: A Critical and Contemporary Review of Shakesperian Literature* (Philadelphia, 1883), 125.

115 Henry Austin Clapp, *Reminiscences of a Dramatic Critic: With an Essay on the Art of Henry Irving* (Boston: Houghton, Mifflin, 1902), 135.

116 Winter, *Life and Art of Edwin Booth*, 199.

117 "Mr. Edwin Booth as Shylock," *New York Evening Post*, February 13, 1861.

118 Calhoun, "Edwin Booth," 84–85.

119 Booth and Grossmann, *Edwin Booth: Recollections by His Daughter*, 83.

120 "The Playhouses," *Illustrated London News*, March 26, 1881, 291.

121 Noah Brooks, "Personal Reminiscences of Lincoln," *Scribner's Monthly*, March 1878, 673–681, 675.

122 Letter to Rev. Mr. Ewer, November 11, 1877, in Booth and Grossmann, *Edwin Booth: Recollections by His Daughter*, 89–90.

123 Winter, *Life and Art of Edwin Booth*, 210.

124 John Scott Colley, *Richard's Himself Again: A Stage History of Richard III* (New York: Greenwood Press, 1992), 112.

125 *The Arcadian*, January 12, 1878, cited in ibid., 111.

126 Calhoun, "Edwin Booth," 83.

127 Odell, *Annals*, 6: 527, cited from *New York Herald*, May 5, 1856.

128 Winter, *Shakespeare on the Stage*, 111.

129 John Ranken Towse, *Sixty Years of the Theater: An Old Critic's Memories* (New York: Funk and Wagnalls, 1916), 192.

130 Winter, *Life and Art of Edwin Booth*, 209.

131 Colley, *Richard's Himself Again*, 109.

132 Forrest had appeared at Ford's Theatre for a week or more in 1862, but it is unlikely Lincoln saw him at that time. For the evidence that Lincoln saw Forrest in *Richard III*, see chapter 3 above.

133 *Spirit of the Times*, June 14, 1877, cited in Richard Moody, *Edwin Forrest, First Star of the American Stage* (New York: Alfred A. Knopf, 1960), 396.

134 Orville Hickman Browning, *The Diary of Orville Hickman Browning*, ed. Theodore Calvin Pease and James G. Randall, 2 vols., Illinois State Historical Library Collections, vols. 20, 22 (Springfield: Illinois State Historical Library, 1925–1933), 1: 216.

135 *Chicago Tribune*, September 17, 1867.

136 George Curtis, Editor's Drawer, *Harper's New Monthly Magazine*, December 1863, 132.

137 *New York Courier and Inquirer*, March 30, 1847, cited in Karl M. Kippola, *Acts of Manhood: The Performance of Masculinity on the American Stage, 1828–1865* (New York: Palgrave Macmillan, 2012), 64.

138 *New York Times*, October 3, 1862.

139 Bruce A. McConachie, "The Theatre of Edwin Forrest and Jacksonian Hero Worship," in *When They Weren't Doing Shakespeare: Essays on Nineteenth-Century British and American Theatre*, ed. Judith Law Fisher and Stephen Watt (Athens: University of Georgia Press, 1989), 3–18, 12.

140 James Rees, *The Life of Edwin Forrest* (Philadelphia, 1874), 55, cited in Garff B. Wilson, *A History of American Acting* (Bloomington: Indiana University Press, 1966), 23.

141 Hackett, *Notes and Comments*, 96.

142 *New York Evening Post*, April 22, 1845, citing an unidentified British review.

143 *New York Evening Post*, October 13, 1868.

144 *Cincinnati Daily Enquirer*, December 7, 1869.

145 William Roscoe Thayer, *The Life and Letters of John Hay*, 2 vols. (Boston: Houghton Mifflin, 1915), 1: 300.

146 *Norwich Aurora*, October 28, 1865.

147 *Daily National Intelligencer*, April 9,1864.

148 *Daily National Intelligencer*, April 12, 1864.

149 Auguste Laugel, "A Frenchman's Diary in Our Civil-War Time—III," *Nation*, July 31, 1902, 88–89; 89.

150 *Cincinnati Daily Enquirer*, December 7, 1869.

151 Ibid.

152 Laugel, "A Frenchman's Diary," 88–89; 89.

153 Ibid.

154 Noah Brooks, "Glimpses of Lincoln in War Time," *Century Magazine*, January 1895, 457–467, 464.

155 Ibid. Lincoln might not have been as enthused had he known that McCullough was a strong Southern sympathizer; he was also a good friend of John Wilkes Booth. See Thomas A. Bogar, *Backstage at the Lincoln Assassination: The Untold Story of the Actors and Stagehands at Ford's Theatre* (Washington, D.C.: Regnery, 2013), 205.

156 Wilson, *A History of American Acting*, 35. "Audiences worshipped Forrest; they liked McCullough" (Kippola, *Acts of Manhood*, 150).

157 Shakespeare, *King Lear*, ed. R. A. Foakes (London: Thomas Nelson and Sons, 1997), 85.

158 Shattuck, *Shakespeare on the American Stage*, 129.

159 In a dinner invitation for "tomorrow evening" dated January 30, 1865, Mary Lincoln wrote of a plan "to attend the theatre to see Forrest in 'Sparticus' [*sic*]" after dinner. Justin G. Turner, Linda Levitt Turner, and Mary Todd Lincoln, *Mary Todd Lincoln: Her Life and Letters* (New York: Alfred A. Knopf, 1972), 200.

160 Kippola, *Acts of Manhood*, 170.

161 Douglas L. Wilson, "His Hour upon the Stage," *American Scholar* 81, no. 1 (Winter 2012): 60–69, 69.

162 Ibid.

163 Artemus Ward, *The Complete Works of Artemus Ward (Charles Farrar Browne)*, edited and compiled by Melville D. Landon (New York: G. W. Dillingham, 1898),

59–60. Dated 1859, the piece was reprinted in the *Brooklyn Eagle*, February 22, 1865.

EPILOGUE: LINCOLN, SHAKESPEARE, AND THE BROTHERS BOOTH

1 James Grant Wilson, "Recollections of Lincoln," *Putnam's Magazine*, February 1909, 515–529, 528–529.

2 It may, however, have been *Richard III* that Lincoln had planned to see. Ford's advertisement, published in newspapers on November 5, announced "Saturday Evening, Nov. 9, last time positively of Richard III." November 9 was a Monday. See *Daily National Republican*, November 5, 1863, 3.

3 Walt Whitman, *Walt Whitman and the Civil War: A Collection of Original Articles and Manuscripts*, ed. Charles Irving Glicksberg (Philadelphia: University of Pennsylvania Press, 1933), 56.

4 Stanley Kimmel, *The Mad Booths of Maryland* (Indianapolis, Ind.: Bobbs-Merrill, 1940), 393. The comment was originally reported by the journalist George A. Townsend in the *New York World*, April 19, 1865; Townsend, however, uses the word "nigger."

5 Cited in Katherine Helm, *The True Story of Mary, Wife of Lincoln: Containing the Recollections of Mary Lincoln's Sister Emilie (Mrs. Ben Hardin Helm), Extracts from Her War-Time Diary, Numerous Letters and Other Documents Now First Published* (New York: Harper, 1928), 243.

6 Michael W. Kauffman, *American Brutus: John Wilkes Booth and the Lincoln Conspiracies* (New York: Random House, 2004), 125. A note in John Hay's *Inside Lincoln's White House* reads, "Lincoln had seen Booth in *Richard III*, *Hamlet*, and other plays." This clearly confuses John Wilkes with his brother Edwin. Hay, *Inside Lincoln's White House: The Complete Civil War Diary of John Hay*, ed. Michael Burlingame and John R. T. Ettlinger (Carbondale: Southern Illinois University Press, 1999), 326n271. See also Joseph George Jr., "The Night John Wilkes Booth Played before Abraham Lincoln," *Lincoln Herald* 59, no. 2 (Summer 1957): 11–15.

7 Hay, *Inside Lincoln's White House*, 111 (November 11, 1863). William B. Styple claims that Tad Lincoln and a friend, the bugler Gustav Schurmann, went by themselves to see Booth in *The Marble Heart* and even chatted with the actor backstage. Styple, *The Little Bugler: The True Story of a Twelve-Year-Old Boy in the Civil War* (Kearny, N.J.: Belle Grove, 1998). The source for this, alas, is unclear, but the friendship between the two boys was real. See "From the Army of the Potomac/Reviews by the President," *Evening Star*, April 10, 1863.

8 "Fanny Seward's Diary," transcript, page 195, "Lincoln and His Circle," University of Rochester Rare Books and Special Collections, http://www.lib.rochester .edu/index.cfm?page=4468&Print=436&image=0-16284.jpg.

9 *Macbeth*, act 2, scene 3, quoted in *Daily National Republican*, April 14, 1865.

10 *Julius Caesar*, act 5, scene 5, quoted in *Evening Star*, April 20, 1865. Ironically, these words are a description of Brutus, Caesar's assassin.

11 *Portland (Maine) Daily Eastern Argus*, April 17, 1865.

12 John Carroll Power, *Abraham Lincoln: His Life, Public Services, Death and Great Funeral Cortege, with a History and Description of the National Lincoln Monument, with an Appendix* (Chicago: H. W. Rokker, 1889), 145; B. F. Morris, *Memorial Record of the Nation's Tribute to Abraham Lincoln* (Washington, D.C., 1865), 183. See Michael Burlingame, *Abraham Lincoln: A Life*, online edition, 2 vols. (Baltimore: Johns Hopkins University Press, 2008), 2: chap. 36, p. 4055, http://www.knox.edu/about-knox/lincoln-studies-center/burlingame-abraham-lincoln-a-life.

13 *King John*, act 4, scene 3, quoted in *New York Herald*, April 21, 1865. The whole quoted passage reads, "All murders past do stand excused in this: / And this, so sole and so unmatchable, / Shall give a holiness, a purity, / To the yet unbegotten sin of times; / And prove a deadly bloodshed but a jest, / Exampled by this heinous spectacle."

14 According to one report, on hearing of Lincoln's death, Jefferson Davis supposedly said, "If it were to be done, it were better to be well done," a paraphrase from *Macbeth*, act 1, scene 7: "If it were done when 'tis done, then 'twere well / It were done quickly." This comes from the statement of John A. Bingham, the assistant judge advocate at the trial of the conspirators. See Bingham et al., *Trial of the Conspirators, for the Assassination of President Lincoln, &C* (Washington, D.C.: G.P.O., 1865), 379. In speaking at the unveiling of Francis Carpenter's *Emancipation Proclamation* painting in 1878, former Confederate vice president Alexander Stephens lamented "the horrible manner of his [Lincoln's] taking off" (*Macbeth*, act 1, scene 7). Alexander H. Stephens, *Recollections of Alexander H. Stephens: His Diary Kept When a Prisoner at Fort Warren, Boston Harbour, 1865, Giving Incidents and Reflections of His Prison Life and Some Letters and Reminiscences*, ed. Myrta Lockett Avary (New York: Doubleday, Page, 1910), 552.

15 Richard Wightman Fox, *Lincoln's Body: A Cultural History* (New York: W. W. Norton, 2015), 53. In Springfield, too, the *Daily State Journal of* April 17, 1865, editorialized, "Nothing but the most uncontrollable and demoniac treason dares assail a man so foully dealt with, or gloat over 'the deep damnation of his taking off.'"

16 The text here is garbled, combining lines spoken by Macbeth and by Banquo from act 2, scene 3 and concluding with lines spoken by Malcolm in act 4, scene 3. The phrase "ill deeds are seldom slow / Nor single—Dread horrors still abound" is from William Davenant's 1664 adaptation of *Macbeth*.

17 Paraphrase from *Macbeth*, act 3, scene 2, in *Gallipolis (Ohio) Journal*, April 20, 1865. The door of Wallack's Theatre in New York, as one witness described it, had on it "a picture of Mr. Lincoln in oil (life size) . . . surmounting a placard, on which are inscribed the celebrated lines from *Macbeth*, spoken with reference to the murder of Duncan, King of Scotland." *San Francisco Daily Evening Bulletin*, May 20, 1865.

18 William R. Williams et al., *Our Martyr President, Abraham Lincoln: Voices from the Pulpit of New York and Brooklyn* (New York: Tibbals and Whiting, 1865), 368. The *Daily National Intelligencer* of April 28, 1865, found lines from *Hamlet* (act 1, scene 5) to condemn the now dead Booth: "Is there hope for the final salvation of such a wretch, 'cut off even in the blossom' of his sin, 'unhousel'd, unanel'd,

no reckoning made,' but sent to his account with all his load of unatoned-for guilt upon his head?"

19 For a full discussion of the many responses to the Lincoln assassination, see Martha Elizabeth Hodes, *Mourning Lincoln* (New Haven: Yale University Press, 2015).

20 John Wilkes Booth, *Right or Wrong, God Judge Me: The Writings of John Wilkes Booth*, ed. John H. Rhodehamel and Louise Taper (Urbana: University of Illinois Press, 1997), 154.

21 Booth, *Right or Wrong*, 149–150.

22 Ibid., 155.

23 In a letter to a friend dated November 11, 1860, Edwin wrote, "I voted (for Lincoln) t'other day—the first vote I ever cast; and I suppose I am now an American citizen all over, as I have ever been in heart." Edwin Booth and Edwina Booth Grossmann, *Edwin Booth: Recollections by His Daughter, Edwina Booth Grossmann, and Letters to Her and to His Friends* (New York: Century, 1894), 155.

24 Reported in the *New York Times*, April 16, 1865. See also Robert T. Lincoln, "Edwin Booth and Lincoln," *Century Magazine*, April 1909, 919–920. According to his latest biographer, Robert probably never mentioned the incident to his parents. The frequently repeated story of Robert romancing Lucy Hale, the daughter of New Hampshire senator John P. Hale and John Wilkes Booth's fiancée, however, has no factual basis. See Jason Emerson, *Giant in the Shadows: The Life of Robert T. Lincoln* (Carbondale: Southern Illinois University Press, 2012), 87, 80–81.

25 David B. Chesebrough, *No Sorrow Like Our Sorrow: Northern Protestant Ministers and the Assassination of Lincoln* (Kent, Ohio: Kent State University Press, 1994), 103.

26 *Daily National Republican*, April 21, 1865.

27 *Daily National Republican*, April 24, 1865, 2nd ed., extra.

28. Nor, evidently, did Booth, though in a letter to William Winter written a few days later, he laments "how tragical and sorrowful have been the events of my life." Edwin Booth to William Winter, April 27, 1879, mss., Y.c.215 (334), Folger Shakespeare Library, published in Edwin Booth and William Winter, *Between Actor and Critic: Selected Letters of Edwin Booth and William Winter*, ed. Daniel J. Watermeier (Princeton: Princeton University Press, 1971), 126–129. For a discussion of this event as it relates to the tensions in post–Civil War America, see Catherine M. Shaw, "Edwin Booth's *Richard II* and the Divided Nation," in *Textual and Theatrical Shakespeare: Questions of Evidence*, ed. Edward Pechter (Iowa City: University of Iowa Press, 1996), 144–164.

29 See "A Startling Scene at M'Vicker's Theatre," *New York Times*, April 24, 1879; and "Booth's Narrow Escape," *New York Times*, April 25, 1879.

30 While playing again in Chicago in 1887, Booth "reportedly made a private visit to a recently unveiled statue of Lincoln in Lincoln Park, where he placed a flower in homage." Daniel J. Watermeier, *American Tragedian: The Life of Edwin Booth* (Columbia: University of Missouri Press, 2015), citing Henry Wysham Lanier, ed., *The Players Book: A Half-Century of Fact, Feeling, Fun, and Folklore* (New York: Players, 1938), 26.

BIBLIOGRAPHY

Abbott, John S. C. *The History of the Civil War in America: Comprising a Full and Impartial Account of the Origin and Progress of the Rebellion.* New York: H. Bill, 1863.

Abraham Lincoln. Based on the play by John Drinkwater; written for television by David Shaw; directed by Paul Nickell. *Studio One.* Columbia Broadcasting System, May 26, 1952. Internet Archive, archive.org/details/StudioOneAbrahamLincoln.

Alford, Terry. *Fortune's Fool: The Life of John Wilkes Booth.* Oxford: Oxford University Press, 2015.

Alger, William Rounseville. *Life of Edwin Forrest, the American Tragedian.* 2 vols. Philadelphia: J. B. Lippincott, 1877.

Alter, Robert. *Pen of Iron: American Prose and the King James Bible.* Princeton: Princeton University Press, 2010.

Anderson, Dwight G. *Abraham Lincoln, the Quest for Immortality.* New York: Alfred A. Knopf, 1982.

Andreas, James R. "Othello's African American Progeny." *South Atlantic Review* 57, no. 4 (November 1992): 39–57.

Andrews, John F. "Shakespeare Aspects of Lincoln Assassination." Interview by Liane Hansen, *Weekend Edition Sunday*, National Public Radio, March 15, 1992.

Angle, Paul M. *"Here I Have Lived": A History of Lincoln's Springfield, 1821–1865.* Springfield, Ill.: Abraham Lincoln Association, 1935.

Archer, Stephen M. *Junius Brutus Booth: Theatrical Prometheus.* Carbondale: Southern Illinois University Press, 1992.

Arnold, Isaac N. *The Life of Abraham Lincoln.* Chicago: Jansen, McClurg, 1885.

Ashby, LeRoy. *With Amusement for All: A History of American Popular Culture since 1830.* Lexington: University Press of Kentucky, 2006.

Badeau, Adam. "Edwin Booth On and Off the Stage." *McClure's Magazine*, August 1893, 255–267.

———. *Grant in Peace: From Appomattox to Mount McGregor, a Personal Memoir.* Hartford, Conn.: S. S. Scranton, 1887.

Baker, Jean H. *Mary Todd Lincoln.* New York: W. W. Norton, 1987.

Bank, Rosemarie K. *Theatre Culture in America, 1825–1860.* Cambridge: Cambridge University Press, 1997.

Barbee, David R. "The Musical Mr. Lincoln." *Abraham Lincoln Quarterly* 5, no. 8 (December 1949): 435–451.

Bartholomeusz, Dennis. *Macbeth and the Players.* Cambridge: Cambridge University Press, 1969.

Bartlett, John. *A Collection of Familiar Quotations: With Complete Indices of Authors and Subjects.* Cambridge[, Mass.]: John Bartlett, 1855, 1856.

———. *The Shakespeare Phrase Book.* Boston: Little, Brown, 1881.

Barzun, Jaques. *On Writing, Editing, and Publishing: Essays, Explicative and Hortatory*. Chicago: University of Chicago Press, 1986.

Basler, Roy. *A Touchstone for Greatness: Essays, Addresses, and Occasional Pieces about Abraham Lincoln*. Westport, Conn.: Greenwood Press, 1973.

Bates, David Homer. *Lincoln in the Telegraph Office: Recollections of the United States Military Telegraph Corps during the Civil War*. New York: Century, 1907.

Benner, Martha L., and Cullom Davis. *The Law Practice of Abraham Lincoln: Complete Documentary Edition*. Champaign, IL: University of Illinois Press, 2000.

Beran, Michael. "Lincoln, *Macbeth*, and the Moral Imagination." *Humanitas* 11, no. 2 (1998). http://www.nhinet.org/beran.htm.

Berkelman, Robert. "Lincoln's Interest in Shakespeare." *Shakespeare Quarterly* 2, no. 4 (October 1951): 303–312.

Bestor, Arthur E., David C. Mearns, and Jonathan Daniels. *Three Presidents and Their Books: The Reading of Jefferson, Lincoln, Franklin D. Roosevelt*. Urbana: University of Illinois Press, 1955.

Bingham, John Armor, Mary E. Surratt, David E. Herold, Lewis Payne, George A. Atzerodt, Michael O'Laughlin, Samuel Alexander Mudd, Edward Spangler, and Samuel Arnold. *Trial of the Conspirators, for the Assassination of President Lincoln, &C*. Washington, D.C.: G.P.O., 1865.

Bogar, Thomas A. *American Presidents Attend the Theatre: The Playgoing Experiences of Each Chief Executive*. Jefferson, N.C.: McFarland, 2006.

———. *Backstage at the Lincoln Assassination: The Untold Story of the Actors and Stagehands at Ford's Theatre*. Washington, D.C.: Regnery, 2013.

———. "The Origins of Theater in the District of Columbia, 1789–1800." *Washington History* 22 (2010): 4–16.

Booth, Edwin, and Edwina Booth Grossmann. *Edwin Booth: Recollections by His Daughter, Edwina Booth Grossmann, and Letters to Her and to His Friends*. New York: Century, 1894.

Booth, Edwin, and William Winter. *Between Actor and Critic: Selected Letters of Edwin Booth and William Winter*. Edited by Daniel J. Watermeier. Princeton: Princeton University Press, 1971.

Booth, John Wilkes. *Right or Wrong, God Judge Me: The Writings of John Wilkes Booth*. Edited by John H. Rhodehamel and Louise Taper. Urbana: University of Illinois Press, 1997.

Bordewich, Fergus M. *America's Great Debate: Henry Clay, Stephen A. Douglas, and the Compromise That Preserved the Union*. New York: Simon and Schuster, 2012.

Boritt, G. S., and Norman O. Forness, eds. *The Historian's Lincoln: Pseudohistory, Psychohistory, and History*. Urbana: University of Illinois Press, 1988.

Braden, Waldo Warder. *Abraham Lincoln: Public Speaker*. Baton Rouge: Louisiana State University Press, 1988.

Braver, Adam. *Mr. Lincoln's Wars: A Novel in Thirteen Stories*. New York: William Morrow, 2003.

Bray, Robert C. *Reading with Lincoln*. Carbondale: Southern Illinois University Press, 2010.

———. "What Abraham Lincoln Read—An Evaluative and Annotated List." *Journal* of the Abraham Lincoln Association, Summer 2007. http://www.historycoopera tive.org/journals/jala/28.2/bray.html.

Briggs, John Channing. *Lincoln's Speeches Reconsidered.* Baltimore: Johns Hopkins University Press, 2005.

———. "Steeped in Shakespeare." *Claremont Review of Books* 9, no. 1 (Winter 2008–2009). http://www.claremont.org/article/steeped-in-shakespeare/#.VNvq gi4rnLV.

Brigham, Johnson. *James Harlan.* Iowa City: State Historical Society of Iowa, 1913.

Bromwich, David. "How Close to Lincoln." *New York Review of Books,* January 10, 2013.

———. *Moral Imagination.* Princeton and Oxford: Princeton University Press, 2014.

———. "Shakespeare, Lincoln, and Ambition." *New York Review of Books* (blog), April 11, 2014. http://www.nybooks.com/blogs/nyrblog/2014/apr/11/shake speare-lincoln-ambition/?insrc=rel.

Brooks, Noah. "Glimpses of Lincoln in War Time." *Century Magazine,* January 1895, 457–467.

———. *Lincoln Observed: Civil War Dispatches of Noah Brooks.* Edited by Michael Burlingame. Baltimore: Johns Hopkins University Press, 1998.

———. "Personal Reminiscences of Lincoln." *Scribner's Monthly,* March 1878: 673– 681.

Brousseau, Elaine. "'Now Literature, Philosophy, and Thought Are Shakespearized': American Culture and Nineteenth Century Shakespearean Performance 1835– 1875." Ph.D. diss., University of Massachusetts–Amherst, 2003.

Brown, John Russell. *Shakespeare in Performance: An Introduction through Six Major Plays.* New York: Harcourt Brace Jovanovich, 1976.

Browne, Ray B. *Lincoln-Lore: Lincoln in the Popular Mind.* Bowling Green, Ohio: Popular Press, 1974.

Browning, Orville Hickman. *The Diary of Orville Hickman Browning.* Edited by Theodore Calvin Pease and James G. Randall. 2 vols. Illinois State Historical Library Collections, vols. 20, 22. Springfield: Illinois State Historical Library, 1925–1933.

Bulman, James C. "Performing the Conflated Text of *Henry IV*: The Fortunes of *Part Two.*" *Shakespeare Survey* 63 (2010): 89–101.

Bunker, Gary L. *From Rail-Splitter to Icon: Lincoln's Image in Illustrated Periodicals, 1860–1865.* Kent, Ohio: Kent State University Press, 2001.

Burlingame, Michael. *Abraham Lincoln: A Life.* Print edition. 2 vols. Baltimore: Johns Hopkins University Press, 2008.

———. *Abraham Lincoln: A Life.* Online edition. 2 vols. Baltimore: Johns Hopkins University Press, 2008. http://www.knox.edu/about-knox/lincoln-studies-center /burlingame-abraham-lincoln-a-life.

———. *The Inner World of Abraham Lincoln.* Urbana: University of Illinois Press, 1994.

Burton, Orville Vernon. "The Gettysburg Address Revisited." In *1863: Lincoln's Pivotal Year,* edited by Harold Holzer and Sara Vaughn Gabbard, 137–155. Carbondale and Edwardsville: Southern Illinois University Press, 2013.

Busey, Samuel C. *Personal Reminiscences and Recollections of Forty-Six Years' Mem-*

bership in the Medical Society of the District of Columbia and Residence in This City, with Biographical Sketches of Many of the Deceased Members. Washington, D.C. [Philadelphia: Dornan, printer], 1895.

Calhoun, Lucia Gilbert. "Edwin Booth." *Galaxy*, January 1869, 77–87.

Campanella, Richard. *Lincoln in New Orleans: The 1828–1831 Flatboat Voyages and Their Place in History*. Lafayette: University of Louisiana at Lafayette Press, 2010.

Cannon, Le Grand B. *Personal Reminiscences of the Rebellion, 1861–1866*. New York: [Burr Printing House], 1895.

Carnegie, Dale. *Lincoln, the Unknown*. New York: Century, 1932.

Carpenter, F. B. *The Inner Life of Abraham Lincoln: Six Months at the White House*. Introduction by Mark E. Neely Jr. Lincoln: University of Nebraska Press, 1995.

———. *Six Months at the White House with Abraham Lincoln: The Story of a Picture*. New York: Hurd and Houghton, 1866.

Carwardine, Richard. *Lincoln*. Harlow, England: Pearson/Longman, 2003.

Chambrun, Charles Adolphe de Pineton, Marquis de. *Impressions of Lincoln and the Civil War: A Foreigner's Account*. Translated by Aldebert de Chambrun. New York: Random House, [1952].

———. "Personal Recollections of Mr. Lincoln." *Scribner's Magazine*, January 1893, 26–39.

Chernow, Ron. *Washington: A Life*. New York: Penguin Press, 2010.

Chesebrough, David B. *No Sorrow Like Our Sorrow: Northern Protestant Ministers and the Assassination of Lincoln*. Kent, Ohio: Kent State University Press, 1994.

Clapp, Henry Austin. *Reminiscences of a Dramatic Critic: With an Essay on the Art of Henry Irving*. Boston: Houghton, Mifflin, 1902.

Clark, Gregory, and S. Michael Halloran. *Oratorical Culture in Nineteenth-Century America: Transformations in the Theory and Practice of Rhetoric*. Carbondale: Southern Illinois University Press, 1993.

Cliff, Nigel. *The Shakespeare Riots: Revenge, Drama, and Death in Nineteenth-Century America*. New York: Random House, 2007.

Clinton, Catherine. *Mrs. Lincoln: A Life*. New York: Harper, 2009.

Cmiel, Kenneth. *Democratic Eloquence: The Fight over Popular Speech in Nineteenth-Century America*. New York: William Morrow, 1990.

Colfax, Schuyler. *Life and Principles of Abraham Lincoln*. Philadelphia: J. B. Rodgers, printer, 1865.

Colley, John Scott. *Richard's Himself Again: A Stage History of Richard III*. New York: Greenwood Press, 1992.

Congressional Globe. 25th Congress, 1st Session. Vol. 5, 1837.

Current, Richard N. "Lincoln after 175 Years: The Myth of the Jealous Son." *Journal of the Abraham Lincoln Association* 6, no. 1 (1984): 15–24.

Curtis, George William. Editor's Drawer. *Harper's New Monthly Magazine*, December 1863, 132.

———. Editor's Easy Chair. *Harper's New Monthly Magazine*, August 1867, 393–397.

Dall, C. H. "Pioneering." *Atlantic Monthly*, April 1867, 403–416.

DeRose, Chris. *Congressman Lincoln: The Making of America's Greatest President*. New York: Threshold Editions, 2013.

Dickey, Stephen. "Lincoln and Shakespeare." In *Shakespeare in American Life*. Folger Shakespeare Library. http://www.shakespeareinamericanlife.org.

Dodge, Daniel Kilham. *Abraham Lincoln, Master of Words*. New York: D. Appleton, 1924.

———. *Abraham Lincoln: The Evolution of His Literary Style*. Champaign and Urbana [Ill.]: University Press, 1900.

Donald, David Herbert. *Lincoln*. New York: Simon and Schuster, 1995.

Dormon, James H. *Theater in the Ante Bellum South, 1815–1861*. Chapel Hill: University of North Carolina Press, 1967.

Downer, Alan S. "Players and Painted Stage: Nineteenth Century Acting." *PMLA* 61, no. 2 (June 1946): 522–576.

Drinkwater, John. *Abraham Lincoln: A Play*. Boston: Houghton Mifflin, 1919.

———. *Lincoln, the World Emancipator*. Boston: Houghton Mifflin, 1920.

Dunlap, William. *Memoirs of the Life of George Frederick Cooke, Esquire: Late of the Theatre Royal, Covent Garden*. 2 vols. New York: D. Longworth, 1813.

Dunn, Esther Cloudman. *Shakespeare in America*. New York: Macmillan, 1939.

Edgett, Edwin Francis, *Edward Loomis Davenport: A Biography*. New York: Dunlap Society, 1901.

Edwards, Herbert Joseph, and John Erskine Hankins. *Lincoln the Writer: The Development of His Literary Style*. [Orono]: University of Maine, 1962.

Emerson, Jason. *Giant in the Shadows: The Life of Robert T. Lincoln*. Carbondale: Southern Illinois University Press, 2012.

Emerson, Ralph Waldo. *The Collected Works of Ralph Waldo Emerson*. Edited by Robert Ernest Spiller, Alfred Riggs Ferguson, Joseph Slater, and Jean Ferguson Carr. 10 vols. Cambridge, Mass.: Belknap Press, 1971–2013.

Falk, Robert. "Shakespeare in America: A Survey to 1900." *Shakespeare Survey* 18 (1965): 102–118.

Fehrenbacher, Don E. *Lincoln in Text and Context: Collected Essays*. Stanford: Stanford University Press, 1987.

Finlay, John. *Miscellanies. The Foreign Relations of the British Empire: The Internal Resources of Ireland: Sketches of Character: Dramatic Criticism*. Dublin, 1835.

Fisher, Judith Law, and Stephen Watt, eds. *When They Weren't Doing Shakespeare: Essays on Nineteenth-Century British and American Theatre*. Athens: University of Georgia Press, 1989.

Foner, Eric. *The Fiery Trial: Abraham Lincoln and American Slavery*. New York: W. W. Norton, 2010.

Forgie, George B. *Patricide in the House Divided: A Psychological Interpretation of Lincoln and His Age*. New York: W. W. Norton, 1979.

Forney, John W. *Anecdotes of Public Men*. New York, 1873.

Fox, Richard Wightman. *Lincoln's Body: A Cultural History*. New York: W. W. Norton, 2015.

French, Benjamin B. *Witness to the Young Republic: A Yankee's Journal, 1828–1870*. Edited by Donald B. Cole and John J. McDonough. Hanover, N.H.: University Press of New England, 1989.

Furtwangler, Albert. *Assassin on Stage: Brutus, Hamlet, and the Death of Lincoln*. Urbana: University of Illinois Press, 1991.

Garraty, John A., and Mark C. Carnes. *American National Biography*. New York: Oxford University Press, 1999.

George, Joseph, Jr. "The Night John Wilkes Booth Played before Abraham Lincoln." *Lincoln Herald* 59, no. 2 (Summer 1957): 11–15.

Goethe, Johann Wolfgang von. *Goethe: The Collected Works*. Vol. 9, *Wilhelm Meister's Apprenticeship*. Edited and translated by Eric A. Blackall in cooperation with Victor Lange. Princeton: Princeton University Press, 1995.

Goodale, Katherine Molony. *Behind the Scenes with Edwin Booth*. Boston: Houghton Mifflin, 1931.

Goodwin, Doris Kearns. *Team of Rivals: The Political Genius of Abraham Lincoln*. New York: Simon and Schuster, 2005.

Gopnik, Adam. *Angels and Ages: A Short Book about Darwin, Lincoln, and Modern Life*. New York: Alfred A. Knopf, 2009.

Gottlieb, Robert. Review of three books on Joseph Jefferson. *New York Review of Books*, October 22, 2009.

Grant, Ulysses S. *The Papers of Ulysses S. Grant*. Edited by John Y. Simon. 32 vols. Carbondale: Southern Illinois University Press, 1967.

Grimsted, David. *Melodrama Unveiled: American Theater and Culture, 1800–1850*. Chicago: University of Chicago Press, 1968.

Grinnell, Josiah Bushnell. *Men and Events of Forty Years. Autobiographical Reminiscences of an Active Career from 1850 to 1890*. Edited by Henry W. Parker. Boston: D. Lothrop, 1891.

Grover, Leonard. "Glimpses of Lincoln in War Time." *Century Magazine*, January 1895, 457–467.

———. "Lincoln's Interest in the Theater." *Century Magazine*, April 1909, 943–950.

Guelzo, Allen C. Review of *Reading with Lincoln*, by Robert Bray. *JALA* 33, no. 1 (2012): 212.

Hackett, James Henry. *Notes and Comments upon Certain Plays and Actors of Shakespeare with Criticisms and Correspondence*. New York: Carleton, 1863.

Hall, Florence Marion. "The Friendship of Edwin Booth and Julia Ward Howe." *New England Magazine*, November 1893, 315–321.

Haring-Smith, Tori. *From Farce to Metadrama: A Stage History of "The Taming of the Shrew," 1594–1983*. Westport, Conn.: Greenwood Press, 1985.

Harkness, David James, and R. Gerald McMurtry. *Lincoln's Favorite Poets*. Knoxville: University of Tennessee Press, 1959.

Harper, Robert S. *Lincoln and the Press*. New York: McGraw-Hill, 1951.

Haswell, Chas. H. *Reminiscences of New York by an Octogenarian*. New York: Harper and Brothers, 1896.

Hay, John. "Abraham Lincoln: Life in the White House in the Time of Lincoln." *Century Magazine*, November, 1890, 33–37.

———. *At Lincoln's Side: John Hay's Civil War Correspondence and Selected Writings*. Edited by Michael Burlingame. Carbondale: Southern Illinois University Press, 2000.

———. *Inside Lincoln's White House: The Complete Civil War Diary of John Hay*.

Edited by Michael Burlingame and John R. T. Ettlinger. Carbondale: Southern Illinois University Press, 1999.

Helm, Katherine. *The True Story of Mary, Wife of Lincoln: Containing the Recollections of Mary Lincoln's Sister Emilie (Mrs. Ben Hardin Helm), Extracts from Her War-Time Diary, Numerous Letters and Other Documents Now First Published.* New York: Harper, 1928.

Herndon, William Henry. *Herndon's Life of Lincoln, the History and Personal Recollections of Abraham Lincoln, As Originally Written by William H. Herndon and Jesse W. Weik, with an Introduction and Notes by Paul M. Angle.* New York: A. C. Boni, 1930.

Herndon, William Henry, and Jesse William Weik. *Herndon's Lincoln.* Edited by Douglas L. Wilson and Rodney O. Davis. Knox College Lincoln Studies Center series. [Galesburg, Ill.?]: Knox College Lincoln Studies Center, 2006.

Hodes, Martha Elizabeth. *Mourning Lincoln.* New Haven: Yale University Press, 2015.

Hodge, Francis. *Yankee Theatre: The Image of America on the Stage, 1825–1850.* Austin: University of Texas Press, 1964.

Holt, Michael F. "Lincoln Reconsidered." *Journal of American History* 96, no. 2 (2009): 451–455.

Holzer, Harold. *Lincoln and the Power of the Press: The War for Public Opinion.* New York: Simon and Schuster, 2014.

———, ed. *The Lincoln Anthology: Great Writers on His Life and Legacy from 1860 to Now.* New York: Library of America, 2009.

———. *Lincoln President-Elect: Abraham Lincoln and the Great Secession Winter 1860–1861.* New York: Simon and Schuster, 2008.

———. *Lincoln Seen and Heard.* Lawrence: University Press of Kansas, 2000.

Holzer, Harold, G. S. Boritt, and Mark E. Neely. *The Lincoln Image: Abraham Lincoln and the Popular Print.* New York: Scribner Press, 1984.

Holzer, Harold, and Eric Foner. *The Civil War in 50 Objects.* New York: Viking, 2013.

Holzer, Harold, and Sara Vaughn Gabbard, eds. *1863: Lincoln's Pivotal Year.* Carbondale and Edwardsville: Southern Illinois University Press, 2013.

Howe, Daniel Walker. *What Hath God Wrought: The Transformation of America, 1815–1848.* New York: Oxford University Press, 2007.

Howe, M. A. De Wolfe, and Annie Fields. *Memories of a Hostess: A Chronicle of Eminent Friendships, Drawn Chiefly from the Diaries of Mrs. James T. Fields.* Boston: Atlantic Monthly Press, 1922.

Hubbard, Henry. *Speech of Mr. Hubbard, of New Hampshire, on the Resolution of Mr. Ewing for Rescinding the Treasury Order, Delivered in the Senate, December, 1836.* Washington, D.C.: Blair and Rives, 1837.

Hughes, Amy. *Spectacles of Reform: Theater and Activism in Nineteenth-Century America.* Ann Arbor: University of Michigan Press, 2012.

Hugo, Victor. *William Shakespeare.* Translated by Melville B. Anderson. Chicago: A. C. McClurg, 1887.

Ireland, Joseph Norton. *Records of the New York Stage: From 1750 to 1860.* New York: T. H. Morrell, 1866.

Jefferson, Joseph. *The Autobiography of Joseph Jefferson.* Edited by Alan Seymour Downer. Cambridge, Mass.: Belknap Press, 1964.

Jefferson, Thomas *The Works of Thomas Jefferson.* Collected and edited by Paul Leicester Ford. 12 vols. New York: G. P. Putnam's Sons, 1904.

Johnson, Samuel. *Samuel Johnson on Shakespeare.* Edited by William K. Wimsatt. New York: Hill and Wang, 1960.

Jones, Thomas D. *Memories of Lincoln.* New York: Press of the Pioneers, 1934.

Kaplan, Fred. *Lincoln: The Biography of a Writer.* New York: HarperCollins, 2008.

Kauffman, Michael W. *American Brutus: John Wilkes Booth and the Lincoln Conspiracies.* New York: Random House, 2004.

Kendall, John S. *The Golden Age of the New Orleans Theater.* Baton Rouge: Louisiana State University Press, 1952.

Kimmel, Stanley. *The Mad Booths of Maryland.* Indianapolis, Ind.: Bobbs-Merrill, 1940.

Kippola, Karl M. *Acts of Manhood: The Performance of Masculinity on the American Stage, 1828–1865.* New York: Palgrave Macmillan, 2012.

Kirkland, Frazar [Richard Miller Devens]. *The Pictorial Book of Anecdotes and Incidents of the War of the Rebellion.* Hartford, Conn., 1866.

Kolin, Philip C., ed. *Shakespeare in the South: Essays on Performance.* Jackson: University Press of Mississippi, 1983.

Kushner, Howard I., and Anne Hummel Sherrill. *John Milton Hay: The Union of Poetry and Politics.* Boston: Twayne, 1977.

Kushner, Tony, and Doris Kearns Goodwin. *Lincoln: The Screenplay.* New York: Theatre Communications Group, 2012.

Lamb, Charles. *The Portable Charles Lamb.* Edited by John Mason Brown. New York: Viking Press, 1949.

Lamon, Ward Hill, and Dorothy (Lamon) Teillard. *Recollections of Abraham Lincoln, 1847–1865.* Chicago: A. C. McClurg, 1895.

Lanier, Henry Wysham, ed. *The Players' Book: A Half-Century of Fact, Feeling, Fun and Folklore.* New York: Players, 1938.

Laugel, Auguste. "A Frenchman's Diary in Our Civil-War Time—III." *Nation,* July 31, 1902, 88–89.

Leach, Joseph. *Bright Particular Star: The Life and Times of Charlotte Cushman.* New Haven: Yale University Press, 1970.

Lee, Douglas Bennett, Roger L. Meersman, and Donn B. Murphy. *Stage for a Nation: The National Theatre, 150 Years.* Lanham, Md.: University Press of America, 1985.

Lehrman, Lewis E. *Lincoln at Peoria: The Turning Point. Getting Right with the Declaration of Independence.* Mechanicsburg, Pa.: Stackpole Books, 2008.

Levine, Lawrence W. *Highbrow/Lowbrow: The Emergence of Cultural Hierarchy in America.* Cambridge, Mass.: Harvard University Press, 1988.

Lincoln, Abraham. *The Collected Works of Abraham Lincoln.* Edited by Roy Prentice Basler. 11 vols. New Brunswick, N.J.: Rutgers University Press, 1953–1990.

———. *Recollected Words of Abraham Lincoln.* Compiled and edited by Don E. Fehrenbacher and Virginia Fehrenbacher. Stanford: Stanford University Press, 1996.

Lincoln, Robert Todd. *A Portrait of Abraham Lincoln in Letters by His Oldest Son.* Edited by Paul M. Angle with the assistance of Richard G. Case. Chicago: Chicago Historical Society, 1968.

———. "Edwin Booth and Lincoln." *Century Magazine,* April 1909, 919–920.

Locke, David Ross. *The Nasby Papers Letters and Sermons Containing the Views on the Topics of the Day, of Petroleum V. Nasby [Pseud.].* Indianapolis, Ind.: C. O. Perrine, 1864.

Lockridge, Richard, and Edwin Booth. *Darling of Misfortune.* New York: Century, 1932.

Lowell, James Russell. "Marlowe." *Harper's New Monthly Magazine,* July 1892, 194–203.

Ludlow, N. M. *Dramatic Life As I Found It; A Record of Personal Experience, Etc.* St. Louis, Mo.: G. I. Jones, 1880.

MacDonald, Joyce Green. "Acting Black: 'Othello,' 'Othello' Burlesques, and the Performance of Blackness." *Theatre Journal* 46 (May 1994): 231–249.

Mann, Horace. *Slavery: Letters and Speeches.* Boston: B. B. Mussey, 1851.

Marder, Louis. *His Exits and His Entrances: The Story of Shakespeare's Reputation.* Philadelphia: J. B. Lippincott, 1963.

Marshall, Gail, ed. *Shakespeare in the Nineteenth Century.* Cambridge: Cambridge University Press, 2012.

Marszalek, John F. *The Petticoat Affair: Manners, Mutiny, and Sex in Andrew Jackson's White House.* New York: Free Press, 1997.

Masters, Edgar Lee. *Jack Kelso: A Dramatic Poem.* New York: D. Appleton, 1928.

McArthur, Benjamin. "Joseph Jefferson's Lincoln: Vindication of an Autobiographical Legend." *Journal of the Illinois State Historical Society* 93, no. 2 (Summer 2000): 155–166.

———. *The Man Who Was Rip Van Winkle: Joseph Jefferson and Nineteenth-Century American Theatre.* New Haven: Yale University Press, 2007.

McConachie, Bruce A. *Melodramatic Formations: American Theatre and Society, 1820–1870.* Iowa City: University of Iowa Press, 1992.

McMillin, Scott. *Henry IV, Part One: Shakespeare in Performance.* Manchester, U.K.: Manchester University Press, 1991.

McMurtry, R. Gerald, "Lincoln Knew Shakespeare." *Indiana Magazine of History,* December 1935, 266–277.

Mearns, David C. "Charlotte Cushman's 'True and Faithful' Lincoln: Some Documents with Some Observations." *Lincoln Herald* 59, no. 2 (Summer 1957): 3–10.

———. *Largely Lincoln.* New York: St. Martin's Press, 1961.

———. "Mr. Lincoln and the Books He Read." In *Three Presidents and Their Books,* by Arthur Eugene Bestor, David C. Mearns, and Jonathan Daniels, 45–88. Urbana: University of Illinois Press, 1955.

Meersman, Roger, and Robert Boyer. "The National Theatre in Washington: Buildings and Audiences, 1835–1972." *Records of the Columbia Historical Society, Washington, D.C.* 71–72 (1971–1972): 190–242.

Meserve, Walter J. "Winter, William." In *American National Biography,* edited by John A. Garraty and Mark C. Carnes, 24 vols., 23: 658. New York: Oxford University Press, 1999.

Miller, Tice L. *Bohemians and Critics: American Theatre Criticism in the Nineteenth Century.* Metuchen, N.J.: Scarecrow Press, 1981.

————. *Entertaining the Nation: American Drama in the Eighteenth and Nineteenth Centuries.* Carbondale: Southern Illinois University Press, 2007.

Moody, Richard. *The Astor Place Riot.* Bloomington: Indiana University Press, 1958.

————. *Edwin Forrest, First Star of the American Stage.* New York: Alfred A. Knopf, 1960.

Morgann, Maurice. *Essay on the Dramatic Character of Sir John Falstaff.* London, 1777.

Morris, B. F. *Memorial Record of the Nation's Tribute to Abraham Lincoln.* Washington, D.C., 1865.

Morris, Clara. *Life on the Stage: My Personal Experiences and Recollections.* New York: McClure, Phillips, 1901.

Moses, Montrose Jonas. *Famous Actor-Families in America.* New York: T. Y. Crowell, 1906.

Moss, M. Helen Palmes. "Lincoln and Wilkes Booth as Seen on the Day of the Assassination." *Century Magazine,* April 1909, 950–953.

Mowat, Barbara. "The Founders and the Bard." *Yale Review* 97 (2009): 1–18.

Mudd, Alysius I. "Early Theater in Washington D.C." *Records of the Columbia Historical Society* 5 (1902): 64–86.

————. "The Theatres of Washington from 1835 to 1850." *Records of the Columbia Historical Society* 6 (1903): 222–266.

Murdoch, James Edward, Thomas Buchanan Read, and George H. Boker. *Patriotism in Poetry and Prose: Being Selected Passages from Lectures and Patriotic Readings.* Philadelphia: J. B. Lippincott, 1864.

Murdoch, James Edward, and J. Bunting. *The Stage; or, Recollections of Actors and Acting from an Experience of Fifty Years.* Philadelphia: J. M. Stoddart, 1880.

Murley, John A., and Sean D. Sutton. *Perspectives on Politics in Shakespeare.* Lanham, Md.: Lexington Books, 2006.

Murphy, Andrew. *Shakespeare in Print: A History and Chronology of Shakespeare Publishing.* Cambridge: Cambridge University Press, 2003.

Neely, Mark E. *The Abraham Lincoln Encyclopedia.* New York: McGraw-Hill, 1982.

Nemerov, Alexander. *Acting in the Night: Macbeth and the Places of the Civil War.* Berkeley: University of California Press, 2010.

Newcomb, Charles King. *The Journals of Charles King Newcomb.* Edited by Judith Kennedy Johnson. Providence, R.I.: Brown University, 1946.

Newstok, Scott L., and Ayanna Thompson. *Weyward Macbeth: Intersections of Race and Performance.* Basingstoke, U.K.: Palgrave Macmillan, 2010.

Odell, George Clinton Densmore. *Annals of the New York Stage.* 15 vols. New York: Columbia University Press, 1927–1949.

Oggel, L. Terry. *Edwin Booth: A Bio-Bibliography.* New York: Greenwood Press, 1992.

Oldroyd, Osborn H. *The Lincoln Memorial: Album-immortelles.* New York: G. W. Carleton, 1882.

Orations of American Orators, Including Biographical and Critical Sketches. New York: Colonial Press, 1900.

Parisian, Catherine M. *The First White House Library: A History and Annotated Catalog.* University Park, Pa.: Published by the Pennsylvania State University Press for the Bibliographical Society of America and the National First Ladies' Library, 2010.

Parsons, Lynn H. *The Birth of Modern Politics: Andrew Jackson, John Quincy Adams, and the Election of 1828.* Oxford: Oxford University Press, 2009.

Pechter, Edward. *"Othello" and Interpretive Traditions.* Iowa City: University of Iowa Press, 2012.

————, ed. *Textual and Theatrical Shakespeare: Questions of Evidence.* Iowa City: University of Iowa Press, 1996.

Pierce, Edward Lillie, and Charles Sumner. *Memoir and Letters of Charles Sumner.* Boston: Roberts Brothers, 1877.

Porter, Charlotte Endymion. *Shakespeariana: A Critical and Contemporary Review of Shakesperian Literature.* Philadelphia, 1883.

Power, John Carroll. *Abraham Lincoln: His Life, Public Services, Death and Great Funeral Cortege, with a History and Description of the National Lincoln Monument, with an Appendix.* Chicago: H. W. Rokker, 1889.

Pratt, Harry E. *The Personal Finances of Abraham Lincoln.* Springfield, Ill.: Abraham Lincoln Association, 1943.

Preston, Mary. *Studies in Shakespeare: A Book of Essays.* Philadelphia: Claxton, Remson and Haffelfinger, 1869.

Randall, James G. *Last Full Measure.* New York: Dodd, Mead, 1955.

Rawlings, Peter. *Americans on Shakespeare, 1776–1914.* Aldershot, England: Ashgate, 1999.

Reeves, Robert N. "Abraham Lincoln's Knowledge of Shakespeare." *California and Overland Monthly*, April 1904, 333–342.

Reilly, Bernard. *American Political Prints, 1766–1876: A Catalog of the Collections in the Library of Congress.* Boston, Mass: G. K. Hall, 1991.

Remarks on the Character of Richard the Third; As Played by Cooke and Kemble. London, 1801.

Reynolds, David S. *Walt Whitman's America: A Cultural Biography.* New York: Alfred A. Knopf, 1995.

Rice, Allen Thorndike. *Reminiscences of Abraham Lincoln by Distinguished Men of His Time.* New York: Harper and Brothers, 1909.

Richmond, Hugh M. *King Richard III.* Manchester: Manchester University Press, 1989.

Rinear, David L. *Stage, Page, Scandals, and Vandals: William E. Burton and Nineteenth-Century American Theatre.* Theater in the Americas. Carbondale: Southern Illinois University Press, 2004.

Robinson, Luther Emerson. *Abraham Lincoln as a Man of Letters.* Chicago: Rilly and Britton, 1918.

Ross, Ishbel. *The President's Wife: Mary Todd Lincoln. A Biography.* New York: Putnam, 1973.

Rusk, Ralph L. *The Literature of the Middle Western Frontier.* 2 vols. New York: Columbia University Press, 1925.

Salgādo, Gāmini. *Eyewitnesses of Shakespeare: First Hand Accounts of Performances, 1590–1890.* New York: Barnes and Noble Books, 1975.

Samples, Gordon. *Lust for Fame: The Stage Career of John Wilkes Booth.* Jefferson, N.C.: McFarland, 1982.

Samuels, Shirley, ed. *The Cambridge Companion to Abraham Lincoln.* Cambridge: Cambridge University Press, 2012.

Schneider, Bethany. "Thus, Always: *Julius Caesar* and Abraham Lincoln." In *Shakesqueer: A Queer Companion to the Complete Works of Shakespeare.* Edited by Madhavi Menon, 152–162. Durham, N.C.: Duke University Press, 2011.

Schurz, Carl, Agathe Schurz, Marianne Schurz, and Carl Lincoln Schurz. *The Reminiscences of Carl Schurz.* 3 vols. New York: McClure, 1907.

Schwartz, Delmore. *Screeno: Stories and Poems.* New York: New Directions Publishing, 2004.

Schwartz, Thomas F. "'—In Short, He Is *Married!*': A Contemporary Newspaper Account." *For the People: A Newsletter of the Abraham Lincoln Association* 1, no. 4 (Winter 1999): 4.

Scovel, James M. "Personal Recollections of Abraham Lincoln." *Overland Monthly,* November 1891, 500.

Shakespeare, William. *The Dramatic Works of William Shakespeare.* 8 vols. (Boston: Phillips, Samson, vols. 1–7, 1849; vol. 8, 1853).

———. *The Dramatic Works of William Shakespeare; with a Life of the Poet, and Notes, Original and Selected.* Boston: Hilliard, Gray, 1836, as it appears on Google Books, http://books.google.com/.

———. *The First Part of King Henry IV.* Edited by Herbert Weil and Judith Weil. Updated ed. Cambridge: Cambridge University Press, 2007.

———. *Hamlet: A New Variorum Edition of Shakespeare.* Edited by Horace Howard Furness. 2 vols. New York: Dover Publications, 1963.

———. *Henry IV, Part I.* Edited by David M. Bevington. Oxford: Oxford University Press, 1987.

———. *Henry the Fourth, Part I.* Edited by Samuel Burdett Hemingway. Philadelphia: J. B. Lippincott, 1936.

———. *King Lear.* Edited by R. A. Foakes. London: Thomas Nelson and Sons, 1997.

———. *King Richard III.* Edited by Janis Lull. Cambridge: Cambridge University Press, 1999.

———. *The Merry Wives of Windsor.* Edited by Charles Jasper Sisson and Charles Harlen Shattuck. New York: Dell, 1966.

———. *New Cambridge Shakespeare.* Edited by Philip Brockbank and Brian Gibbons. Cambridge: Cambridge University Press, 1984–2012.

———. *Oxberry's 1822 Edition of King Richard III, with Descriptive Notes Recording Edmund Kean's Performance Made by James Hackett.* Edited by W. Oxberry; reprinted in facsimile and edited with an introduction and notes by Alan Seymour Downer. London: Society for Theatre Research, 1959.

———. *Richard III.* Edited by Julie Hankey. London: Junction Books, 1981.

———. *The Taming of the Shrew.* Edited by H. J. Oliver. Oxford: Clarendon Press, 1982.

———. *The Tragedy of Othello: The Moor of Venice.* Edited by Alvin B. Kernan. New York: Signet Classic, 1998.

Shank, Theodore J. "Shakespeare and Nineteenth-Century Realism." *Theater Survey* 4 (1963): 59–75.

Shapiro, James, ed., *Shakespeare in America: An Anthology from the Revolution to Now.* New York: Library of America, 2013.

Shattuck, Charles Harlen. *The Hamlet of Edwin Booth.* Urbana: University of Illinois Press, 1969.

———. *Shakespeare on the American Stage: From the Hallams to Edwin Booth.* Washington, D.C.: Folger Shakespeare Library, 1976.

Shenk, Joshua Wolf. *Lincoln's Melancholy: How Depression Challenged a President and Fueled His Greatness.* Boston: Houghton Mifflin, 2005.

Sherman, Robert Lowery. *Chicago Stage, Its Records and Achievements.* Vol. 1, *Gives a Complete Record of All Entertainment and, Substantially, the Cast of Every Play Presented in Chicago, on Its First Production in the City, from the Beginning of Theatricals in 1834 Down to the Last before the Fire of 1871.* Chicago: Robert L. Sherman, 1947.

Sherwood, Robert E. *Abe Lincoln in Illinois: A Play in Twelve Scenes.* New York: Charles Scribner's Sons, 1939.

Sherzer, Jane. "American Editions of Shakespeare: 1753–1866." *PMLA* 22, no. 4 (1907): 633–696.

Skinner, Otis, Edwin Booth, and Mary Devlin Booth. *The Last Tragedian; Booth Tells His Own Story.* New York: Dodd, Mead, 1939.

Smiles, Samuel. *Self-Help: With Illustrations of Character and Conduct.* New York: Ticknor and Fields, 1861.

Smith, Gay. *Lady Macbeth in America: From the Stage to the White House.* New York: Palgrave Macmillan, 2010.

Smith, Sol. *Theatrical Management in the West and South for Thirty Years: Interspersed with Anecdotical Sketches.* New York: Harper and Brothers, 1868.

Smither, Nelle Kroger. *A History of the English Theatre in New Orleans.* New York: Benjamin Blom, 1967.

Sommers, John Jerome. "James H. Hackett: The Profile of a Player." Ph.D. diss., University of Iowa, 1966.

Sprague, Arthur Colby. "Falstaff Hackett." *Theater Notebook* 9 (April–June 1955): 61–67.

———. *Shakespeare and the Actors: The Stage Business in His Plays (1660–1905).* New York: Russell, 1963.

———. *Shakespeare's Histories: Plays for the Stage.* London: Society for Theatre Research, 1964.

Stahr, Walter. *Seward: Lincoln's Indispensable Man.* New York: Simon and Schuster, 2012.

Stearns, Charles Woodward. *The Shakspeare Treasury of Wisdom and Knowledge.* New York: G. P. Putnam and Son, 1869.

Stephens, Alexander H. *Recollections of Alexander H. Stephens: His Diary Kept When a Prisoner at Fort Warren, Boston Harbour, 1865, Giving Incidents and Reflections of His Prison Life and Some Letters and Reminiscences.* Edited by Myrta Lockett Avary. New York: Doubleday, Page, 1910.

Stevens, Walter B. *A Reporter's Lincoln.* Edited by Michael Burlingame. Lincoln: University of Nebraska Press, 1998.

Stoddard, William Osborn. *Inside the White House in War Times: Memoirs and Reports of Lincoln's Secretary.* Edited by Michael Burlingame. Lincoln: University of Nebraska Press, 2000.

———. *Lincoln's White House Secretary: The Adventurous Life of William O. Stoddard.* Edited by Harold Holzer. Carbondale: Southern Illinois University Press, 2007.

Stone, Irving. *Love Is Eternal: A Novel about Mary Todd Lincoln and Abraham Lincoln.* Garden City, N.Y.: Doubleday, 1954.

Stone, Mary Isabella. *Edwin Booth's Performances: The Mary Isabella Stone Commentaries.* Edited by Daniel J. Watermeier. Ann Arbor, Mich.: UMI Research Press, 1990.

Strong, George Templeton. *The Diary of George Templeton Strong.* New York: Macmillan, 1952.

Sturgess, Kim C. *Shakespeare and the American Nation.* Cambridge: Cambridge University Press, 2004.

Styple, William B. *The Little Bugler: The True Story of a Twelve-Year-Old Boy in the Civil War.* Kearny, N.J.: Belle Grove, 1998.

Taliaferro, John. *All the Great Prizes: The Life of John Hay, from Lincoln to Roosevelt.* New York: Simon and Schuster, 2013.

Tarbell, Ida M. *The Life of Abraham Lincoln, Drawn from Original Sources and Containing Many Speeches, Letters, and Telegrams Hitherto Unpublished.* New York: Lincoln Memorial Association, 1900.

Taylor, Gary. *Reinventing Shakespeare: A Cultural History, from the Restoration to the Present.* New York: Weidenfeld and Nicolson, 1989.

Teague, Frances N. *Shakespeare and the American Popular Stage.* Cambridge: Cambridge University Press, 2006.

Thayer, William Roscoe. *The Life and Letters of John Hay.* 2 vols. Boston: Houghton Mifflin, 1915.

Tingley, Donald F. "Ralph Waldo Emerson on the Illinois Lecture Circuit." *Journal of the Illinois State Historical Society* 64, no. 2 (Summer 1971): 192–205.

Tocqueville, Alexis de. *Democracy in America.* Translated by Arthur Goldhammer. New York: Library of America, 2004.

Towse, John Ranken. *Sixty Years of the Theater: An Old Critic's Memories.* New York: Funk and Wagnalls, 1916.

Trollope, Frances Milton. *Domestic Manners of the Americans.* 2nd ed. 2 vols. London: Whittaker, Treacher, 1832.

Turner, Justin G., Linda Levitt Turner, and Mary Todd Lincoln. *Mary Todd Lincoln: Her Life and Letters.* New York: Alfred A. Knopf, 1972.

Vandenhoff, George, and Henry Seymour Carleton. *Dramatic Reminiscences; or, Actors and Actresses in England and America.* London, 1860.

Vaughan, Alden T., and Virginia Mason Vaughan. *Shakespeare in America.* Oxford: Oxford University Press, 2012.

Vaughan, Virginia Mason, and Alden T. Vaughan. *Shakespeare in American Life.* Washington, D.C.: Folger Shakespeare Library, 2007.

Vidal, Gore. *Lincoln: A Novel.* New York: Random House, 1984.

Viele, Egbert L. "A Trip with Lincoln, Chase and Stanton." *Scribner's Monthly,* October 1878, 813–823.

Walsh, William S. *Abraham Lincoln and the London Punch; Cartoons, Comments and Poems, Published in the London Charivari, during the American Civil War (1861–1865).* New York: Moffat, Yard, 1909.

Ward, Artemus. *The Complete Works of Artemus Ward (Charles Farrar Browne).* Edited and compiled by Melville D. Landon. New York: G. W. Dillingham, 1898.

Ward, William Hayes, ed. *Abraham Lincoln: Tributes from His Associates, Reminiscences of Soldiers, Statesmen and Citizens.* New York: T. Y. Crowell, 1895.

Warren, Louis A. "A. Lincoln's Executive Mansion Library." *Antiquarian Bookman* 5, no. 3 (February 11, 1950): 569–570.

———. *Lincoln's Youth: Indiana Years, Seven to Twenty-One, 1816–1830.* New York: Appleton, Century, Crofts, 1959.

Watermeier, Daniel J. *American Tragedian: The Life of Edwin Booth.* Columbia: University of Missouri Press, 2015.

Weber, Karl. *Lincoln: A President for the Ages.* New York: Public Affairs, 2012.

Webster, Daniel. *The Great Speeches and Orations of Daniel Webster, with an Essay on Daniel Webster as a Master of English Style, by Edwin P. Whipple.* Boston: Little, Brown, 1879.

Wells, Stanley, and Sarah Stanton. *The Cambridge Companion to Shakespeare on Stage.* Cambridge: Cambridge University Press, 2002.

Westfall, Alfred Van Rensselaer. *American Shakespearean Criticism, 1607–1865.* New York: H. W. Wilson, 1939.

White, Jonathan. "Did Lincoln Dream He Died?" *For the People: A Newsletter of the Abraham Lincoln Organization* 16, no. 3 (Fall 2014): 1–5.

White, Ronald C. A. *The Eloquent President: A Portrait of Lincoln through His Words.* New York: Random House, 2005.

———. *Lincoln: A Biography.* New York: Random House, 2009.

Whitman, Walt. *Complete Poetry and Collected Prose.* New York: Literary Classics of the United States, 1982.

———. *Walt Whitman and the Civil War: A Collection of Original Articles and Manuscripts.* Edited by Charles Irving Glicksberg. Philadelphia: University of Pennsylvania Press, 1933.

Whitney, Henry Clay. *Abraham Lincoln's Lost Speech, May 29, 1856. A Souvenir of the Eleventh Annual Lincoln Dinner of the Republican Club of the City of New York, at the Waldorf, February 12, 1897.* New York: Printed for the Committee, 1897.

———. *Life on the Circuit with Lincoln. With Sketches of Generals Grant, Sherman and McClellan, Judge Davis, Leonard Swett, and Other Contemporaries.* Boston: Estes and Lauriat, 1892.

Williams, Talcott. "Lincoln the Reader." *American Review of Reviews* 61 (January–June 1920): 193–198.

Williams, William R., et al. *Our Martyr President, Abraham Lincoln: Voices from the Pulpit of New York and Brooklyn*. New York: Tibbals and Whiting, 1865.

Wills, Garry. *Lincoln at Gettysburg: The Words That Remade America*. New York: Simon and Schuster, 1992.

Wilmeth, Don B. "The MacKenzie-Jefferson Theatrical Company in Galena, 1838–1839." *Journal of the Illinois State Historical Society* 60, no. 1 (Spring 1967): 23–36.

Wilmeth, Don B., and C. W. E. Bigsby, eds. *The Cambridge History of American Theatre*. 3 vols. Cambridge: Cambridge University Press, 2006.

Wilson, Douglas L. "His Hour upon the Stage." *American Scholar* 81, no. 1 (Winter 2012): 60–69.

———. *Lincoln's Sword: The Presidency and the Power of Words*. New York: Alfred A. Knopf, 2006.

———. "Prospects for 'Lincoln 2.5.'" *Journal of American History* 96, no. 2 (2009): 459–461.

Wilson, Douglas L., Rodney O. Davis, Terry Wilson, William Henry Herndon, and Jesse William Weik. *Herndon's Informants: Letters, Interviews, and Statements about Abraham Lincoln*. Urbana: University of Illinois Press, 1998.

Wilson, Garff B. *A History of American Acting*. Bloomington: Indiana University Press, 1966.

Wilson, James Grant. "Recollections of Lincoln." *Putnam's Monthly*, February 1909, 515–529.

Wimsatt, William K., ed. *Samuel Johnson on Shakespeare*. New York: Hill and Wang, 1960.

Winkle, Kenneth J. *Abraham and Mary Lincoln*. Carbondale: Southern Illinois University Press, 2011.

Winship, Michael. "Uncle Tom's Cabin: History of the Book in the 19th-Century United States." http://utc.iath.virginia.edu/interpret/exhibits/winship/winship .html.

Winter, William. *Life and Art of Edwin Booth*. New York: Greenwood Press, 1968.

———. *Shakespeare on the Stage*. First Series. New York: Moffat, Yard, 1911.

———. *The Wallet of Time; Containing Personal, Biographical, and Critical Reminiscence of the American Theatre*. New York: Moffat, Yard, 1913.

———, ed. *William Shakespeare's Tragedy of Hamlet*. New York: Printed for William Winter, by Francis Hart, 1879. Online at the Furness Collection, University of Pennsylvania. http://sceti.library.upenn.edu/sceti/printedbooksNew/index.cfm ?textID=hamlet_booth&PagePosition=1.

Wolf, Simon. *The Presidents I Have Known from 1860–1918*. Washington, D.C.: Press of B. S. Adams, 1918.

Wood, Gary V. *Heir to the Fathers: John Quincy Adams and the Spirit of Constitutional Government*. Lanham, Md.: Lexington Books, 2004.

Yonick, Cora Jane. "A History of the Theatre in Springfield, Illinois from 1855 to 1876." Master's thesis, University of Wyoming, 1952.

Young, William C. *Famous Actors and Actresses on the American Stage*. New York: R. R. Bowker, 1975.

Young Mr. Lincoln. Directed by John Ford. Twentieth-Century Fox, 1939.

INDEX

personality of, 87, 103, 105, 182n101
as poet, 88
in *Post Office Mistake, The*, 86
reviews of, 96–100
as self-promoter, 86, 88–89
Shakespeare statue, sponsor of, 88, 102
as theater manager, 88
visits White House, xiii, 77, 81–82, 93,
  94–95, 104–105
"Yankee" roles and, 86, 98
Hackett, James H., and correspondence
  with Lincoln, x, 1, 27–28, 40–41, 44,
  52, 85, 86, 102–104, 110, 120
announces his remarriage, 103
asks Lincoln for diplomatic
  appointment, 103
asks Lincoln for favor, 101
invites Lincoln to see his performances,
  101
publishes letter from Lincoln, 90–93
Hackett, James H., *Notes and Comments
  upon Certain Plays and Actors of
  Shakespeare*, 89
"Actors of Hamlet," 89
comments on *Othello*, 113
"Notes on King Lear," 89, 134–136
sends book to Lincoln, 83
Hackett, John K., 103
Hale, John P., 193n24
Hale, Lucy, 193n24
Hall, Oscar D., 101
Hamlet
cartoon allusions to, 14, 154n51
C. W. Couldock in, 58–59
directions to the players, 72–73
Edwin Booth in, 122
E. L. Davenport in, 109–110
fictional Lincoln references to, xi
Lincoln alludes to, 24, 37, 39, 46
Lincoln comments on, 27, 40–44, 92
Lincoln compared to, x, 92
in Lincoln eulogies, 144
Lincoln identified with Claudius,
  47–48
Lincoln quotes from, 25, 40
Lincoln sees, 109–110, 122–129
Murdoch reads from, 61–62

performed by Illinois Theatrical
  Company, 56–57
performed in Washington, D.C., 108
in political discourse, 6, 8, 10
prayer scene in, 126–128
soliloquies, Lincoln comments on, 89,
  92
Hamner, Thomas, 126–127
Hankins, John, 33
Hanks, Dennis, 28
Harkness, David James, 36
Harlan, James, 48
Harold, David, 147
Hawthorne, Nathaniel, 33
Hay, John M., ix, 29, 48, 50, 91, 104,
  162n99, 182n109
alludes to Shakespeare, 18–19
attends theater with Lincoln, 67, 100,
  182n1
on Forrest, 136
on Hackett, 95, 100, 105
on John Wilkes Booth, 143
Lincoln reads to, 22, 24, 39–40, 48,
  50–51, 77, 85
opinion of Springfield, 55
Hayne, Julia Dean. *See* Dean, Julia
Hayne, Robert Y., debate with Daniel
  Webster, 9–12, 46
Helm, Emilie, 59
Helm, Katherine, 57
Henry IV, Part 1
cartoon allusions to, 14
fictional Lincoln references to, xi
Hackett in, 64, 68, 86, 101, 109
Lincoln finds moral in, 94
Lincoln questions Hackett about,
  94–95
Lincoln quotes from, 94
in political discourse, 8
stage versions of, 94
Henry IV, Part 2
fictional Lincoln references to, xi
Hackett in, 93
Henry V, Lincoln alludes to, 24, 37
Henry VI, Part 1, Lincoln quotes from, 24
Henry VI, Part 3, 77
Lincoln reads aloud from, 22, 24, 50, 85